# ISSUES IN SCHOOL EDUCATION

ENCYCLOPAEDIA OF SCHOOL EDUCATION - I

# ISSUES IN SCHOOL EDUCATION

*By*

**Dr. Marlow Ediger**
*M.S. Education, Ph.D.*
*Professor Emeritus in Education*
*Truman State University*
*Box 417, 201 W, 22nd St*
*North Newton KS 67117*
*United States of America*

*&*

**Dr. Digumarti Bhaskara Rao**
*M.Sc., M.A., M.A., M.Ed., Ph.D.*
*Reader & Research Director*
*R.V.R. College of Education*
*Srinivasa Nagar Colony*
*Guntur–522 006*
*(India)*

DISCOVERY PUBLISHING HOUSE PVT. LTD.
NEW DELHI-110 002

Reprinted – 2019
First Published - 2005

ISBN: 978-93-5056-599-5 (Set)

ISBN: 978-81-8356-025-2



**Issues in School Education**

*Published by:*
**DISCOVERY PUBLISHING HOUSE PVT. LTD.**
4383/4B, Ansari Road, Darya Ganj
New Delhi-110 002 (India)
*Phone*: +91-11-23279245, 23253475; 43596065
*E-mail*: discoverybooksindia@gmail.com
discoverypublishinghouse@gmail.com
*web*: www.discoverypublishinggroup.com

*Printed at:*
Infinity Imaging Systems
Delhi

**This Book
is Humbly Dedicated to**

Prof. Marlow Ediger

Mrs. Mary Ediger

Mr. Bruce Allen Ediger

Mrs. Maureen Ediger

Mr. Kent Dean Ediger

Mrs. Diana Ediger

Ms. Diane Kay Ediger

Mr. Van Marlow Ediger

Mr. Sam Ediger

Mr. Henry Ediger

Late Mr. Jacob Ediger

Late Mrs. Maria Ediger

# Preface

Teacher education is marching ahead with great many ideas and practices. Several educationists from many countries worked for the cause of quality teacher education. One such a great teacher educator is Prof. Marlow Ediger of Truman State University, USA.

Dr. Marlow Ediger is a world famous educationist who exerted all his energies for improving the status of teacher education all through his career. He has expressed his views on various educational affairs in over 250 state, national and international conferences; on radio and television; in over 2500 manuscripts and books published on six continents; and in his thousands of classroom lectures. He is associated with many universities in different capacities in USA and abroad. He is member of several editorial boards of educational journals. He is and was member of so many professional organizations. He is listed in biographical form in several who's who.

This book on such a legendary educator brings forth his views on various areas of education. To know more of his ideas, it is worthwhile to go through the books published by the Discovery Publishing House written by Dr. Marlow Ediger and Dr. Digumarti Bhaskara Rao. His experiences and experiments influenced the careers of his several students.

I am grateful to Prof. Marlow Ediger for kindly permitting to prepare a book and for sending the material and photographs. I also express my thanks to his family members for becoming the source of inspiration.

**Dr. Digumarti Bhaskara Rao**
*Research Director in Education*
*Nagarjuna University*
*dbrao@india.com*

# Contents

*Preface*

**PART 1**

**Biography of Dr. Marlow Ediger**

**PART 2**

**Marlow Ediger's Beliefs in Education**

1. School Climate and Learning 1
2. Portfolios, Students, and the Teacher 9
3. Staff Development Programmes 16
4. Collegial Climate in School 27
5. Quality in the Multicultural Curriculum Excellence and Equity 40
6. Intrinsic Versus Extrinsic Motivation 49
7. Perspectives in Counseling 57
8. Recent Educational Philosophies 62
9. Diagnosis in the Student Teaching Program 74
10. Philosophy of Measurement and Evaluation 84
11. Philosophy and Measurement of School Achievement 92
12. Testing and Measurement of Pupil Achievement 102
13. Statewide Testing and the Innovative Mind 112

14. Psychology in Teaching Mathematics 120

15. Quality and Quantity in the Mathematics Curriculum 142

16. Trends in the Mathematics Curriculum 151

17. Issues/Design in the Reading Curriculum 162

18. Meaning in Reading Symbols Across the Curriculum 169

19. Reading Instruction and the Struggling Reader 175

20. Computers, Technology, and the Reading Curriculum 183

21. Increasing Reading Comprehension 194

22. Assessing Reading in the Science Curriculum 201

23. Reading in Technical Education 209

24. Challenging all Students in the Social Studies 218

25. The Curriculum and Adult Education 227

26. The Psychology of Learning and Adult Education 235

27. The Classics and Adult Reading Interests 240

28. Curriculum Design in Technical Education 248

29. Leadership in Vocational/Technical Education 251

30. Supervision in Vocational Education 262

# PART 1

# Biography of Dr. Marlow Ediger

# Biography of Marlow Ediger

Marlow Ediger was born on October 10, 1927. He received his BS in Education, and the Master of Science in Education Degrees from Kansas State Teachers College (now named Emporia, Kansas State University) in 1958 and 1960 respectively. He received his Doctorate in Education from the University of Denver (Colorado) in 1963. His public school teaching experience included Sand Creek Elementary School, rural Newton, Kansas, 1951-1952; Mennonite School, Jericho, West Bank of the Jordan, 1952-1953; Friends Boys School, Ramallah, West Bank of the Jordan, 1953-1954. Country Side School, near Lehigh, Kansas, 1955-1957; teacher and principal at Lincolnville, Kansas, Public School, 1957-1962; Professor of Education at Truman State University, Kirksville, Missouri, 1962-1992. Professor Emeritus, 1992-present. Speaker in over 200 state, national, and international conventions on Teacher Education. These conventions include the National Council for the Social Studies, National Council Teacher of Mathematics, The National Science Teachers Association, The International Reading Association, and the National Council for Teachers of English, as well as affiliates of these national organizations such as the Missouri Council for the Social Studies, Missouri Council Teachers of Mathematics, Missouri Science Teachers Association, Missouri Reading Teacher's Association, and the Missouri Council Teachers of English Association. Dr. Ediger has also spoken at state teacher education conventions in Minnesota, Iowa, Kansas, Nebraska, California, Arizona, South Carolina, Texas, Oklahoma, Arkansas, Colorado, Pennsylvania, and Tennessee. Abroad, he has spoken at teacher education conventions in Canada, The West Bank in the Middle East, and the Philippines.

Dr. Ediger is a Member of the External Examining Committees to assess PhD theses for the following universities in India: Kerala, Mother Teresa, University of Madras, Utkal, Sambulpar, Alagappa. He is a member of the Editorial Board for the following professional educational journals: *Reading Improvement for Over Thirty Years, Education, Edutracks, The Progress of Education, Journal of Educational Research, The Educational Review*. He has also served previously on the following editorial boards of educational journals: *The Journal of English Language Teaching, Journal of the Karnataka State Education Federation,* and *the Mathematics Teacher.*

Dr. Ediger's biography is listed in Who's Who in America, Who's Who in American Education, Who's Who in the Midwest, Strathmore's Who's Who; Leaders in Education.

Offices held and memberships in educational organisations:

- Vice President and then President in Future Farmers of America (FFA), Inman, Kansas Chapter, 1944-1946. Received a Union Pacific Railroad scholarship to attend Kansas State University, Manhattan, Kansas, 1946.
- Treasurer and then President—Marion County, Kansas Teacher's Association, 1958-1960. Curriculum Committee Chairman, Marion County Teacher's Association, 1960-1961.
- Vice President and then President, American Association of University Professors (AAUP), Truman State University, 1974-1976; Second Vice President, Vice President, and then President of the Truman State University Chapter of Phi Delta Kappa (PDK), 1974-1977.
- Member-Advisory Council of Himalayan Journal of Educational Research and Development, India, 1995.

- *Committee Member*, past and present, of the following organizations for the National Council for the Social Studies: Religion in the Schools, Rural Schools and the Social Studies, Ethics Committee, Publications Committee, Curriculum Committee, Archives Committee.
- Committee Membership in the following organizations, past and present, for the National Council Teachers of English; Vice Chairman and then Chairman of the Rural Language Arts Committee, 1998-2000; Language and Learning Across the Curriculum; Tracking in the Public Schools.
- Member of the Missouri Council Social Studies Board of Control; Member of Board of Directors, Science Teachers of Missouri; Member of Missouri Geography Alliance.
- Member of the following committees, past and present, of the Missouri National Education Association (MNEA): Core Competencies and Key Skills (CCKS); Higher Education Committee; Committee on Public Relations.
- Member of the National Science Teacher's Association (NSTA) Committee on Teacher Education, 1988-1990.
- Member of International Reading Association Committee—Evaluating Student Achievement.
- Awards Received: Mmber in Phi Delta Kappa, an international honorary fraternity whose membership is open upon invitation only, Project Innovation Award for Outstanding Service to the Education Profession; Missouri State Senate Resolution (Jefferson City, Missouri) on being one of the foremost educators in Missouri, 1975; Community Leader of America, award presented by the American Biographical Institute (ABI); Community Leaders of America for Outstanding Service in Teaching, Writing, and Speaking, award presented

by the American Biographical Institute (ABI); Key of Success—Leader in Education, award presented by ABI; International Biographical Roll of Honor, award presented by ABI; Men of Achievement, award presented by the International Biographical Center; Commemorative Medal of Honor, award presented by the ABI.

- Member of the International Reading Association Committee on Evaluating Literacy Standards.
- Membership held in the following professional educational organizations: Association for Supervision and Curriculum Development (ASCD); National Science Teachers Association (NSTA); National Council for the Social Studies (NCSS); National Education Association (NEA Life Member; Member of the Missouri National Education Association (MNEA Life Member); International Reading Association (IRA); National Science Teachers Association (NSTA); National Council Teachers of English (NCTE).
- Dr. Ediger is the author of the following teacher education textbooks:

1. Relevancy in the Elementary Curriculum, 1975, second edition 1991.
2. The Elementary Curriculum, A Handbook, 1977, second edition 1988.
3. Social Studies Curriculum in the Elementary School, 1975, 1980, 1985, 1993, fifth edition 2000.
4. Language Arts Curriculum in the Elementary School, 1983, 1988, 1991, fourth edition 1994.
5. The Modern Elementary School, 1997.
6. Teaching Mathematics in the Elementary School, 1997.
7. Improving the Teaching of Elementary School Mathematics, 1999.

8. The Holy Land, 1998.

9. Teaching Science in the Elementary School, 2nd Edition, 2000.

Dr. Ediger has had more than 2,500 manuscripts accepted for publication in professional educational journals on six continents. Nations in which he has manuscripts published include the United States, India, Canada, Turkey, Romania, Poland, England, France, Norway, Denmark, Sweden, Russia, China, Argentina, Chile.

He co-authored the following teacher education textbooks with Dr. D. Bhaskara Rao, published by the Discovery Publishing House, New Delhi, India.

1. Science Curriculum
2. Elementary Curriculum
3. Language Arts Curriculum
4. Philosophy and Curriculum
5. Psychology and Curriculum
6. Improving School Administration
7. School Curriculum and Administration
8. Modern Elementary School
9. Relevancy in Elementary Curriculum
10. Teaching English Successfully
11. Teaching Science Successfully
12. Teaching Mathematics Successfully
13. Teaching Social Studies Successfully
14. Teaching Reading Successfully
15. Teaching Language Arts Successfully
16. Teaching Science in Elementary Schools

17. Teaching Mathematics in Elementary Schools

18. Teaching Social Studies in Elementary Schools

The above books are given a detailed outlook of Dr. Marlow Ediger on various educational issues and affairs.

Dr. Ediger served as a Sunday School Teacher for over forty years, and was a long time Deacon in the First Presbyterian Church in Kirksville, Missouri. He has written numerous articles on the Teaching of Sunday School.

He is married to Mary Duerksen, a retired teacher of 23 years. They were married on June 2, 1957. Their children are:

- Bruce, (born 1961, and is a computer programmer), wife Maureen, their children are Henry, Harper.
- Kent, (born 1964 and is a chemist) wife Diana Rathmussen, their children are Van Marlow and Samuel George.
- Diane, (born 1969) is a computer programmer.

Much credit in the life of Dr. Marlow Ediger goes to Mary (wife), Bruce (son), Kent (son) and Diane (daughter) as they are the inspiration of his life.

Residential address: Dr. Marlow Ediger, 201 West 22nd Street, North Newton, KS 67117-0417, United States of America.

*Marlow, Elof (brother) and Midred (sister) in 1931*

*Young and Energetic*
*Marlow Ediger*

*Dr. Marlow Ediger & Mrs. Mary Ediger*
*(2 June 1957)*

*Dr. Marlow & Mrs. Mary*
*(1972)*

*Dr. Marlow & Mrs. Mary*
*(1987)*

**The Family of Dr. Marlow Ediger**

***Back row:*** *Kent (Ediger's son), Diana (Kent's wife), Sam (Kent's Son), Bruce (Ediger's son), Henry (Bruce's son), Maureen (Bruce's wife), Diane (Ediger's daughter)*

***Front Row:*** *Van (Kent's son), Mary Ediger and Dr. Marlow Ediger*

*Midred (M. Ediger's sister), Mary (Ediger's wife), Marlow Ediger with his son Bruce, J.E. Ediger (Ediger's father), 22 August 1961*

*Mrs. Maria Ediger and Mr. Jacob Ediger (Mother and Father of Dr. Marlow Ediger)*

# PART 2

# Marlow Ediger's Beliefs in Education

## Your Attention Please

*For making these topics comprehensive, ideas of other educationists have been added to the views of Dr. Marlow Ediger. Majority of the opinions and beliefs in these articles are of Prof. Marlow Ediger.*

# 1

# School Climate and Learning

Teachers and supervisors need to spend a considerable amount of time in improving school climate. With an improved school climate, pupils should learn more than previously. A climate which is conducive to optimizing learner achievement is a must. A negative school climate hinders pupils from achieving and may well also develop inappropriate attitudes. The writer has long felt that a negative school environment makes for lower state mandated test scores and all around lower achievement in the classroom.

## Classroom Attitudes

The classroom setting and its environment needs to be assessed continuously to identify and weed out that which hinders learner progress. Rudeness, for example, makes for undesirable learning situations. People in society have known for a long time that rudeness is an inappropriate way of behaving and yet it is frequently observed in checkout lines, restaurants, as well as in churches. Somehow, the message does not get across that politeness in behavior is a much more pleasant way of human interaction as compared to rudeness. To have to interact with others in school endeavors involving rudeness is indeed very unpleasant and hinders achievement. That might be a salient reason for absenteeism when a polite person is required to do a school project with one or more rude persons in close contact. The polite person may fear to interact with his/her suggestions when the result are rude responses. Teachers may not desire to correct the behaviors of rudeness. The child is the victim in these situations. Attending school then becomes a situation to avoid.

A second kind of negative behavior is intimidation. The intimidator attempts to get away with frightening another pupil by having friends nearby to support the unpleasant deeds. Perhaps, the only friends the perpetrator has are those involved in helping to intimidate others. It is a very unpleasant situation for the one who experiences the intimidation. The perpetrators may do the unpleasant to a pupil when no one else is nearby. The support system for the pleasant pupil is completely lacking. There may be feelings of no one else being there to turn to for offering some kind of help. The intimidators may enjoy harming of their targets. Too frequently, teachers shy away from those doing the intimidating, fearing that classroom interruptions may occur later if attempted corrections are made involving the intimidators (Ediger and Rao: 2003, Chapter Six).

Bullying, a third kind of negative behavior, tends to occur on the playground largely. The bully desires to lord it over others. The bully may be quite strong physically and is able to force others to do what the he/she wants. Pupils tend to fear bullies and give in to what is wanted. Then too, it is very difficult to get out of the way of bullies. Bullies know which targets are easy to use. Selected bullies may like to obtain hush money from the meek. The bully will harm a child if the latter does not pay money in order to avoid being harmed physically, such as being punched until it hurts. Sometimes, the "marks" become obtrusive when kicking the shins is being emphasised. The shins might become quite blue if pay offs are not received in time.

A pupil's lunch money may be "stolen" if he/she does not make pay offs in due time. If the stealer has a friend or two to assist in the "stealing," he is able to commit the action quicker. A threat is added "not to tell anyone". Children who give the hush money to the perpetrator feel very threatened and at all costs avoid telling his/her parents of what is happening. Dreadful consequences have occurred if a child has told a close friend of what has transpired with the intent of getting hush money perpetrators caught. Sometimes the chain of events has been stopped in which the perpetrator has been caught and punished. There is a solid base of support here for victims who tell the right people of hush money being obtained, with threats to be given to those who squeal. Sophisticated approaches are used to extract money under duress from vulnerable individuals. The vulnerable individual, even a grown person of seventeen years of age, may fear to tell parents or other responsible persons of the agony of never eating school lunches. The student has been duly warned of not eating home packed lunches!

Additional harmful approaches used by pupils to deal negatively with each other include the following:

**The put down.**

Highly embarrassing means are used to put an individual in his/her "proper place". The taunts used by the offender "cut deep" into the one being offended. The taunts are highly offensive and the receiver does not wish to hear of these offensive statements. Adults who use the put down and are skilled in doing so use highly offensive statements and if the receiver shows any resentment is asked, "Can't you enjoy a good joke?" The put down is used to even make the perpetrator look good.

**To egg the next person or persons on.**

Two boys may have a disagreement. Each side is egged on to throw the first punch. By this time, a small crowd has gathered and no teacher or supervisor is there to stop the fighting. The blows can become quite vicious. Neither boy is likely to back down from fighting. Both have become victims to the shouts off encouragement of the bystanders. Bruises and cuts began to be seen on one or both of the fighters. The involved boys are the victims in this embarrassing event from which no one wins but both lose, and may lose heavily. The cheering crowd has egged the two boys on to do foolish things which are harmful to both. The next engagement may be easier to encourage. "Cowards" tend not to be liked. A wise peacemaker is difficult to locate within the crowd. Hopefully, an adult will come very soon to break up the fighting or the combatants will pretend to be brave and merely fake wanting to fight.

There are definite things which may be emphasized to minimize rudeness, intimidation, bullying, the put down, and the egg on. A charismatic teacher may be able to demonstrate the detrimental effects of using these approaches to deal with others. He/she might also be able to model correct behavior in dealing with others in a positive manner. A quality learning environment is needed for pupils to do well academically and socially. Something needs to be in the offing to take the place of rudeness as well as curb intimidating behaviors. Objectives, too, need to be decided upon to minimize the "put down" and the "egg on." Within each lesson and unit of study taught, clearly stated objectives need continual emphasis to curtail undesirable behaviors. Teachers need to search for and review the educational literature pertaining to the identified forms of pupil misbehavior. A professional library for teachers in the school setting as well a university teacher education library should provide needed information in solving identified problems. The research done provides learning opportunities for teachers and for pupils to achieve objectives.

Materials for pupils need to be adapted to their own unique levels of achievement. Additional learning opportunities to achieve objectives include films, filmstrips, slides, video tapes, video disks, DVDs. These assist learners in attaining objectives. Objectives should emphasize knowledge, skills, and attitudes ends on rudeness, intimidation, bullying, the put down, and the egg on (Ediger and Rao: 2003, Chapter Eight).

In utilizing materials of instruction, the teacher needs to make learnings interesting, purposeful and meaningful so that it makes sense to learners. Additional standards of teaching to use in implementing the curriculum include:

- Providing for individual differences so that all may benefit optimally from the curriculum.
- Emphasizing reasons for learning so that wholehearted involvement by learners is possible.
- Maximize pupil active involvement in learning, not passive receptivity.

**Evaluation to Measure Achievement**

Videos may be made to ascertain if rudeness is present during a discussion. The point of rudeness in the playback need to be pinpointed and the statements made by the perpetrator needs to be corrected to eliminate the undesirable. Proper ways of saying things may be stressed to replace the undesirable. Recording of discussions may be made rather continuously to notice deficiencies of rudeness and remediation made. Different ways need to be shown on intimidating others. Sometimes, the pupil does not realize he/she intimidates others. Selected dramatisations may make this clear. Intimidating is a subtle way of embarrassing and making others do what the perpetrator wants him/her to do.

Bullying is an overt way of forcing a person to do that which the perpetrator wants him/her to do. The language used, the force demonstrated, and the verbal/nonverbal cues used make bullying relatively easy to identify.

The egg on is easy to emphasize in drama form. For example, several boys may disagree on a path of action. The disagreement gets louder until the fists are to be used. The role play should indicate this with the onlookers encouraging the using of fists. The boys are called cowards if they do not show their bravery. The situation should be life-like and real, but involve a perfectly safe atmosphere.

In the classroom and school lunchroom, pupils may assist in helping to determine when a put down occurs. Appropriate ways of saying things may be emphasised in place of the put down. Individuals need to be careful in refraining from put down use due to its embarrassing intentions. There should be discussions on how the person feels who received the put down. It is harmful to both—the one putting someone else down as well as the victim of the put down. The former may lack friends in many cases and is one to be avoided. The victim develops feelings of revenge and hostility even though he/she may fear to retaliate. The egg on needs to notice the damage that may accrue from getting others to join in on the fight. When both sides are eagerly involved due to the cheering, the results may be emotionally and physically damaging.

For each of the five cases in being the victim discussed above, it is appropriate for the perpetrator to know how extreme the feelings of insecurity are on the part of the victim. The victim then has:

- fears of being alone with no help available.
- fears of being harmed physically.
- fears of not living down the embarrassment and ugly perceptions held by the onlookers.
- fears of having no friends.
- fears of having to face the taunts and injustices of others contiruously.
- fears of disliking the self for not being able to defend the self.
- fears of being left alone with no one to assist or protect the self.

There are problems inherent in democratic living as well as when participating in society. Thus, there will be reservations in interacting with others in the societal arena for the good of society. A democratic society encourages:

- each person to participate in decision making responsibilities.
- each person to have a wholesome attitude toward the thinking of others.
- each person to take part in identifying and solving problems.
- each person to be accepting of others.
- each person to have his/her ideas accepted by others.
- each person to do his/her share of work in society.

A democratic society does not emphasize letting a few people make the decisions and do all the work to improve society. All are to be involved.

The kids at a suburban St. Louis school used to tease each other and keep students out of their exclusive cliques, but now they can be seen chatting at breakfast and helping other with their homework.

Principal Karen Smith credits character education with making the difference. The practice which involves kids getting kids to care more about their school and each other, seems to be working—and not only at Smith's Mark Twain Elementary School in Brentwood.

A study of school-based character education programmes across the nation indicates the effort can work to improve attitudes toward elders while reducing violence, drug use, and risky sexual behavior. What's more, the programmes can help pupils get better grades.... The study found some of the most effective techniques included peer interaction and training directed at a specific skill, such as anger management and conflict resolution. The programmes are also more effective when teachers and staff receive training, according to the study (Latze, 2003).

## References

Ediger, Marlow and D. Bhaskara Rao (2003), *Elementary Curriculum.* New Delhi, India: Discovery Publishing House, Chapter Six.

Ediger, Marlow and D. Bhaskara Rao (2003), *Philosophy and Curriculum.* New Delhi, India: Discovery Publishing House, Chapter Eight.

Latze, Jeff (2003), *Study suggests character education, boosts academics, too,* Kirksville, Missouri Daily Express, page 2.

# 2

# Portfolios, Students, and the Teacher

Much emphasis is placed presently upon the development of portfolios for pupils to show achievement. We believe, it is equally important for teachers to develop portfolios of their own contributions and progress. The teacher should start developing a portfolio upon entering the profession of teaching, perhaps even when being involved in student teaching. Why? We believe, portfolio development provides a vision for teachers as to *what should be* in teaching and learning. The vision presents goals and objectives for the present and for the future. Teachers find it interesting to develop a portfolio sequentially to reflect upon what has transpired. When reflecting, the teacher reviews and analyzes what has been done previously. There is a good chance then that improved performance will be an end result. One can always improve teaching performance when thinking critically and creatively as to what has gone on before in terms of one's own teaching of pupils. Based on these past experience, the teacher may then view *what should* and *can be* in teaching-learning situations. Gilman and Hassett (1995) indicate three broad purpose in and for developing portfolios. The first is that a purpose should be involved. Thus, reasons must be inherent in the making of a personal portfolio. We have heard numerous teachers state that they developed portfolios in order to have a scrapbook on their very own teaching. These teachers also want to pass on to offspring what was done as a classroom teacher. The scrapbooks, if they survive in time, might well have historical purposes as a primary source. A very practical purpose in developing a portfolio is to present information as to what was done in teaching when applying for a new position. Portfolio contents may provide the interviewer an excellent overview of the applicant's ability to teach. Second, portfolio contents (Gilman and Hassett: 1995) chart interests and growth. We find numerous teachers that indicate portfolio development interesting. Thus, it is interesting to look back to see what one did in the past; it is interesting too to see the portfolio grow in size, not that volume alone is salient. Personal growth of the teacher is important when sequentially preparing the portfolio. A professional teacher achieves, grows, and accomplishes at continually higher levels of achievement. The teacher's professional life should move from the actual to the ideal. The ideal is never reached, but it is a goal and vision to attain. The cumulative portfolio permits the teacher to analyze the present situation and move toward further goals in professional teaching. Third, the portfolio (Gilman and Hassett: 1995) present opportunities for higher levels of cognition in that choices are involved in ascertaining that which should go into a portfolio. Portfolio content should challenge teachers to attain in inservice education. Personal means of growth and school staff development approaches may be included in inservice education programmes.

Portfolios have become quite popular in the US. In the state of Vermont, for example, each pupil in school with teacher guidance needs to develop a portfolio to show achievement and progress. Schools and school systems have educated the public on the values of portfolios by having an evening set aside for any interested person to read and comment on available portfolios. There have also been school sponsored fairs where portfolios are on display for viewing. Teachers should certainly learn from diverse sources prior to developing their own portfolios. A survey of educational literature on portfolio development can be very beneficial on portfolio development. Further means of learning about portfolios are to attend related staff development programmes, workshops, university courses and classes, talking and discussing with other teachers about portfolio development, and having one's own portfolio evaluated by an individual or committee who have expertise in the area. Bimes-Michalak (1995) wrote:

> It is easy to see why portfolios have been embraced. According to research and a growing number of teachers, they link assessment to instruction, document growth over time, give ... ownership and responsibility for ... learning, making learning more collaborative, inform instruction, and communicate assessment information to parents, school officials, and the public. They are an assessment tool every classroom needs.

Teacher then need to develop a portfolio covering a period of time, not just for one special occasion or event. The teacher owns the portfolio and is in complete charge of its development. What might go into a portfolio to reveal personal achievement of the classroom teacher? We have the following suggestions to make which have been used by numerous teachers:

1. Snapshots of bulletin board displays which have been used in initiating, developing, and culminating ongoing units of study.
2. Videotapes of pupil-teacher planning of the curriculum.
3. Displays of learner products for other pupils and teachers to observe in the classroom setting. These have been made in slide form, but may appear in other media for the portfolio.
4. Cassette recordings of pupil oral reports given within an ongoing unit of study or lesson.
5. Samples of pupil writing involving diverse purposes. These can in manuscript/cursive style or on software packages.
6. Journal entries written by the teacher covering excursions taken into the community.
7. Anecdotal records on diagnosis and remediation of pupil difficulties in learning.

8. Test scores of pupils taught.
9. Diary entries and logs written by pupils pertaining to what was achieved in ongoing lessons and units of study.
10. Summaries of parent-teacher conferences.

Further items that might be placed in a teacher portfolio include professional meetings attended, talks given at professional meetings, articles written for publication, and new procedures emphasised in teaching and learning.

Engel (1994) discusses the need far a new paradigm in evaluation of achievement. Paradigms pertain to the ways we think and act ultimately. Paradigms present a model to follow. Pertaining to assessment, Engel wrote the following:

> Authenticity can be seen as consistency in time—between what is happening now and what is intended for the future. An action is authentic when aligned with its long term purposes—when one can look toward the future and see the connections between the means and the end. In assessment, authenticity implies the results can be trusted partly because the methods support long-term purposes. Authenticity can be contrasted with expedience. The former is justified by a long term view; the latter by a short term perceived need.

Teachers in developing their very own portfolios need to have long range goals. Portfolios cover what has transpired in time. The contents therein pertain to items emphasizing personal growth in teaching and learning. A variety of approaches are used by the teacher to present data of contextual situations involving interacting with pupils in the school setting. Purpose is involved here in that accurate portrayal of the teacher's role and responsibilities as a professional is presented in portfolio form. The evaluator of the portfolio desires to perceive the objectives of the teacher in teaching pupils, the learning opportunities provided so that learners attain the stated ends, as well as appraisal procedures used by the teacher to ascertain pupil achievement in the school curriculum.

Tyler (1949) raised four vital questions pertaining to curriculum development. These are:

1. Which objectives should pupils achieve?
2. Which learning activities should be provided so that pupils might achieve these objectives?
3. How should the object matter be organised for pupil acquisition?
4. How should pupil achievement be evaluated?

We believe that these four questions need to be answered by all educators. They are vital to consider in the area of curriculum improvement. Answers to salient questions and problems provide necessary data in portfolio development. There are a few additional questions that need answers. These are the following:

1. How might balance among objectives be emphasised in teaching and learning? The concept of balance among objectives pertains to stressing cognitive, affective, and psychomotor ends.
2. How should learning opportunities be sequenced for pupils? Thus a logical or psychological sequence may be in evidence.
3. How may a multi-media approach be emphasised as learning opportunities for pupils in the curriculum? A multi-media approach is emphasised to guide each pupil to achieve optimally, not for the sake of doing so.
4. Which procedures should be used to appraise learner progress?

The procedures involve using portfolios along with teacher written test, standardised tests, discussions, learner products, behavioral journals, dairy and log entries, as well as teacher observation to notice pupil achievement.

When viewing Tyler's (1949) questions as well as those we have listed in sequence, there are needed answers which might well provide information for a portfolio. A problem then arises as to how thick the portfolio should be. We believe the best answer to this question is to choose for inclusion what is truly relevant and vital. Perhaps, a trusted colleague might offer suggestions here. We would see no problem in two or more teachers developing a portfolio cooperatively. Cooperative development of a portfolio could be excellent when involved teachers are members of a teaching team. The point of developing a portfolio is to convey achievement on teaching to interested persons. Brown and Irby (1995) provide three reasons for portfolio development--to encourage reflection for improvement, to assist career advancement, and to be an alternative assessment tool.

We believe too that portfolios may be developed as a matter of personal interest and humble pride of achievements made in the educational arena. Certainly, pride is involved when one is pictured in the local newspaper showing how 100 days in the new school year were celebrated. The picture then in the local newspaper shows the many ways one's pupils have learned what makes for a set of 100 items. Much price too comes from having received high ratings from an observational visit made to the classroom by the school principal. These awards and rewards definitely should become a part of the portfolio. They are relevant items to include. As the teacher reflects upon portfolio contents, he/she will devise criteria in terms of what to include and what to omit, particularly when a portfolio might appear to become voluminous.

## Conclusion

Wolf (1996) summarizes teacher portfolio development and use when writing the following:

Why the interests in teaching portfolios? Although portfolios can be time consuming to construct and cumbersome to review, they also can capture complexities of professional practices in ways that no other approach can.

Not only are they an effective way to assess teaching quality, but they also provide teachers with opportunities for self reflection and collegial interactions based on documented episodes of their own teaching.

Essentially, a teaching portfolio is a collection of information about a teacher's practice. It can include a variety of information, such as lesson plans, student assignments, teachers' written descriptions and videotapes of their instruction, and formal evaluation by supervisors...

A teaching portfolio should be more than a miscellaneous collection of artifacts or an extended list of professional activities. It should carefully and thoughtfully document a set of accomplishments attainment over an extended period of time, and, it should be an ongoing process conducted in the company of mentors and colleagues.

## References

Gilman, David A., and Marie Hasset (1995). More than Work Folders: Using Portfolios for Educational Assessment. *Clearing House* 68, 310-313.

Bimes-Michalak. Beverly (1995). The Portfolio Zone. *Education Digest,* 60, 53-57.

Brown, Genevieve, and Beverly J. Irby (1995). The Portfolio: Should it Also Be Used By Administrators? *The NASSP Bulletin.* 79, 82-85.

Engel, Brenda S. (1994). Portfolio assessment and the New Paradigm: New Instruments and New Places. *The Educational Forum.* 59, 22-29.

# 3

# Staff Development Programmes

Much is written in educational literature pertaining to staff development. It appears that writers stress staff development for each innovation presented. For example, if the interdisciplinary curriculum needs emphasis, then staff development is needed. Or, if full inclusion is wanted, then staff development should be in evidence. We believe the first issue in staff development is how many sessions should be devoted to staff development when writers bring in new ideas in teaching and at the same time advocate staff development for implementing that idea. Is it necessary to have staff development for each new or innovative idea adopted in teaching and learning? Might teachers be trusted with implementing the new concept(s) on their own?

## Further Issues in Staff Development

Who should determine what should be emphasised in staff development? A common vision is being emphasised as to what our schools should be like as a result of this vision. How is the vision to be achieved? A staff development program, in part, may help. Ediger (1988) recommends that staff development programmes have three integrated parts, such as a general session, small group or committee endeavours, and individual study. Teachers here should determine what is to be emphasised in the general session to identify problem areas, they should volunteer as to which committee to work on to solve problems, and then work individually on a problem of their very own choosing. The teacher and teaching here are at the center of the stage in staff development. Principals and supervisors are their to assist teachers in working toward solutions of problem areas.

Toward the other end of the continuum, supervisors and principals, after consultation with teachers, may desire to bring in a certain programme whereby staff development is necessary. The teachers are trained and educated to use a certain model in teaching after a quality programme of training. This approach at staff development has unique features that the first did not possess. The latter procedure in staff development is more principal/supervisor oriented, even though there was consultation with teachers about the new approach. Second, a commercial approach or one proposed by a team of educators was emphasised. The ideas for problem areas to be solved basically did not come from local teachers. Third, teachers must develop into having completely new teaching styles. The teaching model selected for staff development and implementation might not intrinsically be wanted by teachers. There may be a different procedure in teaching desired by teachers. Fourth, an external training team may be involved in the training of teachers. Trainers then come from outside the local school system or district. Fifth, trainers sequence experiences for teachers in staff training sessions. A logical approach is then involved in sequencing experience for trainees.

## What Should Training Sessions Stress?

The objectives of instruction may be changed or modified. Generally cognitive objectives have received major emphasis in the curriculum. There are different levels of pupil achievement in the cognitive domain. Changes may be made from stressing the lower level cognitive objectives to those emphasizing higher levels of thinking. Bloom's (1956) is still popular in discussing objectives from the lower to higher levels of cognition. His sequence is the following: recall of factual information by learners, comprehension of what has been recalled, application or using what has been learned, analysis involving critical thought, synthesis stressing unique ways of putting the information together after analysis, and evaluation of what has been learned in terms of standards or criteria. Staff development programmes may stress teachers having children move for lower to higher cognitive objectives using Bloom's taxonomy. Learning opportunities need to be designed to guide pupils in thinking at a more complex level in ongoing learning opportunities. Feedback from teachers to members of the staff development programme should be in the offing after the teacher has used higher cognitive objectives in the classroom.

There is much discussion in education about having pupils apply what has been learned. Perhaps, a staff development programme will stress the level of application in ongoing training sessions. Teachers then put to use ideas developed and acquired in the staff development programme to the regular classroom. These teachers report back to the training session how the ideas worked out in the classroom.

Modification of objectives stressed in teaching and learning may also emphasize minimizing cognitive and advocating affective ends in teaching. Affective objective put more emphasis upon attitudes that pupils need to develop. Hopefully, quality attitudes will assist pupils to achieve cognitive objectives more effectively. Krathwohl stressed five levels of affective objectives in moving from the lowest to the higher levels. These are the following: paying attention to relevant content presented, responding to content with feeling or emotion, responding to content in a value oriented way, organizing values and feelings into a structure, and characterizing the attitudes in terms of being consistent and following a pattern. A quality affective curriculum emphasizes pupils developing positive feelings and values.

A learning stations philosophy might well stress an affective curriculum. Here, the teacher together with pupils develop an adequate number of stations as well as tasks for each station. Pupils might then choose which tasks to complete and which to omit. Decision-making by learners is important. Ideally, pupils choose tasks which possess interest and perceived purpose. Motivation for learning should be higher if the pupil has had input into what he/she has planned and wishes to learn. The learner also is involved in planning and selecting—two concepts which no doubt are at the heart of democratic thinking. The learner chooses from among alternatives and he/she is affected by choices made, from among alternatives. Involvement by pupils in selecting objectives, learning activities, and appraisal procedures emphasizes increasingly democratic living. Also the attitudes of the pupil determine, in part, what will be learned. A psychological curriculum stresses pupils sequencing their very own learning opportunities; opposite of a psychological curriculum is a logical curriculum whereby a teacher arranges the order of learning for pupils.

In noticing that a almost complete absence of statements advocating democracy and democratic ideals from policy makers. Fenstermacher (1995) write the following:

> ...We hear a great deal about readying the next generation of workers for global competition, about being first in the world in such high status subjects as math and science, and about having world class standards for what is learned in school. We hear almost nothing about civic participation or building and maintaining democratic communities, whether these be neighborhoods or governments at the local, state, or federal levels. The advancement of democratic ideals and institutions goes largely unmentioned, taken for granted or insufficiently important to rank up their with such world-shaking events as our playing Avis to Japan's Hertz.

Workshops and staff development programmes might then be arranged for the teacher to stress democracy as a way of life with the inclusion of affective objectives.

A third change in the curriculum may reflect the use of psychomotor objectives. Here, the school curriculum stresses the use of the gross and finer muscles of the learner. Harrow (1972) listed six levels of psychomotor objectives. These are the following:

1. Reflex movement
2. Basic fundamental movements, including locomotor, non-locomotor manipulative movements.

3. perceptual abilities containing several subcategories:

    (*a*) Kinesthetic discrimination that refers to body awareness, body image, body relationship of surrounding objectives in space.

    (*b*) Visual discrimination including visual awareness, visual tracking, visual memory, figure ground differentiation, and perceptual constancy.

    (*c*) Auditory discrimination including auditory activity, tracking, and memory.

    (*d*) Tactile discrimination

    (*e*) Coordination.

4. Physical abilities including endurance, strength, flexibility and agility.

5. Skilled movement including simple adaptive skill, compound and complex adaptive skill.

6. Non-discursive communication including expressive movements and interpretive movements.

In emphasizing psychomotor objectives, the teacher assists pupils to become actively involved in making, constructing, artistic endeavours, doing, and other forms of using physical movement and motion. Psychomotor objectives may be used in any curriculum area and receive more emphasis in teaching and learning as compared to cognitive and affective ends of instruction (Earnest, 1995).

Staff development programmes may be needed to change from a cognitive or affective objectives emphasis to one stressing the psychomotor domain. Psychomotor objectives truly emphasize an activity centered curriculum for pupils. I supervise student teachers and regular teachers in the public school setting. In teaching a unit on "Weather and How It Affects Us," pupils with teaching team guidance discussed and constructed a barometer, a wind vane, a hygrometer, and an anemometer. Each object was goal centered, planned, constructed, and appraised in terms of criteria.

**Learning Opportunities to Achieve Objectives**

In changing from previously used activities and experiences to a new approach takes effort, knowledge, skill and motivation. If pupils are to use modern technology in the curriculum, it may truly revolutionize the curriculum depending upon the amount of change being empathised. In using the word processor, worldwide web and internet, graphing techniques, CD ROM's, video disks, among other items, teachers may need to experience two to three years of quality staff development programs. Objectives need to be determined for pupils to achieve sequentially in using modern technology. Progress by pupils may well be slow, but sure with good teaching, in using technology to achieve objectives.

Second, staff development programmes might well be extensive if an interdisciplinary curriculum is to be in evidence. An allied arts programme of instruction may well emphasize a team teaching approach. Allied arts attempts to integrate art, music, dance, drama, poetry, and architecture, among other possibilities. Thus, a teaching team consisting of the following teachers, each qualified in his/her area of expertise—an art, a music, a physica. education, and a literature or English teacher—must be in the offing. If possible, an architecture from the community might be hired part time. If the school system has an architect, it becomes easier for this person to work on the team to plan the objectives, learning opportunities, and evaluation procedures then would otherwise be the case. Staff development programmes might then include members learning to plan together, developing means of curricular integration of content, and evaluating to ascertain the effectiveness of the teaching team. Team teaching has built in inservice education opportunities since members may learn from each other during planning sessions.

Third, cooperative learning, as activities and experiences for pupils to achieve objectives, may need staff development programs. The goals of the staff development programme might stress how to form groups for cooperative learning, how to work effectively as a teacher with diverse groups in the classroom, and how to apprise pupil performance within a group. The classroom teacher needs to believe in cooperative learning for it to become effective in the classroom setting.

There needs to be a caring attitude towards each other in cooperative learning endeavors. Pupils who feel neutral to each other or possess feelings of hostility might well fail to become good members of a committee in cooperative learning endeavors. Noddings (1995) wrote the following:

> The greatest structural obstacle, however, may be simply legitimizing the inclusion of themes of care in the curriculum. Teachers in the early grades have long included such themes as a regular part of their work, and middle school educators are becoming more sensitive to developmental needs involving care. But, secondary schools—where violence, apathy, and alienation are most evident—do little to develop the capacity to care. Today, even elementary teachers complain that the pressure to produce high test scores inhabit the work they believe is central to their mission: the development of competent and caring people. Therefore it would seem that the most fundamental change required is one of attitude. Teachers can be very special people in the lives of children, and it should be legitimate for them to spend time developing relations of trust, talking with students about problems that are central to their lives, and guiding them toward greater sensitivity and competence across all the domains of care.

Fourth, peer coaching may be used to assist teachers to hone and perfect teaching skills in any curriculum area. Two teachers working together may observe each other's teaching and discuss the quality of objectives to be stressed, the aligning of learning opportunities with the objectives, and evaluation to ascertain if the objectives have been achieved by pupils. Showers and Joyce (1996), strong advocates of peer coaching, wrote the following:

> When staff development becomes the major vehicle for school improvement, schools should take into account both the structures and content of training, as well as changes needed in the workplace to make possible the collaborative planning, decision making, and data collection that are essential to organisational change efforts. As we ponder ways to ensure that training/ coaching fuels the school renewal process, we are also examining how the culture of the school can increasingly provide a benign environment for collective activity.
>
> A cohesive school culture makes possible the collective decisions that generate schoolwide improvement efforts. The formation of peer coaching teams produces greater faculty cohesion and focus and, in turn, facilitates more skillful shared decision making. A skillful staff development programme results in a self-perpetuating process for change as well as new knowledge and skills for teachers and increased learning for pupils.

Peer coaching might then be used to improve the quality of learning opportunities for pupils as well as select objectives and evaluation procedures for learners. Learning opportunities (Ediger, 1994) should emphasize that pupils experience:

1. **Meaningful lessons and units of study.** With meaning, pupils understand and comprehend that which was contained in ongoing learning opportunities.

2. **Interesting content and skills in the curriculum.** With interest, the pupil and the curriculum become one, not separate entities. Pupils attend and achieve from ongoing lessons and units of study.

3. **Purpose in learning.** With purpose in learning, pupils accept reasons for attaining relevant facts, concepts, and generalisations presented....

4. **Sequence in learning.** With quality sequence, pupils relate newly acquired content with that previously achieved. Previous knowledge attained provides readiness for the new objectives to be achieved...

5. **Balance among objectives stressed.** Thus, knowledge, skills, and attitudes—three kinds of

objectives need to be achieved by students. These objectives interact and are not in isolation from each other. For example, if pupils possess positive attitudes, they should achieve needed knowledge and skills more readily.

Traditional organisation of learning opportunities stress using textbooks heavily, workbooks, work sheets, and recitation methods of instruction. A separate subjects curriculum tends to be in evidence with traditional approaches in teaching. Moving away from the separate subjects curriculum is correlation, then fusion, and finally the interdisciplinary curriculum. Skill in planning is needed to move away from the usual ways of teaching to that which harmonizes more so with learner growth and development characteristics. Each pupil is to realize optimal development in knowledge, skills and attitudes or the affective dimension. A multimedia approach is recommended in teaching to provide for individual differences.

**Evaluation of Pupil Prograss**

Traditional procedures of evaluating pupil achievement has been to use standardised and norm .referenced testing. Teacher written test items have also been used much in the past to ascertain pupil progress. These procedures are still recommended to determine pupil achievement. However, addition procedures must be used. Teacher observation needs to be used to notice learner progress in contextual situations. Thus, within a given activity, the teacher notices how well each pupil is progressing. Assistance is given to pupils as is necessary. Pupils might then continue to work in context on the project or activity being pursued.

A relatively recent development is for pupils with teacher guidance to develop a portfolio of achievement and progress. In the portfolio the pupil places samples of activities completed. These include written work, at projects, snapshots of construction experiences, videotapes of dramatic endeavors, and cassette recordings of speech activates, among others. The portfolio may also contain test results, journal entries, rating scales, rubrics, and checklists to indicate learner progress and achievement. Materials for the portfolio must be carefully chosen; otherwise it may become too voluminous. Contents in the portfolio are to show interested persons accomplishments of the involved pupil. A variety of learning opportunities experienced by a learner must show its related accomplishments to others who are interested in seeing the individual pupil's achievements.

Kane and Khattri (1995):

> Some questions related to performance assessment remain to be answered by future research. They have to do with basic and secondary issues in educational reform. What knowledge and skills are students expected to domonstrate after a certain period of schooling? What other systematic reforms must be undertaken in order for assessment reforms to be effective? Which assessment formats are most useful for which specific purposes? The greatest challenge ahead lies in designing systems of school reform that synergistically support the core educational functions of teaching and learning for which teachers are the most powerful "engine."

## References

Bloom, Benjamin S. (1956). *Taxonomy of Educational Objectives, Handbook one—Cognitive Domain.* London, England: Longmans Publishing House.

Earnest Vimala (1995). *The relative effectiveness of teaching volumetric experiments in chemistry using Simpson's taxonomy of educational objectives for the psychomotor domain—an experimental study,* Ph.D. Thesis. University of Madras, India, pp. 4-21.

Ediger, Marlow: Simpson Publishing Company, pp. 117-126.

Ediger, Marlow (1994). "Early field experiences in teacher education," *College Student Journal,* 28:302.

Fenstermacher, Gary D. (1995). "The absence of democratic and educational ideals from contemporary educational reforms initiatives," *Educational Horizons,* 73:70.

Kane, Michael B., and Nidh Khattri (1995). "Assessment reform," the *Phi delta kappan*, 77:32.

Krathwohl, David, et al. (1956). *The Taxonomy of Educational Objectives, Handbook two, Affective Domain.* London, England: Longmans Publishing House.

Noddings, Neil (1995). "Teaching themes of care," *Phi delta Kappan.* 76:679.

Showers, Beverly and Bruce Joyce (1996). "The evolution of peer coaching," *Educational Leadership,* 53:16.

# 4

# Collegial Climate in School

Much has been spoken about at teacher education conventions as well as manuscripts published on collegial relationships among teachers. Recommendations are that teachers work together cooperatively with others in curriculum development. Each pupil is to receive the best education possible. To do this, teachers need to work harmoniously with colleagues, parents, the lay public, school administrators, as well as with students. Schools are social institutions with many people working and studying therein. Quality human relations must then be in the offing. There are numerous approaches whereby teachers may work collaboratively with others.

## Team Teaching

Being a member of a teaching team requires collaboration, not competition. The team works together as a unit and for the good of becoming a professional group of educators. Generally, there is a team leader, but this need not necessarily be the case. A team of two to four teachers on a team might well plan for the best objectives for pupils to achieve, quality learning opportunities for pupils to achieve objectives, as well as valid, reliable instruments to evaluate learner achievement. No one here may have been designated as the leader of the team; leadership emerges as the planning moves forward for implementation. Situational leadership is then being emphasised.

If a leader is designated for the teaching team, he/she might receive extra salary for duties encountered. The designated leader chairs all or almost all of the sessions involved to plan for instruction. The leader assists participants to work together well with each other and participate actively in the planning sessions. Each team member has responsibilities in teaching/assisting in large group sessions, committee endeavors, as well as in individual projects and activities. The team determines the objectives, learning opportunities, and appraisal procedures for a given set of pupils.

The teaching team must be able to reach consensus, if possible, in the decision-making arena. A good leader is able to secure the participation of all members of a team. Feelings of belonging and security are felt by team members. The talents of each member are recognised and used. Esteem needs are then being met. Team members are to become knowledgeable in planning for and implementing procedures for instruction. Knowledge about quality teaching together with the ability and skills to interact positively with others is needed for team members to function well. Friction among team members hinders effective participation by all in planning for instruction.

The strengths of each team member should be used in team teaching be it in large group, committee, or individual endeavors. Team teaching then strongly emphasizes using abilities and skills of each member to do the best job possible of teaching.

We will state three advantages and disadvantages of using collegial methods of instruction in team teaching. The advantages are:

1. More than one mind should be better than one mind in planning for instruction.
2. Team members have a chance to learn from each other, as compared to a single teacher in the self-contained room. In planning sessions; built in inservice education is then inherent.

3. Weakness may be minimised among team members when using the talents of teachers to teach in large group, committee, or individual pupil endeavors.

Weaknesses are the following:

1. Members may disagree strongly on educational philosophy and psychology to the point that a unified team is not possible.
2. Authoritarian persons hinders a team from stressing that all participate in planning objectives, learning activities, and evaluation procedures.
3. Team members have not learned to work together in planning and teaching sessions.

There are numerous areas of collegiality for teachers, and other school personnel to participate in. Hoerr (1996) wrote:

> Sufficient time must be allocated for collegiality. Whether the time comes before school or after school meetings, at lunch time, over dinner, at evening meetings, or on weekends depends on a given faculty's availability and preference. When is unimportant. The important thing is that teachers and administrators meet frequently enough and for sufficiently long periods to enable them to discuss their educational philosophies, long term issues, and ways they can work together....
>
> Once the time for collegiality has been carved out, someone—perhaps the principal, initially—needs to set an agenda and focus the discussion. Collegiality stems from discussions about students, instruction, and curriculum, and such discussions take significant chunks of time...
>
> Change is best viewed as a series of concentric circles, starting small and expanding. Inviting everyone to participate at the start is importan. From this beginning, a nucleus of interested teachers will no doubt emerge—people who are willing to take risks, to look at their roles differently, and to get involved with schoolwide issues...
>
> But principals need to realize that, if teachers are going to invest their time and energy, they need to be heard and to make a difference on substantive issues...

## School-University Collaboration

Public schools and university educators need to work together in curriculum development. Thus public school teachers have opportunities to influence the direction of courses taught on the campus, field experiences provide by the university for future teachers, as well as student teaching and internship experiences. University personnel have opportunities to bring in new ideas in elementary and secondary school teaching. They can provide assistance in workshops, faculty meetings, and staff development programmes in the public schools. Both the public school teachers as well as university personnel have their knowledge and skills available to guide in developing a quality curriculum for public school pupils.

Public school teachers have their practical skills to share in collaborating with university professors of education. They are engaged in the actual planning for and teaching of pupils. These teachers have experienced the every day interactions with pupils. How to organize for instruction, how to group learners for teaching and learning, as well as how to work in the area of discipline has been the role and lot of public school classroom teachers. University professors of education tend to be well versed in the theory, philosophy, and psychology of teaching pupils. They tend to deal more with the abstractness of learning as compared to the concrete situations of present day classroom teaching. Both need to interact with each other to share experiences and grow thereform. Clark (1996) wrote the following pertaining to collaboration:

> ...collaboration programme should focus on the major areas of staff development/inservice training, curriculum revision, upgrading, instructional materials and equipment, and improving educational management—all central to developing a responsive academic and vocational education delivery system.

### *Advantages of school-university collaboration*

1. Both may receive new perspectives in teaching pupils.

2. Growth and development of public school teachers and university professors may be enhanced while learning from each other.

3. New ideas in curriculum improvement may be an end result.

*Disadvantages*

1. There might be too much of superior/subordinate feelings in the relationship.

2. Time may be a crucial factor in working together. A suitable time for both might be difficult to come by due to distance as well as other inservice programmes in operation, particularly in the public schools.

3. Increased stress being placed on collaboration might hinder working together harmoniously with so many different groups.

**Pupils and Cooperative Learning**

There are educators who claim high pupil achievement when teachers guide pupils in working on committee endeavors. When pupils work in teams, they share ideas and learn from each other. The shared ideas may come from a variety of learning opportunities involving problem solving. Learners of diverse ability levels are serving in a group experience. Thus, heterogeneous grouping is involved. The teacher serves as a guide and stimulator to encourage pupil learning. Pupils learning to work together well becomes a major objectives of instruction. Advocates of cooperative learning quote much research to corroborate their thinking on assisting pupils to attain well in school.

Advocates of cooperative learning believe that stressing pupils working together on projects and activities will make for better cooperation later when individuals are employed at the workplace. They emphasize the importance of harmoniously working together as indicated by employees and managers in the world of work. The ability to cooperate and work together on joint enterprises are salient concepts to emphasize in cooperative learning.

*Advantages*

Advantages given for cooperative learning endeavours are the following:

1. Life consists of many group endeavors be it at the work-place or in recreational social situations.
2. Pupils needs to work and play well with other presently since continuous progress is needed in the area of quality human relations.
3. Individuals should be able to work well with others since strife, hostility, hatred, and other forms of negative social behavior hinder more optimal learner achievement in all facets of life.

*Disadvantages*

Disadvantages of heavily stressing cooperative learning in the school curriculum include:

1. Pupils individually possess different learning styles; working individually on an assignment is a favorite learning style of pupils.
2. There should not be an either-or dichotomy in organizing for instruction. Thus, it is not either working cooperatively or individually, but both may well be stressed in teaching and earning situations.
3. It is extremely difficult to appraise learner progress when a group or committee is being evaluated for progress on learning.

Ediger (1994) wrote the following pertaining to questions raised by pupils after a set of slides had been shown in unit teaching:

> Pupils appeared to possess high enthusiasm for studying the new social studies unit as evidenced by the questions raised and

> interest shown. Discipline problems here were nonexistent. Learners guided by the student teacher and the cooperating teacher brainstormed possible hypotheses for answers to each of these five questions. The list of hypotheses was quite long and covered two class periods of time devoted to teaching the social studies. Rules followed in brainstorming were to not duplicate on ideas presented previously, nor to place value judgements on hypotheses presented. Each hypothesis was written on the chalkboard. If an hypothesis was not clear to pupils, clarification of responses were asked for.

Pupils were then asked by the student teacher which committee they would like to serve on when thinking of testing the hypotheses given by pupils for one of the five problems areas listed above, during the brainstorming sessions...

Leadership emerged within each committee; no one was designated as the chairperson. Pupils were to stay on the topic when securing data sources. Each was to have ample opportunities to use relevant sources of information. Respect for each learner within a committee was a must. Each committee discussed information sources to test hypotheses for their chosen problem area. Learners seemed to be quite knowledgeable to where to look to find needed information. In evaluating committee endeavors of learners, the following appear salient:

1. Enthusiasm for learning was high.
2. Pupils enjoyed brainstorming methods of teaching.
3. Acquisition of subject matter followed pupil purpose in that learners were heavily involved in choosing facts, concepts, and generalisations to attain.
4. Pupil attitudes were positive throughout the unit which stressed problem solving. Critical thinking was necessary when accepting or not accepting information in answer to problems.
5. Creative thinking during brainstorming emphasised novelty and uniqueness of ideas. Positive affect was an end result when learners developed their very own responses.

## Working Collaboratively in School Research

Numerous educators emphasize the importance of teachers and university personnel working collaboratively on educational research. The research conducted generally pertains to action research whereby problems in the local school setting are identified and solutions sought. University personnel need to be highly knowledgeable of research design and statistical procedures. Public school teachers work on the "firing line" in actual teaching and learning situations. The action research would then be conducted in the public school setting with its practical problems that arise. Answers to problems and questions would be sought through appropriate methodology in research. Cooperative endeavors need to be involved including university professors and public school teachers in conducting the research. Teachers might then learn from university professors in methodology in conducting research. Professors may learn more about the school curriculum and problems encountered in teaching pupils.

### *Advantages*

Advantages of cooperative endeavors in conducting action research include the following:

1. Public school personnel and university professors may learn from each other pertaining to curricular problems as well as research procedures. Curriculum and research become one, not separate entities.

2. The concrete with its objective, learning opportunities, and appraisal procedures is integrated with the abstract including its research design and statistical procedures of treating data.

3. Practical curricular problems might be solved or minimised with action research.

### *Diadvantages*

Disadvantages of conducting action research involving public school teachers/university professors include the following:

1. Public school teachers might feel minimised due a lack of knowledge pertaining to conducting action research. A hierarchy of university professors being "superior" to pupil school teachers may be difficult to ameliorate.

2. Democratic atmospheres might be difficult to implement when higher education and public school personnel attempt to harmonize efforts in curriculum improvement.

3. Public school teachers may find it difficult to spend much time on conducting research since they have little time during the school day to spend on research endeavors. Staff development programmes, inservice education and faculty meetings also take considerable time from the teacher's total hours in a day.

Pertaining to challenges involving school-university partnership, Swanson wrote:

> The second challenge of all the partnerships encountered is the need to develop professional expertise and self esteem among all educators. By definition, systematic reform requires managing multiple reform efforts simultaneously. As a result, extensive professional development is needed for both university- and school-base educators in a number of subject matter areas: subject matter knowledge, pedagogy, understanding of the change process, and leadership skills.

## A Common Vision and Consensus

All educators need to have a vision of *what might be* in education. Thus, there is a feeling that the school is achieving at a certain level but should attain at a more optimal rate. It is good to possess visions and dreams of the ideal and strive in that direction. One might, of course, never achieve the ideal, but the desire to do so is there. There are diverse philosophies of education that make for diversity such as problem solving, subject centered curricula, decision-making strategies, and the measurement movement whereby pupils are to attain predetermined educational objectives. These schools of thought disagree from each other in terms of what pupils are to attain and which kinds of learning opportunities should be in the offing. Then too there are various psychologies of learning that teachers, administrators, and support personnel believe in. Humanists believe in pupils making choices as to what to learn as well as the means of learning. They tend to stress a psychological curriculum for learners. Pupils then order or sequence their own experiences with teacher guidance. Behaviorists advocate a logical curriculum in which the learning opportunities are arranged by the teacher(s) in ascending order of complexity so that measurable objectives are attained by pupils.

Even though there are diverse philosophies and psychologies of instruction, there needs to be common ground in which a vision appears as to *what should be* in education. Or should there be multiple beliefs in terms of what the goals of the school should be?

It takes much study and knowledge to come up with a theory of the ideal to which a school needs to strive. Ignorance and bliss should not be the rule here, but rather study, thought, and evaluation of educational content and the school curriculum should result increasingly so in experts power or knowledgeable people making decisions.

***Advantages***

There are advantages in having a common vision pertaining to *what should be* in an ideal school. These are the following:

1. School personnel basically agree on what pupils should learn and achieve. Basic agreements or pupils K-12 can incorporate quality scope, sequence, and continuity.
2. The basics in the curriculum may receive the attention that is needed.
3. Conflicting objectives have less chance of being implemented.

***Disadvantages***

1. Teachers become conformists rather than creative thinkers.

2. People think differently; therefore there will be differences in visions perceived by educational personnel.

3. Whose vision is to prevail? Should teachers or administrators have their say so largely, in curriculum matters? What role do parents play here?

Sometimes diversity is prized highly in education. Diversity is necessary so that a broad curriculum is available to provide for differences among learners.

**In Summary**

Speakers and writers communicate ideas frequently on the necessity of collaborative endeavors involving school personnel. Collaborative endeavors are then necessary to achieve a quality curriculum for pupils. These collaborative endeavors include, among others, team teaching, school-university collegiality, cooperative learning for pupils, research performed cooperatively by public schools and university personnel, and stressing a common vision for schools and school districts.

Toward the other end of the continuum is individual choices to be made by involved persons. Existentialism as a philosophy of education emphasizes the individual mking choices in an openended environment. The individual teacher then may or may not wish to be a member of a teaching team. Those teachers desiring to do so would engage in improving the curriculum through university collaboration. We believe that in a classroom, an increased emphasis might be placed on existentialism as a philosophy of education. Here, a learning stations approach in teaching may be stressed. There needs to be an adequate number of stations with each having enough tasks so that individual pupils may choose which to complete and which to omit. The pupil is the chooser, not the teacher. The teacher is a guide, a stimulator, and a motivator. There needs to be an adequate number of tasks so that a psychological curriculum is in evidence. Learners then sequence their very own learning opportunities. Sequence resides within the pupil in learning, not the teacher. A second approach here might be to have teacher/pupil planning of objectives, learning activities, and evaluation techniques. Thus, the teacher plans with each pupil that which the latter desires to learn. A third approach includes use of contracts. Here, the pupil with teacher guidance determines what to study. The agreement here is put into contract form, dated and signed by pupil and teacher. The due date for fulfilling the contract is also written in the agreement. The pupil has heavy input in term of what he/she wishes to study and learn.

Disadvantages for each of the above named plans of collaboration need to be appraised. Weaknesses of each plan diagnosed may then become a focal point in attempting to make necessary modifications. The modifications might well minimize selected weaknesses. For example, team teaching may have members of a team who disagree much on educational philosophy and psychology to teaching. If team members viewed this situation as opportunities for growth rather than hostility, disagreements might become healthy and make room for thinking skills and better human relations. Individuals might desire to volunteer to be members of teams thus taking care of problems, in degrees, of human relations. Krajewski (1996) wrote the following pertaining to problems faced in the school setting:

> All problems should be viewed as opportunities, and each solution brings more challenging opportunities. Generally, decisions made as close to the implementation levels possible provide a sharper focus and a broader input base. Be a facilitator; exciting things can happen with good guidance. Let go; let your ideas fly.
>
> Recently, I visited a school where teachers claim to have the decision-making power and consider the principal to be "just around," And he was around—around the classrooms, the lounge, and the library. He felt the entire school was his office and, in a soft spoken voice, he used gentile methods and warm praise to celebrate the excellence of the school and its staff.

The above quote indicates that problems are there to be identified and solved. Problems should not be there to shy away from difficulties encountered, be it the teachers or the principal of the school.

As a further example pertaining to weaknesses of a plan, in conducting school research in the public schools with university personnel involved, there may be attempts in stressing democratic tenets in collaborative endeavors. As a team, public school teachers and university professors have as a major goal respecting each other in research designs developed and implemented. Inservice education here for public school teachers, in particular, could assist in bridging gaps in research knowledge. Furthermore, the roles of teachers and professors could be clearly defined. The role of teachers would pertain to organizing their classroom for detailed involvement in the research whereas university personnel would provide expertise on the plan of the research study, statistical treatment of data, and general knowledge and skills in conducting research. At the same time, teachers and researchers learn from each other.

In many cases, the weaknesses mentioned for each plan of collegiality discussed above may be diagnosed and remedied.

## References

Clark, Donald (1996). "Industry—Education Collaboration that Works." *The Educational Digest,* 31: 60-63.

Ediger, Marlow (1994). "Social Studies and the Affective Dimension," *Journal of Instructional Psychology*. 21: 220.

Hoerr, Thomas R. (1996). "Collegiality" *Phi Delta Kappan,* 77:381.

Krajewski, Bob (1996). "Enculturing the School: The Principal's Principles, *National Association Secondary School Principals' Bulletin*. 80:5 and 6.

Swansons, Judy (1996). "Systematic Reform in the Professionalism of Educators", *Phi Delta Kappan,* 77:38.

# 5

# Quality in the Multicultural Curriculum Excellence and Equity

It is vital to have quality in the multicultural curriculum. Excellence and equity are also necessary ingredients. To have the concepts of quality, excellence, and equity, there are vital components to emphasize in curriculum development. The curriculum needs to be planned thoughtfully and carefully with each learner achieving as much as possible. The objectives section is of prime importance. There needs to be rational balance among knowledge, skills, and affective ends. Knowledge objectives need careful consideration in that they contain salient structural ideas. These ideas when achieved by students provide major generalisations for student use in relating new ideas thereto. The generalisations need to be accurate and provide much information on diverse cultures. Subordinate contain achieved might then be related to the main ideas.

Skills objectives emphasize students applying knowledge in useful situations. Thus, students should use information on many cultures when working together with others of diverse races and creeds. There are a plethora of useful skills to stress by students when working harmoniously together. Acceptance, critical and creative thinking, problem solving, and hands on approaches in learning are vital.

Attitudinal objectives emphasize feelings that one person has toward others and is exemplified with empathy, helpfulness, wanting to learn from others, kindness, and thoughtfulness (Ediger, 2002, 7-10).

**Learning Opportunities to Achieve Objectives**

A variety of learning opportunities need to be used to assist students to achieve objectives in multicultural education. These learning opportunities need to be developmental and provide for individual differences. Students and the teacher need to discuss proper attitudes toward others of diverse racial groups. These standards should be listed and posted in the classroom. Referring to these standards is a must to notice classroom climate and individual achievement in attitudes.

Reading experiences are highly significant to emphasize. Books need to be available on a variety of topics dealing with diverse cultures. Also, they must be on the reading level of the involved reader. The student might choose which book(s) to read sequentially. He/she may also select the assessment procedure used to ascertain progress. Many will wish to have a conference with the classroom teacher to discuss ideas read. There are diverse ways for student use to show achievement from having read a book. The teacher may discuss discussion possibilities with pupils. Adequate stress should be placed upon a set of readers having read the same paperback on current issues in racism. The teacher will want to assess student achievement on attitudes toward people of other races. Hopefully, continual improvement will be shown. The ideal is to accept others as equals in all situations. Books for students to read might include the following:

- Clements, Andrew (2002), The Jacket. New York: Simon and Schuster for Young Readers.
- Green, Jan (2000), Talking About Racism. Austin, Texas: Steck-Vaughn Company.
- Katz, Karen (1999), The Colors of Us. New York: Henry Holt and Company.

- Mitchell, Lori (1999), Different Just Like Me, Watertown, Massachusetts: Charlesbridge Publishing Company.
- Monk, Isabell (1999), Hope. Minneapolis: Caroirhoda Books.
- Parks, Rosa (1992), Rosa Parks, My Story. New York: Dial Books.
- Torres, Leyla (1993), Subway Sparrow. New York: Farrar, Straus, and Giroux.
- Wyeth, Sharon (1998), Tomboy Trouble. New York: Random House.

A special section in the library should house reference books for teachers to use in teaching about racism and multicultural education.

Daily newspaper and weekly news magazines may be used to read articles and discuss problems in equity in society, be it in jobs, housing, education, wages, and salaries. Inequities need identification and issues discussed freely. Here is where respect for each student and his/her ideas are important. A fair, open place for each committee's discussion must be in the offing. Biases need to be addressed and solutions sought through problem solving. Minority groups, in particular, must feel that they are being listened to and accepted. Criteria, listed on the chart, for treating each person fairly need to be referred to periodically. Students need guidance to assess the self in emphasizing growth toward being accepting of individuals and groups of diverse racial groups.

Students need to study units dealing with other cultural groups in the nation. For example, committees may be formed to develop indepth studies of the Old Order Amish whose value system is quite different from other subcultures in the United States. Each committee then may choose to inquire about a certain facet of Old Order Amish culture, such as in the following categories:

- **Means of transportation.** The use of horse and buggy or carriage is emphasised instead of the modern automobile.

- **Means of earning a living.** Amish formerly farmed, but due to scarcity of farm land, many go into other kinds of work. These kinds of work include carpentering; construction work; carpet laying; as well as weaving beautiful blankets, place mats, rugs, and carpets using scrap materials only or largely.

- **Cottage industries are salient.** Making carriages, harnesses, and horse collars; sewing aesthetically pleasing blankets for selling; baking cakes, roles, cookies, bread, and dough nuts; making candy, for example, one Amish owned candy factory employs eight women of their own faith making 500 pounds of peanut clusters, 800 pounds of bon bons, and 500 pounds of peanut brittle each day. A truck hauls the candy each day to places of selling.

- Farming is done with draft horses which pull ploughs for ploughing the fields, disks for disking the farm land, and a drill for seeding the crops. These scenes may be compared with those of modern farming operations (Ediger, 2001, 743-751). Internet sources are excellent for obtaining information on the Old Order Amish.

Students need to develop interest in and be accepting of other cultures. These cultures may be highly unique such as the Old Order Amish. All people need respect, acceptance, and a realisation of how needs are alike of all peoples such food, clothing, and shelter. How needs are met may vary from culture to culture.

Different patterns of grouping may be used in teaching students of diverse racial groups. It is good to have in each group students of diverse racial groups. This presents excellent opportunities to learn from each other and practice desirable behaviors of acceptance toward others. Homogeneous grouping emphasizes uniformity of achievement in what is to be studied. Heterogeneous grouping stresses students being of mixed achievement levels. Both may be emphasised in ongoing units of instruction. A major goal here is to have students learn from each other as well as develop positive attitudes. Satisfying experiences among racial groups are musts! Sometimes, each student may work on an individual project or activity. With different learning styles inherent among students some may prefer to work by the self at times. At other times, small group and collaborative experiences may be preferred. Individual differences and needs must be met in a harmonious manner among students of different racial groups. Approaches in grouping practices must be kept flexible.

A variety of activities assists students to achieve as optimally as possible. Construction projects, art experiences, and dramatic activities emphasize a hands on approach to learning whereas reading and writing stress abstract experiences. Multiple intelligences theory stresses that there are a plethora of intelligences possessed by students and one size does not fit all. These intelligences possessed may be stronger in one area individually and include the following:

- Verbal/linguistic with emphasis upon reading and writing. Each student needs opportunities to read subject matter on famous leaders, past and present, involving those from different racial groups;
- Visual/space with art products and processes showing student achievement in learning about people from diverse cultures;
- Logical/mathematics in which learners may reason and think logically about solving problems between/among selected racial groups;
- Musical/rhythmical whereby students learn to sing and compose music pertaining to specific racial groups. Dance activities are also salient in the rhythmic realm;

- Intrapersonal in which a student pursues tasks individually as compared to interpersonal intelligence whereby learners desire to work collaboratively on a group project;
- Bodily/kinesthetic involve experiences pertaining to physical prowess as in quality athletic and game skills. Here, learners may achieve in learning to play games and sports endeavors of other cultures;
- Scientific which emphasizes objectivity and develops skills in objective thinking as in science activities (See Gardner, 1993).

In each of the above named multiple intelligence learning opportunities, students need to grow in working harmoniously with individuals of diverse racial groups. Showing respect toward other learners is of utmost importance. Being members of heterogeneous racial groups with stress placed on goal attainment must be emphasised. There are a plethora of learning opportunities stressing multiple intelligences.

Journal writing harmonizes well with multiple intelligences theory of learning as well as in providing for individual differences. Each student is owner of personal journal writing being stressed. The contents of a journal may contain personal impressions of what was learned in a given lesson or unit of study. Thus, in a news clipping discussed in class, the student may write about discrimination in salaries between men and women paid in the workplace as well as among diverse racial groups. By writing content in the journal, the student has a better chance to assess involved problems. Directly related to journal writing is a slightly more structured approach such as writing diary entries. The diary entries are dated and a student may record on a daily basis what was learned, for example, about Rosa Parks and Martin Luther King, Jr., which was not known before.

Portfolio development by a student with teacher guidance may supplement information from state mandated tests to reveal learner achievement. In the portfolio, the following products and processes, selected at random, may be filed by a student:

- Book report written, such as on Caesar Chavez, a leader in obtaining migrant worker rights.
- Diorama made on Mexican workers coming into the United States and doing impoverished kinds of low paying work. Considerable research needs to be done in planning for the diorama. If the product is too large for containment in a port folio, a related snapshot may substitute.
- A mural may be made of crowded older buildings in a slum area and being replaced with modern updated structures.
- Use of software and computer assistance having simulation content on racism involving minority students problems in choosing a profession, finishing requirements, and then looking for a workplace position (Ediger, 1997).

**Evaluation of Achievement**

There should be a variety of means used to appraise student achievement. Teacher observation with the use of recommended criteria needs adequate emphasis. The teacher may observe rather continuously how each learner is improving his attitudes toward other races and cultures. The observational results may be used to improve sequence in learning, remedy deficiencies in knowledge and skills obtained, and as well as objectives to be stressed in teaching.

Teacher self evaluation is salient to use. Approximately ten criteria may be listed with the teacher responding to each using a five point Lickert Scale. Items to be listed for the self evaluation might well include the following:

- I try to understand each student's cultural needs.
- I try to treat each student fairly and equitably.

- I try to learn as much as possible about racial injustices.
- I try to be a model to students in class in revealing respect for all peoples.

Essay test items may be used to appraise learner achievement. Results from the essay test should be used to improve student knowledge, skills, and attitudes in accepting individuals of other racial groups. Essay test items need to be written clearly so students understand what is wanted. There needs to be definite objectives which the teacher wishes to assess pertaining to learner achievement in improved racial attitudes.

Classroom discussions may be used to appraise student participation. Within the discussion, students may reveal understandings, skills, and attitudes pertaining to subject matter learned, feelings generated, and eagerness to learn about issues and problems pertaining to race in society.

Committee endeavors may be appraised in terms of effort put forth by participants, acceptance of peers, and democratic procedures used. The committees need to work in the direction of having good human relations.

Construction and art projects may be assessed in terms of neatness, understanding of inherent ideas, and uses made of the completed products. The quality of interaction among committee members is very important to assess.

Problem solving may be appraised in terms of relevancy of identified problems, motivation in working toward solutions, and cooperation shown in working with peers.

Critical thinking may be assessed in terms of indepth perception of ideas, as well as relating ideas gleaned and applied to other thought situations. Appreciation of obtaining carefully thought through ideas should improve attitudes among the races.

Creative thinking may be assessed in terms of growth in this area of the student's total development. An increase in novel, unique and originality of ideas need to be forthcoming.

## References

Ediger, Marlow (2001), "Studying the Old Order Amish," *Education,* 121(14), 743-751.

Ediger, Marlow (2002), "Measurement Theory Versus Constructivism. *Journal of Research in Education,* 1(1), 7-10.

Ediger, Marlow (1997), *Teaching Reading and the Language Arts.* Kirksville, Missouri: Simpson Publishing Company.

Gardner, Howard (1993), *Multiple Intelligences: Theory into Practice.* New York: Basic Books.

# 6

# Intrinsic Versus Extrinsic Motivation

There is still much debate pertaining to motivating students in reading achievement. Thus, should students feel motivated from within or intrinsic motivation? Or, is it better to have extrinsic motivation whereby external stimuli are used to help learners to achieve more optimally in reading? This paper will attempt to analyze the two points of view when motivating student progress in reading achievement.

## Intrinsic Motivation in Reading

Intrinsic motivation is an ideal whereby from within the student is desiring to do more reading and at an increased level of difficulty. A model to present here is individualised reading. With individualised reading instruction, the teacher needs to have an maple supply of library books in the classroom from which each student may choose what to read sequentially. The learner is the chooser, not the teacher of the individual books a student wishes to read.

Library books need to be on different topics or genres. Why? Students possess different interests in what is chosen to be read. A wide variety of subject matter must then be available for student reading. Interest is a powerful factor in learning. With interest, effort is put forth in reading and learning. In addition to interesting library books which may be selected sequentially for individual reading, the student may also make choices based on his/her present reading achievement level. A student then may read more complex levels of library books, than others, due to possessing increased skills to identify words in context as well as being able to process more complex information. The act of reading requires students individually to be fluent in word recognition and comprehension (Ediger, 2000, Chapter Four).

After reading a library book, the student may have a conference with the teacher to assess knowledge acquired, skills developed, as well as attitudes revealed from having read a library book. Information may be recorded by the teacher when making comparisons with the next conference to be held to notice learner progress and achievement. The conferences are informal and should add to developing interest for student reading. Obstacles need to be put aside when encouraging learner interest in reading. Intrinsic motivation is then involved in a quality reading curriculum (see Ediger, 1994, 178-180). Advocates of intrinsic motivation in reading minimize the following:

1. Formal testing to notice achievement. These may include standardised and state mandated testing which advocates feel may decrease interest by the student in reading.

2. Required textbooks whereby all students in a classroom read the same sequential stories regardless of learner interests and abilities.

3. A philosophy of sameness for all students in the reading curriculum with a "one size fits all" set of beliefs.

### Testing to Motivate Reading Achievement

The testing and measurement movement is strong in desiring to have extrinsic motivators to increase student reading achievement. State legislators, the governor, and state departments of education officials wish to document how well students are doing in reading. To document reading achievement, state mandated testing needs to be in the offing for all students. Each state mandated test needs to have accompanying objectives of instruction. These objectives, available to teachers, provide direction in terms of what is to be taught. The tests are aligned with these objectives so that validity is possible in testing, meaning that students have had access to learnings related to the test items.

To obtain reliability, pilot studies need to be made to take the kinks and weaknesses out of the test items. Vague, hazy test items might then be eliminated from the test. Test/retest, alternate forms, and/or split half reliability data from pilot study results provide information on how consistently the state mandated test measures learner achievement (See Ediger, 2000, 22-31).

Problems in state mandated testing might well be the following:

1. They may not be valid unless the teacher has a copy of the related objectives of instruction and follows them religiously in teaching students.

2. They provide a test score only, to show student achievement in reading.

3. They do not provide adequate information from student test results to use in diagnosis and remediation.

4. They generally stress use of multiple choice test items which are highly factual in their writing.

5. They do not provide opportunities for students to be creative in responding to test items.

State mandated tests omit completely what students have achieved on a day to day basis in reading or how well students do in reading in life like, functional situations.

Motivation in desiring to become a good reader comes from extrinsic sources due to state departments of education having cut off points in order for students to be successful achievers in reading. Which extrinsic motivational devices are used to spur students on to become better readers and teachers to do a better job of teaching reading?

1. Publishing report cards in the media whereby a state compares different school district's achievement in reading, among other curriculum areas. Comparisons are then made among school districts, making it competitive to out do others in the curriculum.

2. Threats of state takeover of a school/district if student achievement is at an unacceptable rate.

3. Withholding of state moneys for those school districts having low student achievement.

4. Paying teachers based on student test achievement, a form of merit pay.

5. Taking away teacher tenure if test results of students are continually low. This may be carried one notch further with teacher dismissal for low student achievement.

6. Teacher accountability rules whereby a teacher is accountable for have students achieve state mandated objectives by doing well on the related tests.

7. Withholding high school diplomas in high stakes testing if students fall below the level of receiving a pass mark.

8. Not permitting a student to pass to the next sequential level of schooling if he/she fails a state mandated grade level test.

9. The teacher giving candy and other rewards to students who met a predetermined standard in class, generally determined through a cut off point on a teacher written test.

10. Educational bankruptcy laws in which a state can declare a school or school district bankrupt in school achievement. Actions are then taken by the state to remedy deficiencies.

Each of the ten listed times above deal with external forces in a state to improve what is perceived to be deficient on the local school level. Extrinsic motivation is then used to manage the curriculum in order that schools improve in teaching students. Extrinsic motivation is used to motivate students, teachers, and administrators to do better than what has been achieved previously in teaching and learning situations.

**Intrinsic Motivation and Reading Instruction**

Intrinsic motivation depends upon the learner from within wishing to dc more reading. Ideally, there is no compulsion here. Learners select reading materials to read sequentially based on person interest and effort to consume that which is interesting and meaningful. The teacher, of course, needs to assist in motivating students to do more reading. The following are methods of motivation:

1. Develop a neat, attractive bulletin board for all to see. The contents of the bulletin board has a caption, illustrations, print discourse under each illustration, and new library book jackets displayed at intervals. Bulletin board displays need to be changed at different times to develop and maintain student interest in reading.

2. Introduce new books in the library by telling something interesting about its contents to students. Show illustrations in the library book as interesting items in the story being shared.

3. Read aloud sections of a library book to whet student appetites for reading its contents.

4. Have selected students participate in reader's theater in order to motive learners to read the contents of the involved library book.

5. Let students individually indicate interesting library books to others in class by pantomiming selected sections of a book.

6. Organize a few students to engage in creative dramatics in front of the class to encourage reading of the book being dramatised.

7. Encourage peers to read aloud to each other in small groups to motivate interest in reading that book.

8. Use peer teaching to introduce new library books to others within a group setting.

9. Use committee endeavors to discuss library books read and to stimulate each other to do more reading.

10. Have teacher aids read to students using appropriate methods to encourage reading see also Cunningham and Allington 1999).

There are a plethora of approaches which may be used to motivate students intrinsically to engage in reading. With intrinsic motivation psychology, the reading teacher desires to have students want to read and realize how interesting the act of reading can be. The home needs encouragement to have materials available for student reading. Also, parents need to read to themselves as a model for student emulation. The school setting might wish to model reading by emphasizing Sustained Silent Reading (SSR). Here, at designated times, everyone in a school reads to themselves. This provides a further model for student emulation. From within the student then observes and participates in numerous reading activities and experiences.

**Extrinsic Motivation in Reading**

With extrinsic motivation in teaching reading, the teacher plays a key role in the classroom. This is in addition to state mandated testing and its external procedures stressed in developing better readers. Thus, the reading teacher may use the following to raise the bar in reading achievement:

1. Have high expectations with increasingly complex measurably stated reading objectives for student attainment.

2. Reward students for achieving at a certain specific level in attaining the measurably stated objectives. The rewards may consist of inexpensive prizes, tokens to

exchange for these prizes, a longer recess period, and a popcorn party toward the end of the school day for award winners, among others.

3. Test and measure frequently with teacher written tests. Upping test scores should be a motivator for students.

4. Assist students to develop line graphs showing progress in reading achievement. Seeing the line go up on the graph should be a motivator for students to achieve higher level objectives.

5. Give a certificate to each student for having read a certain number of library books per week or biweekly. Standards are to be announced ahead of time so that each student may know how many books to read to obtain a certificate.

6. Place a happy face or sticker for each item answered correctly from a workbook page in reading.

7. Give praise to a student answering a reading compression questions correctly covering content from the basal reader.

8. Provide carefully guided reading instruction to keep students on task and achieving optimally in ongoing reading lessons.

9. Emphasize the use of teacher written worksheets to check reading comprehension each day. Inked rubber stamps may be used to stamp achievement on each sheet for students doing exceptionally well when responding to worksheet items.

10. Stress doing well in reading with slogans placed on the classroom wall to encourage student to do well in learning to read. These external approaches are to motivate student reading.

## Closing

Most reading teachers will use a combination of intrinsic and extrinsic devices (see Ediger, 1999, 222-228) to motivate student reading achievement. However, selected teachers will lean more toward the intrinsic motivation psychology than others, as well as vice versa. Teachers need to experiment with both and decide which approach works best in motivating reading achievement. Perhaps, Learning Styles Theory (see Searson and Dunn (2001) will help to decide which students do better with either intrinsic or extrinsic approaches of motivation in reading achievement. Multiple Intelligences Theory might also help determine how students wish to show how much as well as what has been learned in reading. Testing then may not be the only procedure (see Gardner, 1993).

## References

Cunningham, P.M., and R.L. Allington (1999), *Classrooms That Work: They Can All Read and Write.* New York: Longmans.

Ediger, Marlow (1999), "The Principal, Teachers, and the Philosophy of Education," *Experiments in Education,* 27 (12), 222-228.

Ediger Marlow and Digumarti Bhaskara Rao (2000), *Teaching Reading Successfully.* New Delhi, India: Discovery Publishing House, Chapter Four.

Ediger, Marlow (1994), "The School Administrator and Curricular Concerns," *The Progress of Education,* 73 (8), 178-180.

Ediger, Marlow (2000), "Portfolios and the Middle School Student," *Michigan Middle School Journal,* 24 (2), 22-31.

Gardner, Howard (1993), *Multiple Intelligences: Theory Into Practice.* New York: Basic Books.

Searson, Robert, and Rita Dunn (2001), "The Learning Styles Teaching Model," *Science and Children,* 39 (5), 22-26.

# 7

# Perspectives in Counseling

The school counselor needs to be a caring person that desires the best for each pupil. A caring counselor assists learners to attain optimally in knowledge, skills, and attitudes in the school curriculum. Concern for pupil achievement in all facets of development is an ideal. The ideal must be emphasised as much as possible. Ideals become objectives to attain. Activities and experiences need to be in the offing to guide in attaining goals. A quality programme of evaluation should be stressed to assess how well goals have been achieved.

## Counselor Perspectives

The pupil becomes the focal point in implementing the curriculum. Guiding optimal learner progress then becomes the number one objective in the perspective of the counselor. Counselors must work harmoniously with teachers and administrators to emphasize this goal. A leadership role by the school counselor is needed to stress faculty members and the principal working on common goals emphasizing learner optimal progress.

A workshop conducted by the school counselor may aid in developing a needed perspective to assist pupils achieving as much as possible individually and within committee settings. A suitable theme for the workshop needs to be chosen. The theme may well stress guiding optimal pupil achievement. An open-ended approach might then be in evidence in determining sequence in the workshop. Thus, in the general session, participants may identify relevant problems for solution that stress assisting learners to attain optimally. The following are examples of problems that participants in the workshop may select for solving;

1. How to determine present levels of achievement of each learner so that an appropriate sequence of instruction can be emphasised.

2. When to use different psychologies of learning such as behaviorism, humanism, and/or gestalt schools of thought in the educational psychology arenas.

3. Where in the instructional sequence to emphasize problem solving, measurably stated objectives, projects methods of teaching, and idea or subject centered curriculum, and a learning centers philosophy of instruction.

4. Which approach to appraising learner progress would be most effective? Included would be the testing and measuring procedures, portfolio methods, subjective methods (these could incorporate rating scales, check lists, discussion quality, and committee work criteria), as well as teacher observation of learner progress.

5. How to meet individual needs of pupils. Here, participants may which to examine new programmes of education which assists in providing for individual differences among pupils.

The needs of workshop members must be considered thoroughly when choosing problem areas for consideration by participants. At the same time the guidance counselor assists workshop participants to clarify problems selected in terms of recommended psychologies of learning. By following desired theories off learning, teachers should be able to guide more optimal pupil progress in the classroom.

After problems, relevant for solving, have been selected from the general session, workshop participants should choose which committee or committees they would like to work on. For example, a group of four teachers may wish to study how to determine where each pupil is achieving presently. Reference sources need to be adequate in number in order to locate necessary information to solve the identified problem. Reference sources should include recently published professional teacher education text books, current educational journals, and uptodate audio visual materials which stress content directly related to the chosen problem area, identified in the general session. Members in a committee need to follow definite standards in order that an effective group is in evidence. These standards include respecting the thinking of others, staying on the topic being pursued, having content discussed circulate within the committee (interaction rather than coactions), and clarifying ideas presented. Committees should report to the entire workshop on progress being made in terms of methods and procedures obtained to guide pupils in the classroom to attain more optimally. Other committees might then learn from these reports, be they progress or final reports. Ample time should be given to discuss questions raised by participants pertaining to content in the report(s). Committee members learn from each other during the entire time devoted to the workshop. Questions raised assist the reporting committee to clarify and refine answers to questions. Additional research may be necessary as a result of questions raised.

In addition to the general session and committee endeavors, each participant has a unique problem area to solve. Personal problems unique to the participant needs identification and possible solutions sought. Consultant service should be available throughout the workshop. Consultants can be especially beneficial for participants when a personal problem in teaching is chosen and needed solutions sought. The guidance counselor must choose quality consultants to assist workshop participants. The guidance counselor himself/herself must be a caring, helpful person who assists, helps, coordinates and works harmoniously with workshop participants.

The writer has attended many workshops and has recorded problem areas faced by classroom teachers. The following appear to be very salient;

1. how can I work more effectively with parents to help each pupil learn as much as possible?
2. what might I do to have learners attend more carefully to the ongoing lesson presentation?
3. with numerous plans and procedures continually available for teaching, how should I evaluate the worth of each?
4. what can I do to implement tenets of cooperation learning more thoroughly?
5. which philosophy of instruction has the most merit, predetermined measurably stated objectives of instruction or an integrated, interdisciplinary curriculum? There are strong proponents for either side of this issue.

**Faculty Meetings**

Faculty meetings can be an appropriate means of determining how well the new ideas obtained from the workshop have worked out in the classroom setting. After the workshop has been completed, faculty and staff, as well as school administrators should desire to know what effect those meetings have had on teaching-learning situations. Hopefully desired content from the workshop will be used in the curriculum. In faculty meetings then, teachers have ample opportunities to report how well any acquired idea has worked when implemented. If for example, a teacher tried out basic ideas acquired on cooperative learning in teaching pupils, he/she should discuss with clarity how this new approach worked out in class and what is recommended in terms of implementing the new procedure of teaching. It is excellent if teachers and administrators ask questions of the presenter so that ideas are clarified and modifications made as needed. The role and expectation of the guidance counselor is to assist, coordinate, and encourage. He/she wishes the best possible achievement from pupils. The counselor is a caring and kind person, assisting all to work for the good of the pupil.

## Closing

School counselors should provide leadership in guiding teachers and administrators in providing the best objectives, learning opportunities, and appraisal procedures possible in the curriculum. A workshop approach might well assist teachers to provide interesting, meaningful, and purposeful learning opportunities in the curriculum. Facilities and materials for use at a workshop should be conducive in having participants attain as optimally as possible.

# 8

# Recent Educational Philosophies

The curriculum needs to be developed thoughtfully and carefully. The considerations of student interests, purposes, and talents need ample study in order to develop the implemented curriculum. Students differ from each other in a plethora of ways. These need ample consideration in achieving a quality curriculum. Parental assistance need also to be incorporated into curriculum development. Proper methods and philosophies of instruction also might well help pupils to achieve, develop, and grow.

## Essentials in the Curriculum

There is a school of thought which emphasizes that pupils attain essential, not learner chosen knowledge. The thinking is that the basics need identification and implemented in teaching and learning situations. Necessary knowledge for now and in the future must be emphasised in teaching and learning situations. There are selected knowledge and skills which then need identification and implementation in the classroom. The identified essential knowledge is to be taught to all pupils. Knowledge and skills identified are taught to develop the educated individual who can apply what has been learned for the personal self and for the future job, occupation and vocation selected. Major emphasis should be placed upon expository kinds of reading. Reading in the different subject matter areas should assist pupils to acquire knowledge, useful now and at the future workplace.

Grammar and writing need to emphasize a core of spelling words which research has shown to be salient for all learners. These words are used frequently by pupils in writing and stress utilitarian goals. Grammar needs to emphasize those learnings which guide pupils to write more clearly and more meaningful in the communication arena. Grammar is to be studied not for its own sake but for purposes of conveying ideas to others. The parts of speech and how words are to be used in sentences must be stressed. There is a structure to the English language consisting of sentence patterns, and diverse kinds of dependent clauses. Proper sequence in writing sentences helps the reader to attach sequence in what is being read.

Oral communication provides the basis for writing. What is said aloud can also be written down. Oral communication skills should emphasize clarity in pronunciation. Thus words need to be clearly enunciated. Appropriate stress, (saying individual words louder or quieter) breaks the monotony of saying each succeeding word within sentences. Stress in oral communication is like a crescendo in music.

Words should be pitched higher or lower depending upon what makes for good communication. Proper pitch should be stressed in oral communication. Thus, words need to be pitched higher or lower, depending upon what is needed for effective oral communication. A monotone voice is difficult to listen to for even a very short period of time. Musical scores contain notes on a scale to show the different levels of pitch in singing a note or playing it on a musical instrument. Linguists generally identify four levels of pitch from highest to lowest in oral communication. Juncture or pauses should be stressed adequately within a word, or within a sentence, as well as within sequential paragraphs. Too frequently, pupils do not pause adequately, as needed, and thus words and sentences are joined together needlessly, whereas there needs to be adequate juncture or pause(s). Pupils need much assistance in oral communication since practical skills are necessary to convey ideas effectively, now as well as in the future.

Reading is certainly a basic and should stress a demanding curriculum of understanding content read. Phonics instruction will assist the pupil to unlock unknown words. Phonics is to be separated from whole language approaches. With phonics instruction, the learner can become an independent reader. If a word is not identified in reading print, use of phonics will help pupils to read, and read more fluently. There are a core of words which pupils need to master. These words are met up with again and again in reading. The core words in reading are to be considered as basics. All kinds of information can then be read independently with a quality programme of the basics.

A quality mathematics curriculum can well provide for a basics programme of instruction. Addition, subtraction, multiplication, and division objectives can be determined whereby pupils learn what is essential. Frills and fads need to be eliminated. The scope and sequence of mathematics then may emphasize the four basic operations on number. Pertaining to essentialism, the founder William Chandler Bagley (1938) advocated the following:

1. Strong discipline in the classroom with appropriate standards for pupils to achieve.

2. A separate subjects curriculum. Opposite of the separate subjects curriculum would be to relate mathematics with other academic areas such as social studies.

3. Student interest should be played down and a more demanding mathematics curriculum be stressed.

4. A stable mathematics curriculum, rather than one of continuous modification and change.

5. Vital subject matter taught using basal textbooks rather than an activity centered curriculum.

7. A teacher determined curriculum rather than using pupil-teacher planning in curriculum design.

Bagley opposed the following trends in education:

1. The complete abandonment in many school systems of rigorous standards of academic achievement.
2. The disparagement of system and sequence in learning and a dogmatic denial of any value in, even any possibility of learning through, the logical, chronological, and causal relationship of learning materials.
3. The wide vogue of the so-called "activity movement."
4. The discrediting of the exact and the exacting studies.
5. An increasingly heavy emphasis upon the "social studies."
6. Using the lower schools to establish a new social order.
7. The "curriculum revision" movement and its vagaries.

Essentialist then advocated a school setting whereby, in the discipline arena, teachers teach and pupils learn. They stressed, too, that pupils study subject matter systematically rather than pupils engaging in an activity centered curriculum. Each academic discipline should be taught separately, not stressing integration of subject matter. The curriculum should be stable and not emphasize curriculum revision continuously. Life in society changes rather rapidly and schools need to provide stability in the curriculum. Life is demanding and cannot stress only or largely that which is of interest.

Science and social studies should also emphasize clarity in stated subject matter objectives. The scope and sequence in subject matter should be clearly spelled out. A no nonsense approach should be stressed in teaching and learning. There are exact standards which pupils need to achieve, regardless of interest involved. Pupils need to achieve subject matter knowledge in school and not experience entertainment only or largely. A stable curriculum is to be emphasised rather than one with continuous change.

**An Activity Centered Curricula**

Activity centered advocates, in developing the curriculum, tend to de-emphasize using basal textbooks for teaching and learning situations. They advocate using a variety of learning opportunities to provide for individual differences. Thus, an activity centered curriculum may stress construction activities for pupils to show what is being learned. A learning by doing approach is emphasised. In a construction activity, for example, pupils may make models pertaining to what has been or is being taught. Additional items to construct dealing with related units of study might include the following:

1. Anemometers and wind vanes pertaining to a science unit titled, "The Weather and How it Affects Us."

2. A Conestoga wagon in a social studies unit on "The Westward Movement." The latter may be used in creatively dramatizing what settlers did as they moved to California.

It is important to notice in the above two named activities active involvement by pupils in learning is being emphasised. They do not learn only from a basal textbook, but from a variety of reference sources to make anemometers, wind vanes, and the Conestoga wagon. The basal text is used as a resource, as are other developmental materials of instruction. Learning by doing stresses the following:

1. Doing art projects relating to an ongoing activity.
2. Dramatizing concepts and generalisations acquired.
3. Problem solving involving a dilemma situation.
4. Movement, interaction of learners, and motion in learning become purposeful and paramount.

Within each project, pupils need to have a purpose or reason(s) for participation. They need to carry out the purpose, followed by assessing the final product or process.

William Heard Kilpatrick (1871-1964), late professor of Columbia University in New York City, was a leading advocate of the project method. He emphasised pupils do the following flexible steps (Wahlquist, 1942).

1. Pupil purposing or having one or more reasons for doing the project.
2. Pupil planning of how to do the project.
3. Pupil execution in caring out the plans.
4. Pupils judging of the final product in terms of desired criteria.

Pupils may work individually or preferable collectively in working on the project. Intellectually skills are developed in doing the project. Intellectually, pupils need to read background information on the project so that adequate knowledge is present. They need to write summaries, outlines, diary entries on a day to day basis while working on the project, do summaries of articles read, and keep a log to summarize the diary entries. Good attitudes are an outcome of a positively developed project. Social abilities might well be achieved as a result of working with others. Holism is stressed as pupils work together on a project which stresses an integrated curriculum.

**The Measurement Movement**

The measurement movement stresses the importance of teachers being able to document what pupils have learned. To measure a distance, for example, where accuracy is involved, a measuring tape may be used. Depending upon the accuracy needed, the readings from the tape should provide quite accurate measurements. There will be small amounts of error from one measurement to the next when repeated measurements of the same distance are involved. But the sequential measurements will be very close as compared to estimating the distance.

Toward the early 1900s, Edward Lee Thorndike and his colleagues applied the measurement concept to measuring pupil achievement in spelling, handwriting, arithmetic, and other academic subject matter areas. Presently, there are standardised tests, criterion referenced tests and state mandated tests devised to measure pupil achievement in all academic areas. All states in the union by the school year 2005-2006 are to have state mandated tests in place to measure learner achievement and progress. If a pupil fails the state mandated test, he/she might not receive a high school diploma. This indeed would be quite a penalty for any pupil in the early 21st century.

To achieve satisfactorily on the state mandated test, the teacher needs to teach pupils to achieve well on each test. The curriculum then needs to be aligned carefully with each test item. Pupils do better on a test if the curriculum is aligned with the state mandated test. Why are measurably stated objectives to be used in teaching and learning situations?

1. The accountability of teachers can best be determined with measurably stated objectives, resulting in a precise score from pupils such as a Percentile, to notice how well a pupil has done under a teacher's teaching. Teachers are to be held accountable for pupil achievement.

2. Percentiles are relatively easy for a teacher or parent to understand.

3. With percentiles, pupil comparisons with each other may easily be made.

4. Failing schools may be sorted from those doing well in pupil achievement.

5. Remedial work may be stressed with those pupils not achieving on a satisfactory level, based on state mandated test results.

**The Feeling Dimension in Learning**

The feeling or attitudinal dimension is very important to evaluate. Existentialism is a philosophy which is very closely related to feelings taught and developed/possessed of/by the pupil. It is very difficult to measure pupil achievement of inherent feelings. The author when being a doctoral student in Curriculum and Instruction, as his major, used the California Test of Personality (CTP) to measure if public schools pupils did better academically and socially in the classroom with or without the assistance of university student teachers. The CTP, as does any personality test, have a high standard of error in test results. Thus, the actual score received on a CTP test can vary much from one measurement taken to the next on the same or alternative form of the test. This variation can make for considerable fluctuation in interpreting the results of a pupil's test results. Then too, generally, there are few test items on a personality test making for problems in reliability.

Existentialism stresses the importance of feelings possessed by a pupil, but does not recommend testing to ascertain these feelings. In fact, existentialism is a very open ended curriculum with much pupil freedom in the making of choices and decisions as to what to learn.

Existentialists emphasize that a person first exists and then must find his/her essence or purposes in life. These purposes are not given to the person, but must be found. To find these purposes, there may be dread, anxiety, fear, alienation, and loneliness. Each person is "thrown" into the world and then needs to find reasons for life and living. Feelings are subjective as well as knowledge is subjective. The objectivity of science is not found in existentialism. What then might make up the major part of the existentialist curriculum?

1. Literature which deals with the human condition.
2. History which stresses the consequences of decision-making.

Pupils with teacher assistance need to study about the human condition in literature and history to locate problems in the making of decisions. They need to think of alternatives to the decisions which were made. Feelings in the making of decisions must be noted. Choices of reading materials should be left to the individual pupil. In discussion groups, each pupil needs to feel free in the making of choices to alternative decisions than those made. Hindering the flow of discussion on ideas discussed, relating to the topic, is to be discouraged. Authentic decisions must be made. Responsibilities for choices made, vicariously or real, rests with the learner.

**The Classics Curriculum**

A classical curriculum emphasizes the importance of pupils studying content which has survived in importance, in time and in place. This is an attempt at identifying core knowledge for pupils to acquire. Other names for a classics curriculum are perenialism, and The Great Books philosophy of education. Recently written literature read might not be important or even be forgotten after a short duration of time, perhaps after a few years or even months. Literary writings, for example, of Robert Louis Stevenson, Henry Wadsworth Longfellow, Mark Twain, William Shakespeare, Nathaniel Hawthorne, among others, have endured in importance and provided excellent literature in terms of style, content, and meaning. The content might well have positive values as well as standards of morality for pupils to learn. Advocates of the Classics believe strongly that:

1. Good literature reveals its importance and quality as it is judged to be good with its enduring merit.
2. Good literature does not outlive its usefulness.
3. Good literature is read by scholarly people as the years keep showing its relevance and beauty in language use.
4. Good literature, such as the classics, has its utilitarian values today.
5. Good literature possesses needed standards of characterisation, setting, plot, sequence, and novel use of language.

Great minds of the past have ideas which reveal worth and merit today, such as Plato's *Republic*. In his ideal nation, Plato divided the worker population into there categories—rulers, soldiers, and artisans. The very highest of citizens in terms of ability and talent were the rulers or governmental officials of the ideal republic. These people had attended school for the longest period of time of any in the republic. The rulers were to see that the best rules, laws, and regulations were in the offing for citizens. Below that of being in the ruler's' category were the warriors. The warriors were guardians of the *Republic*. They were the soldiers and policemen in guarding the ideal state from enemies, foreign and domestic. The lowest group in Platonic society were the artisans who provided for the physiological needs of all people such as food, clothing, and shelter. These were considered as being menial tasks by Plato. From a discussion on the contents of the *Republic,* pupils may debate the following, as an example:

1. Can people in society be divided into three categories, only, as Plato indicated?
2. How can pupils be educated so that they can indicate their talents in a tripartite division?
3. What do you believe would make for an ideal republic or nation?

Implications from the Classics in curriculum development are the following:

1. A liberal arts curriculum assists a learner to explore knowledge and, perhaps, find his/her niche in life.
2. Vital content is acquired which has been evaluated in space and time. The unimportant is then weeded out in the process.
3. Clear communication with others is then possible when all college students have a two to four year programme of liberal arts instruction with a common body of classical knowledge.

4. General education, like the classics, needs to be obtained prior to choosing a vocation, job, or profession. General education provides the necessary prerequisites in pursuing studies for a job, occupation, or profession.
5. A common body of knowledge for all college students occurs when a core curriculum is being emphasised such as the Great Books of the Western World.
6. The mind or mental facets of a pupil need to be developed with imbibing the thinking of the great minds of the past who have demonstrated achievements and accomplishments.
7. What is deemed to be important for pupil learning has been developed by advocates of core knowledge for all to acquire.

Accordingly, educational intellectualism tends to be past orientated and to emphasize stability—the continuity of the great enduring, enduring ideas, over time. In general, the eternal ideas are best represented in the abiding masterworks of the world's greatest of the world's greatest minds as these are conveyed through the cultural heritage of mankind. The overall goal of education is to identify, preserve, and transmit essential Truth (that is the essential principles that govern the underlying meaning and significance of life). More specifically the intermediate role of the school 'as a particular social institution is to teach students how to think (that is, how to reason) and transmit the best thought (the enduring wisdom) of the past.

In contemporary education, philosophical conservatism expresses itself primarily as educational intellectualism and theological intellectualism, Philosophical intellectualism is best represented in America today. by such individuals as Robert Maynard Hutchins and Mortimer Adler, who are both primarily concerned with metaphysical wisdom in the traditional Aristotelian sense and who both tend to place great emphasis upon traditional liberal arts education in the spirit of the "Great Books" (O' Neil, William F., 1981).

## References

Bagley, William Chandler (1938), "An Essentialist Platform in the Advancement of American Education," *Educational Administration and Supervision*, 24: 241- 256.

O' Neil, William F. (1981), *Educational Ideologies*. Santa Monica, California, p. 168.

Wahlquist, John T. (1943), *Philosophy of American Education*. New York: The Ronald Press Company, 223- 224.

# Diagnosis in the Student Teaching Program

The student teacher needs to be guided to make continuous progress to become a high quality teacher in the public schools.

## General Areas in Diagnosing Achievement

There are selected observations made of student teacher performance which need to be analysed in order to work toward more optimal achievement. First, a student teacher may face only a part of the classroom while teaching. It is important to observe and communicate with all pupils in the classroom. If only a few are observed, the others may well feel left out of teaching/learning situations. In addition, the student teacher needs to invite all pupils in a classroom to participate actively such as in a discussion. There are eager beavers who might wish to answer all questions raised by the student teacher in an ongoing lesson. However, the reluctant participator also needs to be engaged in learning. The student teacher needs to seek involvement by these pupils also. Pupils who are withdrawn, shy, or hesitant need recognition when they are wholeheartedly engaged in a discussion. In a democracy, all pupils need to be engaged in learning and achieving.

Second, pupils need to be rewarded for work well done, not the few only, but also others in the classroom need to experience rewarding sessions. It is ideal for learning to be its very own reward. Selected children may need more encouragement than others in order to be motivated to higher levels of achievement. These pupils need to experience reinforcement for achievement in ongoing lessons and units of study. The reinforcement may come in the form of verbal praise. Each pupil in the classroom should feel positively toward the curriculum. This can be done, in part, through reinforcement of improved achievement of a pupil. The self concept of the learner is of utmost importance in that he/she feels that task completion is a definite possibility. Self efficacy is necessary in order that each pupil feels he/she can achieve optimally. The student teacher needs to develop feelings of self worth within each pupil.

Third, the student teacher needs to assist each pupil when the assistance is necessary. The right kind of assistance, too, must be given. Student teachers increasingly need to possess professional knowledge and skills which can be of great benefit to assist pupils in the classroom. Careful observation is necessary of each pupil's achievement in order to provide help in ongoing activities. The assistance needs to be given in a respectful, caring way. Each pupil must be valued and accepted. Playing favorites among pupils is and should be frowned upon.

**Determining Reading Levels**

A student teacher needs to be able to provide pupils with needed assistance in specific learning situations. The ultimate goal in teaching is for pupils to become independent learners, but to do so, assistance is necessary for young people to become fully functioning individuals. The student teacher with cooperating teacher assistance need to possess professional understandings pertaining to help which should be given in a judicious manner, as needed, to pupils. Word recognition skills do provide problems to some children in learning to read well. If a pupil is stuck on a plethora of words, comprehension will indeed go downhill. A flexible standard to use in determining if a textbook, or other reference material, is on the reading level of individual pupils, is the use of an informal reading inventory. Here, the student teacher may use the basal text as a device to ascertain the reading level of a pupil. This method, known as the informal reading inventory (IRI), attempts to ascertain if the script is meaningful and understandable to pupils. The student teacher/cooperating teacher should mark off 100 running words in the text at random. If a pupil can identify correctly 95 out of 100 running words, the text is on the learner's reading level provided that three out of four comprehension questions covering content read are answered correctly. There are two dimensions here involving word recognition and comprehension. If the pupil can do the 95% level of identifying words correctly and the 75% comprehension standard, the text is on his/her reading level. This leaves room for pupil learning to identify five new words out of one hundred and also leeway to improve in comprehension with one of our questions to be answered correctly covering subject matter read. This is, then, the instructional level of reading.

If a pupil reads correctly all the words in the selection and answers all questions correctly, then the text is on the learner's recreational level of reading. The recreational level is excellent for independent reading of library books such as in individualised reading and sustained silent reading (SSR). To consider the frustrational level of reading, the pupil identifies fewer than 95% of the running words and answers fewer than 75% of the questions asked of learners. There are standards to follow when using the IRI to ascertain pupil's reading levels:

1. The pupil should not have practiced reading the selection before the IRI is taken.

2. The pupil should not have listened to content read by someone else from the selection prior to the informal IRI test.

3. The teacher needs to record the kinds of errors made in word recognition, such as omitting words, substituting words, repeating words pronounced

correctly, not paying attention to punctuation marks, reading very haltingly, among others, which hinder comprehension.

4. The questions asked of pupils in checking comprehension should involve not only recall, but also higher levels of cognition.

5. Each pupil needs to understand the purpose of giving the IRI. The purpose is to use the results in choosing appropriate reading materials for individual pupils as well as to provide information to the teacher about the kinds of assistance which should be provided to each learner.

By involving the student teacher in giving the IRI, he/she becomes cognizant of problems involved in guiding pupils to become better readers. Reading is a highly salient skill for pupils to develop in school and in society. There is much reading which a pupil does in all academic areas, be it elementary, middle school, high school, or university levels. Reading well is also important for personal development and increase interests possessed.

## Specific Help Provided to Pupils

The student teacher needs to become proficient in making observations of pupil achievement. These observations should include assistance which help pupils to become better readers. A pupil may then need help in word recognition skills. Pupils individually or in groups who are deficient in using phonics to identify consistently spelled words can be given learning activities in harmonizing grapheme/phoneme relationships. There are entire words which are spelled phonetically. Others have parts within a word which have consistency between symbol and sound. Some words are lacking almost entirely of having consistency in symbol/sound relationships. The latter need to be learned by sight in order to become words which are recognised immediately. This will tend to take more time as compared to words which contain sound/symbol relations. For good readers, eventually all words need instant recognition as sight words when readiness is in evidence. But, to do so phonetically spelled words must be presented as those having grapheme/phoneme relationships in whole or in part. Assistance is there in word recognition when pupils need help to identify unknown words. The help comes from the teacher who assists pupils to learn and use phonics.

Syllabication skills are salient for pupil mastery. A word which appears to be unknown might be recognised when a prefix, suffix, or both are removed from an unknown word. A prefix such as "un" might be removed from the unknown word and the child identifies that which was not known. A suffix removed from the unknown word, such as "er" makes it meaningful to the child. Syllabication skills mastered by the learner make it possible to identify many words which appeared to be new words.

Use of context clues to identify unknown words may well be the most meaningful to the child. Here, the pupil ponders which the correct word will be for the unknown, realizing it must make sense in relation to the other words in the sentence or paragraph. Any good reader realizes that when reading of words is continued, the ensuing content will assist in clarifying what just previously was not meaningful. This is true of identifying unknown words or ideas. There is a 'straightening out' of what was not meaningful previously. Context clues are indeed important to use when attempting to identify unknown words.

When pictures and illustrations are heavily used in a basal reader or library book, the reader should use these not only to obtain concepts and facts, but also to identify unknown words. If a young child cannot identify an unknown word, He/she may look at a picture on that same page and this may provide the clue to identify the unknown.

Selected children may use configuration clues to identify unknown words. This approach is rather limited in application, but it may assist certain children to recognize unknown words. The teacher may try assisting pupils to use configuration clues to identify the unknown word. Words do differ from each other in length, tallness of letters within the word, and letters which go below the line.

**Comprehension of Content Read**

The purpose of learning word recognition skills is for the pupil to comprehend that which was read. There are a plethora of comprehension skills which need to be taught to pupils in reading. Reading for factual information is one kind of comprehension. This kind of comprehension may be stressed for pupils to secure important facts, not trivia. facts might be thought of as the building blocks for higher levels of comprehension. Pupils may be asked to read for population figures, capitol cities of nations, gross national products of a series of countries, as well as agricultural crops grown.

Pupils should also read to obtain relevant concepts. Inside of each concept are a variety of facts. The facts become related to form a broader idea such as a concept. Important concepts to read for might include agriculture, livestock, feed, pasture land, tilled land, rotation, erosion, and terraces Concepts may be consolidated to make for a generalisation. If pupils, for example, read to secure a generalisation, the following question might provide the incentive: What causes erosion of soil used for farming? Information read by learners may end up with a generalisation such as the following: Wind and heavy rainfall causes top soil to erode. Inside of the generalisation are concepts such as wind, rainfall, top soil, erode.

Reading to acquire a main idea is another type of comprehension to emphasize as a skill. Main ideas are broader than generalisations and tend to stress one sentence when this kind of comprehension is emphasised. With appropriate readiness, the teacher may say, "Can you tell me in one sentence what brought the Middle Ages to a close?" The inclusive sentence must tell holistically what brought an era to a close. The new era was the Renaissance and followed the Middle Ages.

Additional kinds of comprehension to stress in context are the following:

1. **Reading to follow directions.** Here, the pupil should be able to tell in his/her own words what is to be done, when directions have been read. It is necessary to have a clear understanding of directions on how to do something. Too frequently, pupils have read directions hastily, only to misunderstand that which was read and thus make for an inaccurate product.
2. **Reading to appraise ideas read.** Student teachers need to assist pupils to evaluate what has been read. Thus, the materials read need to be analysed in terms of being accurate and relevant. Perhaps, an additional criterion may involve being able to separate content read in terms of being fantasy versus reality. To be able to separate subject matter into component parts is indeed worthwhile when proper standards are used.
3. **Reading to synthesize ideas.** Relating ideas read into a component whole is necessary. Otherwise, there will be much isolated knowledge and bits of information which are too difficult to remember. Being able to synthesize information tends to do away with unrelated ideas. There is, then, an organisation of ideas which provides integration and wholeness.
4. **Reading to apply ideas.** Here, the student teacher needs to help pupils to locate information so that it can be used in a practical situation. If a pupil is to present an oral report to the class on a specific topic, he/she needs assistance to find the correct source and understand the content therein so it may be applied in a useful situation and that being to present the oral report to classmates. To be useful, the subject matter needs to be organised properly and sequentially.

**Plans in Grouping Pupils for Instruction**

Student teachers need to be well versed in grouping pupils in the classroom for effective reading instruction. The plan used should assist each pupil to achieve as much as possible. Flexible grouping is needed so that pupils experience a variety of settings to increase optimally in reading progress. The homogenous/heterogeneous dilemma in grouping for reading instruction may be dismissed by having learners be in groups which benefit the pupil as much as possible in reading achievement. A very flexible procedure is to arrange reading materials at learning centers. Each center may have a title such as animal stories, nature, health, and so on. The library books for five or six learning centers should be written on different levels of achievement for slow, average, and fast readers. Learners individually may choose which books to read sequentially. The student teacher may assist in making the selection if a child is not able to settle down to read a library book. Each center may have a picture and caption to introduce pupils to the kind or titles of books inherent at each center. Pupils individually may select those books to read which are interesting and purposeful. Chosen library books may also be used in sustained silent reading (SSR). These are highly informal reading programs.

Second, individualised reading may be used in teaching and learning situations. Here again, the pupil chooses a library book from among others. Following the reading of the chosen book, the pupil may have a conference with the teacher. The pupil discusses content read with the teacher. The teacher listens to a pupil read aloud to check reading skills. Information on the pupil's achievement in reading may be recorded and dated for reference purposes.

Third, basal readers may be used. An accompanying manual can provide much information for the teacher to use in teaching such as objectives, learning opportunities, and evaluation procedures. There is emphasis placed upon phonics instruction as well as holistic procedures in reading. The student teacher may choose initially to follow the manual rather closely and later on be more creative in its use. Pupils with basal reader use may be grouped in terms of achievement such as fast, average, and slow readers. Groups may be changed in membership as the need arises.

The teacher needs to appraise pupil reading skills and comprehension. The questions used to appraise comprehension should be on different levels of cognition, not factual information only or even largely. Diverse evaluation procedures may be used such as true/false, matching, completion, short answer, and essay. Feedback from learners provides the teacher with necessary information to improve the reading curriculum.

Fourth, highly scripted readers may be used in reading instruction. These readers with accompanying manuals contain clearly written statements for the teacher to use in the reading curriculum. There is little leeway for the teacher to use his/her own ideas in teaching and learning situations. The script is written by the authors to maintain uniformity by all teachers using the reader. The precise wording can be followed readily by classroom teachers. Mistakes can be greatly minimised in teaching procedures, as provided by the authors. These tend to be teacher proof materials for teachers to use in teaching.

Big Book approaches may be used for teaching reading to young readers, in particular. The Big Book is large enough for all involved in reading instruction to see. Thus, five or six pupils may be seated directly in front of and face the Big Book. There is readiness activities whereby pupils are asked to look carefully at the illustrations and predict content for the story. Together with the teacher, pupils may read aloud the subject matter. First, the teacher reads aloud as pupils follow the print, followed by pupils and the teacher reading aloud together as the latter continues to point to words being read. The read aloud activity may be pursued as long as desired. In this way pupils may master each word by sight and not be hindered with phonic drills and practice. Comprehension and enjoyment are key ideas in teaching with the Big Book use.

### Assessment of Reading Progress

The student teacher needs to possess a good repertoire of assessment procedures to determine pupil progress. Teacher observation is an excellent procedure to use with appropriate criteria in mind for the assessment process. Teacher observation may be used in the following ways:

- Notice fluency in oral reading of a pupil. This will involve helping pupils to:

1. Avoid repeating what has been read correctly in oral reading.
2. Pay careful attention to punctuation marks.
3. Omission of words, inserting of words and misidentification of words.

- Diagnose specific problems in word attack skills to be taught, i.e. configuration clues, phonics, syllabication, among others.
- Remedy weaknesses in comprehension skills such as increasing ability to comprehend facts, to read critically and creatively, and to solve problems.

Informal teacher written test items may be written to measure pupils achievement in reading. Each test item needs to be written clearly so pupils understand what is wanted for the response. If a pupil provides a different answer that is correct in the test but is not on the teacher's answer key, credit, of course, should be given for the answer given by the learner. Ample attention should be given to essay tests to evaluate pupil achievement in reading. Essay tests provide opportunities for pupils to be creative in responding. The quality of writing may also be assessed in addition to the content in the response to an essay test item. The teacher needs to be certain that pupils include, in the response for an essay test question, salient content. Additional kinds of teacher written test items include true/false, matching, short answer, and completion.

**Conclusion**

The student teacher joins the cooperating teacher in assisting optimal pupil achievement. He/she needs to develop into being a professional teacher who can help pupils do well in school and in society.

# Philosophy of Measurement and Evaluation

Diverse approaches are available to teachers in measuring and evaluating pupil achievement. Since numerous procedures are available, different philosophies are available in the appraisal arena.

A quality teacher does a good job of appraising pupil progress with excellence in the appraisal arenas. Teachers are in a better position to sequence learning opportunities for pupils. Each pupil then has improved chances to experience sequential learning opportunities.

Realism, Measurement Driven Instruction and Evaluation Realism as a philosophy of education is inherent in Measurement Driven Instruction (MDI). MDI has a rather strong following among educators. It may be in evidence with state mandated objectives and tests, Instructional Management Systems (IMS), and mastery learning. Each of these procedures stresses the use of precise objectives. These ends are specific. After instruction, it can be measured if a pupil has/has not attained a specific objective.

Objectives here are chosen in terms of relevancy and specificity. Thus, it is vital to know if a pupil has/has not achieved an objective. Objectives are accepted for teaching based on their being stated in measurable, observable terms. That which is subjective and internal to the pupil is not capable of being measured or observed.

MDI objectives are predetermined. They have been written prior to instruction. No pupil input is emphasised in developing the curriculum with MDI. Instructors/test writers are in the best position to write precise, measurably stated objectives together with tests that align with the written ends. The alignment of tests with the objectives emphasizes the significance of validity. Learning opportunities are then chosen by instructors to assist pupils to attain the specific objectives. Each pupil is measured in achievement against the precise ends stressed in teaching and learning situations. If the test measures consistently when test-retest or split-half reliability is used, the concept of being reliable may be attached to the measurement instrument. For tests to emphasize quality in their construction, validity and reliability, as measurement concepts, need to be in emphasis.

MDI, as a philosophy of measurement and evaluation, does not stress:

1. The use of broad, general objectives in teaching-learning situations.
2. Pupil/teacher planning of objectives, learning opportunities, and appraisal procedures.
3. Pupils sequencing their own activities and experiences in a psychological curriculum. MDI advocates a logical curriculum in that instructors order objectives sequentially for pupil achievement.
4. Instruction pertaining to that which cannot be measured such as internal interest, purposes, and meanings that pupils develop.
5. An activity centered curriculum, such as pupils engaging in construction and processing activities.

Wahlquist (1942) wrote the following pertaining to objectivity, specificity, and realism and realism as a philosophy of education:

> Realists generally agree in stressing the need of making philosophy scientific. A major part of the realist programme of reform consists in emphasizing the close relationship of philosophy

> to the sciences. There are those who think that the proper procedure for philosophy is to utilize the methods of abstraction perfected in mathematics and made the basis of all scientific investigation. Generally realists agree that the method of scientific analysis is the fundamental approach. The ultimate determinant of an idea is regarded as something external to the personality, and not dependent upon it. Consequently, truth must be discovered by objective means, as free as possible from the subjectivity of the experimenter. The realist is interested in the temperature of the room as registered by a gadget, not the impressions of the persons in the room.

Experimentalism, Problem Solving, and the Pupil Flexible steps in problem solving procedures in teaching and learning situations are openended, not absolute nor precise. A model for pupils with teacher guidance engaging in problem solving may be the following:

1. Identification and clarification of the problem.
2. Selection and appraisal of information needed to solve the problem.
3. Development of a related hypothesis.
4. Using the hypothesis in a lifelike situation.
5. Revision and modification of the hypothesis if needed.

Problem solving methods of instruction emphasize pupils with teacher guidance identifying lifelike problems. These problems are relevant in society and are not predetermined by educators for pupils to solve.

Pupils interest, curiosity, and purpose need to be developed so that problems/questions are identified. Lecture/heavy use of explanations in teaching do not suffice. Rather, inductive methods of teaching are advocated, whereby pupils choose a problem and use diverse reference sources to select subject matter to solve the problem. Subject matter is not set out in advance for pupil acquisition, but rather is instrumental for learner use in problem solving. From a stimulating learning environment, the learner identifies one or more problems. From information gathered using a variety of reference sources, the pupil arrives at a generalisation to tentatively solve the problem. The generalisation is a hypothesis and subject to trying out to check its feasibility.

Problem solving methods do not stress:

1. Measuring each specific step of attainment in flexible problem solving. Much of what transpires in problem solving occurs internally within the learner.
2. A predetermined curriculum for pupils. Rather problems emerge as ongoing learning opportunities are experienced.
3. Teachers making assignments for pupils continuously such as using textbooks and workbooks as learning activities.
4. A deductive approach in teaching. With deductions, subject matter moves from the teacher to the pupil with content presented by the former to the latter.
5. A highly structured curriculum which is carefully sequenced by teachers and other educators.

Pupils achievements may be evaluated through teacher observation. Paper/pencil tests be they norm referenced or criterion referenced, do not measure pupil skills in problem solving. Rather, in a contextual situation, pupils with teacher guidance identify and solve problems. Realistic, life-like situations provide opportunities for pupil problem solving activities. Evaluating of pupil progress is flexible and openended. Teacher observation and pupil self evaluation may be used to appraise the quality of processes and procedures used by learners in problem solving. Pertaining to the thinking of John Dewey, late leading advocate of experimentalism, Atkinson and Maleska (1965) wrote the following:

> To a follower of Dewey, education has two sides—psychological and social; neither may be subordinated or neglected. The

psychological nature of the child forms the basis for his education—it is the teacher's responsibility to make full use of his natural, spontaneous activities. Describing original nature as being spontaneously impulsive rather than passive, Dewey divided impulses into four kinds: the social impulses of communication and conversation; the constructive impulse to make things; the impulse to investigate things; and the impulse of artistic or creative expression.

With these impulses in mind, said Dewey, the school must be changed from a place of sedentary listening to one for active doing or working. The teaching process be planned to allow the child to learn wherever possible by his own experiences and, it that way, to acquire the habit of thinking. A proper solution to any problem demands intelligent thinking which becomes the principle factor in the ability to cope with new situations.

Dewey felt that when the psychological and social approaches to learning are separated, there is produced either a forced or external education in which freedom of the individual is subordinated to a preconceived notion of what society should be, or else a barren and formal development of the mental powers in which the learner has little idea of the use to be made of what is being learned.

## Humanism, Individual Decision Making and Evaluation

Individual Decision-making presets a third model in the philosophy of evaluation. A learning centers approach might be emphasised. An adequate number of tasks for the diverse centers needs to be in the offing. Here, the pupil sequences his/her own tasks. Those tasks not possessing perceived purpose and interest may be omitted. There are more tasks available than what any one pupil may be able to complete. Pupils may choose problem solving as well as nonproblem solving endeavours. The pupil needs to be able to select and complete ordered learning opportunities. Teachers need to evaluate each pupil on his/her abilities to choose quality tasks sequentially. The tasks chosen provide pupil motivation to achieve, develop, and do well. Subjective criteria are used here by the teacher to appraise pupil performance.

In addition to the learning centers approach, individual decision-making may further be stressed in individualised reading. Regardless of the academic area involved, pupils may use self-selected reading materials, rather than basal texts. Or, self-selected reading materials are used to supplement the basals. If library books are chosen by the pupil, the teacher needs to appraise learner's ability to select and read the complete library book. After the library book has been read, the pupil and the teacher should have a short conference to assess comprehension. A few salient comprehension questions may be asked of the learner. Thus, from a variety of library books containing diverse content and being on different reading levels, the pupil selects sequential library books to read.

Individual decision-making philosophies of instruction do not:

1. Stress a teacher developed curriculum, consisting of predetermined objectives, learning opportunities, and appraisal procedures.
2. Advocate a logical curriculum in which the teacher arranges, sequentially, learning opportunities for pupils.
3. Emphasize a highly structured curriculum. With pupil decision-making, openness and flexibility are key concepts in curriculum development.
4. Require a textbook/workbook philosophy of instruction. Rather, a variety of instructional media to meet pupil needs, interests, and purposes are salient.
5. Propose predetermined objectives for learner attainment.

Instead, goals emerge as pupils with teacher guidance pursue learning opportunities involving choice.

Pupil achievement then is evaluated in terms of quality decisions made, sequential tasks completed stressing worthwhile experiences, as well as learner motivation in achieving, growing and developing.

Mc Neil wrote the following:

Humanists believe that the function of the curriculum is to provide each learner with intrinsically rewarding experiences that contribute to personal liberation and development. To humanists, the goals of education are dynamic personal processes related to the ideals of personal growth, integrity, and autonomy. Healthier attitudes toward self, peers, and learning are among their expectations. The ideal of self-actualisation is at the heart of the humanistic curriculum. A person who exhibits this quality is not only cooly cognitive, but is also developed in aesthetic and moral ways, i.e. one who does good works and has good character. The humanist views actualisation growth as a basic need. Each learner has a self that is not necessarily conscious. This self must be uncovered, built up, and taught.

## Conclusion

Diverse philosophies are in evidence pertaining to measuring and evaluation learner progress.

1. Measurement driven instruction advocates the use of precise objectives in teaching and learning situations. Alignment of learning activities and appraisal procedures with the objectives is vital. A highly structured curriculum is then in evidence. Pupil progress is measured in terms of achieving the precise ends. Norm referenced and criterion referenced tests are major approaches in determining objectively that which each pupil has learned.

2. Problem solving methods harmonize with that which exists in society. In the societal arena, persons identify and solve problems, be they major or minor in nature. Teacher observations emphasizing quality flexible criteria are necessary to evaluate learner progress in problem solving. The teacher appraises the quality of problems chosen, of hypotheses developed, of approaches used to assess each hypothesis, and of necessary revisions of hypotheses. Objective results of pupil achievement cannot be secured due to an openended curriculum being in evidence whereby pupils with teacher guidance choose relevant problems of intrinsic worth. Each flexible step or procedure in problem solving is based upon a learner's or a

committee's experience, not upon objectivity or a priori (prior to experience), criteria. Subject matter used to solve problems might be objective in nature such as in arithmetic, algebra, and geometry. Criterion and norm referenced tests may be used where to measure pupil achievement.

3. Pupils individually making choice in school, be it problem solving or other types of activities and experiences. Quality, openended criteria need to be utilised by the teacher to appraise decisions made by pupils. With pupil choices and decision making in the curriculum, there are no valid tests for measuring progress for all learners in a classroom. Rather such items as pupils deciding on purposeful learning activities to pursue, being on task, possessing positive attitudes, and working creatively individually and with others become important criteria for evaluating learner progress. Where right or wrong answers are obtained by the pupil in a given learning opportunity, objective scoring is then possible such as in mathematics.

## References

Atkinson, Carroll, and Meleska, Eugene T. *The story of education.* New York: Chilton Books, 87 and 88.

McNeil, John T. (1990). *Curriculum* Fourth edition. Glenview, Illinois: Scott, Foresman, Brown Higher Education, 5 and 6.

Wahlquist, John T. (1942). *The philosophy of American Education.* New York: The Ronald Press Company, 56.

# Philosophy and Measurement of School Achievement

There are diverse schools of thought on how pupils should be measured or evaluated to show academic achievement in the school setting. Teacher written tests have been used for a least 150 years. There appears, in the past, to have been a lack of knowledge on basic techniques to use in measuring/evaluating learner achievement and progress. Presently, there are student university level textbooks containing guidelines for teachers to use in writing test items. Thus, classroom teacher may receive much assistance then in writing diverse kinds of test items.

## Teacher Written Tests

High quality teacher written tests might well possess the best validity of all test writers since they are right in the classroom and might well write test items pertaining to what was taught whereas test writers for state mandated tests are rather far removed from the local classroom. The state writers of test items do not know the children for whom the test was written and thus, cannot provide for individual differences among learners who will be taking the test. Validity is a very salient concept in testing pupils in that learners need to have opportunities to achieve what is in the state mandated objectives. The state mandated objectives can become more valid if the state standards or objective directly relate to the taught curriculum. The classroom teacher may then align the written test items with the stated objectives, in a unit of study.

Test items written by the teacher to cover what was taught might consist of true/false, or multiple choice items. If the test items covered by the teacher in teaching pupils are of high quality, meaning they are very clearly written and no guesswork is involved in their interpretation, high reliability should then also be in the offing. This means that pupils should receive a similar score the second time the same test is taken. With quality reliability then, the test measures consistently when pupils take the same test twice (test/retest reliability), unless learner fatigue sets in.

There is also split half reliability when the test is taken only once and the odd numbered items are compared with the even numbered test items in terms of correct responses from pupils taking the test. The resulting statistic is called split half correlation.

A reliability figure can come about also when a comparison between alternative forms of a test taken by a set of pupil is made. The alternative forms reliability, if high, indicates the two tests are of comparable difficulty and cover similar subject matter from the same unit taught. No matter on what level, local or state, the test items are written, they should possess quality validity and reliability. Again, validity pertains to subject matter taught and measured in terms of learner achievement. Validity then emphasizes what was taught, pupils had opportunities to learn. What is taught then needs to relate to the identified objectives of instruction. Hopefully, very important objectives were emphasised in teaching pupils. Reliability stresses obtaining consistency of pupil results from testing. Inconsistent test results means that a pupil was, for example, on the 25th percentile the first time a test was taken and the eightieth percentile the second time the same test was taken. This does not tell us anything about a pupil's performance or achievement. If a pupil is on the fiftieth percentile both items the same test was taken, then out of every 100 pupils who took the same test, fifty were above and fifty below the median (or average) percentile. The mean is the average score for all pupils taking the test whereas the median is the middle most score. The mode is the most frequent for those who took the test..

The early years of the twentieth century were conspicuous in the application of science to all phases of business and industry. It was applied not merely to the invention of new products and processes but to the details of organisation and management designed to promote economy and efficiency. Experts trained in "scientific management" studied carefully the performances of workers on the job with results so fruitful in economy and efficiency that many can be seen in "job analysis" possibilities of application not only to vocational education but to the reform of other aspects of education as well. All that was needed, it seemed, was to identify the specific outcomes by assuring that pupils engage in the activities certain to eventuate in the proper habits and skills, information, attitudes, and the like. The new emphasis upon the selection and organisation of subject matter received definite formulation in 1918 with the National Commission for the Reorganisation of Secondary Education. The commission stated the areas of concern or the functions of the secondary school, in the form of the Cardinal Principles of Education. Its preliminary statement read: In order to determine the main objectives that should guide education in a democracy, it is necessary to analyze the activities of the individual. Normally he is a member of a family, of a vocational group, and of various civic groups, and by virtue of these relationships, he is called upon to engage in activities that enrich family life. To render important vocational services to his fellows, and to promote the common welfare." (Thayer, VT: 1970).

## Commercial Tests Used to Measure Pupil Achievement

Commercial companies develop standardised achievement tests, also called norm referenced tests (NRT). These are used rather frequently to measure pupil achievement. There are different elements that go into the development of standardised achievement tests since the conditions for test taking are to be the same for all pupils. The following factors are then to be the same:

1. Time limits enforced for taking each test.
2. Subject matter tested on for each set of pupils taking the designated test.
3. Directions given to pupils for test taking.

Professional writers write the test items for a specific curriculum area or areas. These test items then are responded to by pupils in a pilot study. Feedback from the pilot study provides knowledge, to the test writers, of the quality of each test item. Computerised scoring using the same key further standardizes the test in that conditions are the same for all involved in taking the test. When writers of the test items see the computerised printout from pilot study results, they notice which test item was too easy and all responded correctly to that test item. Or the other extreme whereby all responded correctly to a test item. Where all responded correctly or incorrectly to the same test item makes it either too easy or too difficult. Then too, pupils results are not spread out adequately. Generally, the lowest and the highest 5th percentile scores in a pilot study are eliminated to take care of extreme scores. When an adequate number of pilot studies have been run, then a spread of scores will result from the first to the 99th percentile. Standard tests are designed to spread out pupils' scores from high to low. Each academic or curriculum area will have data on pupils' scores and their equivalency in the Manual of the standardised test.

Quality validity and reliability will be discussed in the manual and how these were determined. The test writers are quite far removed from the local classroom in ascertaining which test items should be written and included on the test. The test will be administrated in various parts of the United States to pupils from diverse levels of achievement. Local pupils who have taken the standardised test will have their scores compared with those in the Manual (who were in the final pilot study) to notice the related percentile level.

## Criterion Referenced Tests

To take care of the predetermined methods of spreading scores out from high to low, as did advocates of standardised testing, criterion referenced testing (CRT) was invented and brought into the measurement movement. The CRTs have objectives available which teachers may use as guidelines for instruction. CRTs are pilot tested to take out vaguely written test items. Clearly written, meaningful test items should be in evidence. As is true of standardised tests, CRTs also tend to use multiple choice test items. Together with the stem, each distractor of the four in a multiple choice test item needs to be plausible. The four responses should be of similar length. No clues should be given as to which is the correct response.

Learning opportunities selected by the teacher should be aligned with the objectives of instruction. After an instructional period of time, the CRT is used at a designated interval to measure pupil achievement. The state generally determines when the tests are to be administered. These tests are to be administered on grades three through eight. There might be cutoff points for a pupil passing CRT tests for each grade level in order to be promoted to the next higher grade level. Exit exams of the CRT may need to be passed in order to receive a high school diploma. Sometimes, there have been computer glitches which provide wrong information to the pupil and his/her parents as to having passed a CRT. The pupil is then held back one school year unless someone challenges the test results and enough pressure is put onto the school system or testing company who scored the tests. Generally, these are highly unusual cases in which a pupil did excellent daily class work, but "failed" the CRT exit test due to computer glitches.

Differences between the standardised test and the criterion referenced test are the following:

1. The standardised test has no objectives for the teacher to use in guiding the selection of subject matter for pupils to study.

2. The standardised test spreads pupils from high (99th) to low (1st percentile). As many pupils as can achieve well can reach the highest percentile in a CRT.

3. Multiple choice test items, only are used on both standardised testing and CRTs. Machine scoring does not assess essay test results.

4. Standardised tests are quite mechanistic in their writing whereas CRTs are more open-ended.

**The Portfolio**

There are a plethora of educators who state that testing and measuring of pupil achievement is a rather narrow approach to evaluation of pupil achievement and progress. What about evaluating the every day products and processes revealed by pupils of daily school work? Here the portfolio comes into being. Each pupil may then prepare a portfolio with teacher guidance. The portfolio contents may be dated and the name of the involved pupil placed on the outside. Portfolio contents might well include the following:

1. Written work of the pupil such as summaries, outlines, poems, plays, essays, diary entries, logs, book reports, and reviews.

2. Art work consisting of murals, water coloring, pencil sketching, making of dioramas and models, as well as drawing individual pictures. Snapshots may be taken of the product if it is too large to place inside a portfolio.

3. Video tapes of personal committee work, dramatisations, cassette recordings of book reports and oral reading.

4. Teacher written test results and self-evaluation results using appropriate criteria.

The portfolio should not become too voluminous, but should pinpoint salient, representative work of the learner. The portfolio should be read by two or three competent individuals using standards which truly do state the worth of this evaluative device. Evaluators need to use rubrics in the assessment to make for increased reliability among evaluators. The rubric, in broad terms, needs to:

1. Show pupil growth, or lack thereof, in each academic area of the curriculum.
2. Pinpoint strengths and weaknesses of pupil achievement.
3. Assess qualities of neatness, effort, and sequence.
4. Show ownership and pride of the preparer.
5. Assist the learner to appraise the self with increased skill.
6. Help the learner to analyze, think, and create.
7. Guide the pupil in desiring to increase achievement.
8. Motivate the pupil to develop increased skill in individual and committee endeavors.
9. Emphasize that the pupil reflect upon what is and what can be achieved with a vision toward higher accomplishments.
10. Empower the learner to grow, achieve, and develop in each and all intelligences.

The portfolio can be an excellent way to report pupil progress to parents. It needs to be well organised so that a responsible viewer might receive the information needed. A quality Table of Contents might well assist viewers such as parents to locate information needed. The parent, for example, may wish to view the appropriate portfolio section to notice how well the son or daughter is doing in mathematics. The parent may then ask the teacher questions pertaining to the following, involving subtraction:

1. Which problems does the child reveal in "take away" problems?
2. Is the child writing numerals and words more legibly than what is in the present portfolio?

3. How well does the child understand the concepts of regrouping and renaming?
4. How well is the child able to work together with classmates in the mathematical arena?
5. How effectively does the child reason in mathematics? logical thinking is a major goal in mathematics.
6. Is the child improving in using problem solving skills?
7. how well is the learner doing in thinking critically?
8. To what degree does the child reveal *creativity* in finding unique solutions to problems?
9. How well does the learner reveal intrinsic interests in doing mathematics? The pupil then uses mathematics on his/her own as well as complete classroom assignments satisfactorily.
10. How are portfolio results used to improve the mathematics curriculum?

**Issues in Measurement and Evaluation**

There are a plethora of issues in the measurement and evaluation of pupil achievement. Selected approaches are highly informal and yet they do have tremendous merit. One of these approaches is teacher observation of learner progress. Teacher observation is done rather continuously of pupil progress. As the classroom teacher is teaching, he/she can observe if a pupil is diligent, prompt, exacting, and responsible. These observations need to be recorded later. If possible they may be recorded in dated, journal entries written by the observer.

Brief observations may also be recorded in anecdotal record form and dated. With a succession of observations made, a pattern of pupil behavior will be formulated by the observer. The observations made are for teacher reference, alone and may be used in planning the curriculum to assist each learner to achieve as optimally as possible. Observations made indicate, for example, which child needs more assistance in phonics, syllabication skills, use of context clues, in creative and critical thinking, as well as in problem solving. Teacher observations may be helpful to use on a daily basis to guide optimal learner achievement.

**Formative and Summative Evaluation**

Formative evaluation is done by the teacher to assess what pupils have learned and what is left to learn in an ongoing unit of study. The ongoing unit of study has not been competed as yet. The teacher wants to find out how well pupils are achieving the objectives of the science unit being taught. Are there corrections which need to be made before the unit of study has ended? The teacher does not wish to wait until the end of the unit of study to ascertain how well pupils have done while corrections can still be made. Testing and teacher observation may be used as assessment procedures.

Toward the other end of the continuum, summative evaluation emphasizes that the unit of study has been completed. Decisions need to be made now as to which modifications need to be made the next time the unit is taught. The following considerations must be made:

1. Are there additional objectives which should be stressed in the instructional arena?
2. Should selected objectives be modified or culled?
3. Might pupils achieve more if the sequence of learning opportunities were changed?
4. Are there an adequate number of attitudinal or skills objectives being emphasised within the unit of study?
5. Should more objectives reflect higher levels of cognition?
6. Are pupils engaged in adequate committee work?
7. Do pupils show initiative in working by the self?
8. Are pupils evaluating the self adequately in achieving objectives?

9. What can be done to assist pupils to appraise the self more adequately?

10. Which methods of instruction should be used to reflect needs of handicapped pupils?

Formative evaluate occurs during the time a unit is taught. Changes may then still be made in the present unit being taught. There are identified deficiencies whereby instruction might still occur to remedy inadequacies of pupil achievement in the unit being taught. Summative evaluation assesses learner achievement in the complete unit of instruction. Here, teachers evaluate what should be done differently when the unit is taught again. Deficiencies need to be pinpointed and remedied.

**Teacher Accountability and Evaluation**

Along with the testing and measurement movement has come teacher accountability concepts. With state mandated objectives, teachers are to be held a accountable for pupils achieving these identified ends. Through pupil testing and measuring, it is to be noticed if the teacher has done a good job of teaching. If the teacher has taught well, it is expected that pupil achievement of objectives will show up in test results. There is a certain logic involved in equating teaching well with pupil achievement. However, the teacher is not the only being who influences pupils. The home, the community, religious institutions, among others, do affect the pupil's values and standards. Then too, a single test is not adequate to show pupil achievement. Multiple institutions in society, too, need to be held responsible for learner achievement. A plethora of evaluative techniques need to be used to notice pupil progress and achievement (Ediger and Rao, 2003).

## References

Ediger, Marlow and D. Bhaskara Rao (2003), Philosophy and Curriculum. New Delhi, India: Discovery Publishing House.

Thayer, V.T. (1970), Formative Ideas in American Education. New York: Dodd, Mead and Company, Inc., p. 224.

# Testing and Measurement of Pupil Achievement

Students of education have noticed the tremendous emphasis being placed upon testing and measuring of student achievement. News media frequently criticizes pupil achievement in terms of test results achieved. It appears that these test scores cannot go high enough to please news reporters and writers of news items. Testing and measuring pupil achievement are sensitive items to accomplish. Teachers and school administrators may be very critical of items contained in a test. They also might well criticize the time allotted for giving the many tests to pupils as well as that more than a state mandated test needs to provide data on pupil achievement. One test then is not adequate to show what pupils have learned.

The author will analyze diverse procedures to appraise learner achievement using realism, existentialism, experimentalism, and idealism as different philosophies of appraisal.

## Realism and Assessment of Student Progress

Realists believe that one can know the real world as it truly is, in whole or in part. Thus, for example, chemists have identified 107 elements which make up the natural environment. Each compound can be stated in terms of the inherent elements. Sugar then contains the following elements: C6 H12 06 (C = carbon, H = hydrogen, and O = oxygen). The exact number of atoms in a molecule of sugar such is 6 atoms of carbon, 12 of hydrogen, and 6 of oxygen. Measurable amounts, involving accuracy, are in each compound, such as sugar.

The model of science and mathematics with its precision has been applied to determining student achievement. Standardised tests such as The Iowa Test of Basic Skills are used to measure learner achievement and progress. There may be a single percentile given for student achievement from taking the total test. For each component part, such as mathematics, there may be a separate percentile from the other academic areas and skills as measured by The Iowa Test of Basic Skills. A percentile is a single numeral indicating how well the student is achieving.

When the measurement movement in education came forth in the early 1900s, E. L. Thorndike, Professor at Columbia University in New York City, stressed the thesis that "whatever exists, exists in some amount, and if it exists in some amount, it can be measured." Thorndike and his associates developed tests to measure handwriting progress, arithmetic achievement, and student learning in general. The measurement movement survived in time/place and is extremely important presently to use in ascertaining student achievement. Pertaining to E. L. Thorndike, Thayer (1970) wrote: The early years of the twentieth century were conscious in the application of science to all phases of business and industry. It was applied to not merely the invention of new products and processes but to the details of organisation and management designed to promote economy and efficiency. Experts trained in scientific management studied carefully the performances of workers on the job with results so fruitful in economy and efficiency that many came to be seen in "job analysis" possibilities of application not only to vocational education but to the reform of other aspects of education as well. All that was needed it seemed, was to identify the specific outcomes by insuring that pupils engage in the activities certain to eventuate in the proper habits and skills, information, attitudes, ideals, and the like.

Realism as a philosophy of testing and measurement is very much in evidence in the following concepts: behaviorally stated objectives, measurement driven instruction (MDI), as well as report cards (to compare school districts in achievement within a state). Programmed learning strongly emphasizes the measurement movement such as in the following writing by Harris and Sipay (1985):

> Programmed materials are designed so that the user (1) encounters a series of small tasks in which success is very likely; (2) is involved in the learning process through actively responding: (3) perceives immediate feedback as to the correctness of each response. In theory, programmed materials should greatly facilitate individualised instruction because they allow each student to work almost independently with materials suitable for his or her needs, proceeding at a pace commensurate with ability and interest.

State departments of education, governors of states, as well as state senators and representatives have strongly recommended that each state establish standards (objectives) for students to attain. Tests are written to determine if the objectives, and how many, have been achieved by students. The recently passed legislation by the US House and Senate, signed by the President, as attached to the Elementary and Secondary Education Act (ESEA) emphasizes the following:

1. State mandated tests be developed which measure student achievement in the language arts, science, mathematics, and the social studies.

2. These tests are to be given in grades 3-8 and in grade ten.

3. Student test results are to be broken down in terms of gender, race, and income levels. Students who fail the state mandated tests three years in a row will be given a voucher to attend a school of their choice. Educationally bankrupt schools whose students fail to

achieve adequately on the state mandated tests may be taken over by the state.

4. Information from test results are to be provided to teachers so they may use it to help students achieve more adequately on the next grade level.

5. Gaps in student achievement between/among the races, income levels, and minority groups are to be eliminated.

Realism then as a philosophy of education emphasizes that measurable results from pupils can be obtained to state precisely how well a student is achieving. Comparisons may be made in ascertaining how well pupils and school districts are achieving within a state. Precise information from student test results make it possible to accurately compare one student with another as well as one school district with another.

## Existentialism and Student Achievement

Existentialists believe that each person should learn to make choices, from among alternatives, in society. There should be no compulsion, ideally, in making these choices. In the school setting, then, pupils need to learn to make decisions. Decision making, for example, may involve the selection of reading materials in a programme of individualised reading. There needs to be an adequate number of library books on diverse genera for students when choosing what to read. With existentialist philosophy, the library books should contain content on the human experience in all of its manifestations. The dread to make many choices in life, the anxiety, the tensions, the fears, and the emotions which make a person human must be thoroughly reflected in the decisions made of what to read. The pupil, alone, needs to choose content to read and then share ideas gleaned in a conference with the teacher or with peers. The pupil needs to select what to discuss. The teacher may take notes on comprehension skills achieved by the learner. Comparisons may be made by the teacher with later conferences to notice pupil achievement. The teacher needs to notice how the pupil is achieving in the area of existentialist thinking. Such concepts as the following need to be understood and emphasised by the pupil: freedom, choice, dilemmas, human condition, death, living, dread, alienation, awesomeness, and anxieties. A central idea in existentialist thought is the need to personally develop reasons for living; the purpose or reasons for living are not given to any individual but must be sought.

Existentialism does not advocate:

1. The use of predetermined objectives for pupil achievement, rather the objectives emerge within and from the individual.
2. Testing to determine achievement, rather the pupil determines what to learn and which content to pursue. The teacher is a guide and stimulates learning.
3. External motivation, but rather believes the individual is motivated from within.
4. The learning of subject matter to the minimizing of pupils focusing upon the feelings or affective dimension of human beings. Rather, feelings are the most important part of the human condition.
5. Objectivity of subject matter, but rather content acquired by the pupil is unique and *subjective* to the involved individual.

Pertaining to existentialist thinking, Harper (1955) wrote the following:

> Existentialism, as the name implies, is a philosophy of human existence. It arose early in the nineteenth century in response to a cultural climate in which Soren Kierkegaard observed that men had forgotten what it means to exist. Men had leaned what it means to be one in a crowd, to be a mass; they had forgotten what it means to be an individual, that is what it means to die, to suffer, to decide, to love. They had forgotten what it means to stand apart, as each man is born to stand apart, from the rest of the universe and from one's fellows...

## Experimentalism and Pupil Achievement

Experimentalists believe that one cannot know ultimate reality as it truly is, but he/she can experience it. The experiences will not be perfect in knowing ultimate reality, but in degrees come close enough to what is reality so that the individual can function effectively in society. Experiences emphasize the need for change in society. With experiences, problems are identified which need solving. John Dewey (1859-1952) was a leading advocate of experimentalism as a philosophy of education. Among his many writings, Democracy and Education (Dewey, 1916) states his beliefs on teaching pupils. In his laboratory school at the University of Chicago, Dewey tried out his experimentalists beliefs in practical situations. Problem solving was a major method of instruction emphasised in the curriculum. Here, pupils with teacher assistance identified a problem in a contextual situation. The problem is delimited so that it possesses clarity. Information is gathered in answer to the problem. The information is analysed with critical thinking involved. An hypothesis results which is tentative and subject to testing in a life-like situation. The hypothesis is revised if necessary. Problem solving is stressed as being the complete act of thought.

Experimentalists believe in integrating school and society. Thus, what is important in society, such as problem solving, is also to be emphasised in the school curriculum. School and society are not to be separated, but become integrated entities. Experimentalism believes in assessing pupils to do the following:

1. Using subject matter to solve problems. Subject matter is not to be learned for its own sake, nor to achieve predetermined objectives.

2. Identifying problem areas in context as the unit of study progresses.

3. Acquiring facts, concepts, and generalisations as a problem area is being solved.

4. Evaluation consists of using relevant sources of information to solve a problem as well as to test an hypothesis in a functional situation.
5. Being actively involved in problem solving, not passive recipients of knowledge. Interest in learning makes for student effort in achieving, growing, and developing.

Pertaining to John Dewey, Atkinson and Maleska (1965) wrote the following:

> To Dewey education has two sides—psychological and social: neither may be subordinated or neglected. The Psychological nature of a child forms the basis for his education—it is the teacher's responsibility to make full use of his natural, spontaneous activities. Describing original nature as being spontaneously impulsive rather than passive, Dewey divided impulses into four kinds: the social impulses of communication or conversation; the constructive impulse to make things; the impulse to investigate things; and the impulse of artistic or creative expression.
>
> With these impulses in mind, said Dewey, the school must be changed from a place of sedentary listening to one for active working or doing. The teaching process must be planned to allow the child to learn whatever possible by his own experiences and, in that way, to acquire the habit of thinking...

### Idealism and Pupil Achievement

Idealists believe in a subject centered curriculum. Idealism might well have been called idea-ism since it advocates an idea centered curriculum. Worthwhile idea centered objectives need to be carefully selected for pupils to attain. One cannot know ultimate reality as it truly is, but persons can receive ideas from the natural and social environment. Mind is real and needs to be developed. An alert mind is necessary to attain ideas pertaining to the natural/social environment. Mental development is then of utmost importance since ideas are to be achieved by pupils. Generalisations are more important to learn as compared to learning specifics, although the specifics support the broad ideas. Ideas need achievement rather than direct knowledge pertaining to external world, which is unknowable. Idealists believe in selected concepts being apriori. That is to say that selected ideals (here, idealism has the connotation of stressing ideals to be achieved) have always been true in time and space. Words such as truth, honesty, goodness, beauty, justice and courage, have been true apriori, or always. The *will* must be used to achieve the abstract, since interest alone on the student's part is not adequate. To make progress in learning might well emphasize doing the unpleasant.

To achieve ideas and ideals, reason is necessary on the part of the learner. The reasoning person develops ideas and ideals which transcend sense data. Beyond sense data (seeing, smelling, hearing, touching, and tasting) are purposes and values which assist to attain the ideals of the apriori. For many idealists beyond the here and the now is God. This life may not be the finality of one's deeds and acts. The here and the now may be a testing ground for the hereafter, also called heaven. Thus beyond sense perceptions, many vital happenings transpire. Human beings are at the apex of living things. They are much higher and more significant as compared to what is called animal life.

Idealism emphasizes the coherence theory in testing statements. Thus, a true statement is one which fits in logically with others. Reason is used to test the involved logic. Pertaining to idealism, Brubacher (1966) wrote:

> The most prolific work on the idealistic philosophy of education in the twentieth century was Herman Harrrell Horne (1874-1946). At a time when idealism was rapidly fading as the dominant American theory of education, Horne managed to draw together the various strains of idealism into their more systematic educational exposition. In addition to much that is already familiar, he made two points of his own. One is his volition and effort in learning. The pupil is like a plant, he agreed with Friedrich Froebel, in that his reasons are self-active. But the child is unlike the plant, Horne continued, in that he can withhold his response. Hence, the ultimate responsibility for getting an education rests on the will of the pupil. All education, therefore, is self education; it is the result of voluntary effort put forth by a self-active mind. If not, then like Immanuel Kant (1724-1804),

> Horne urged that the pupil put forth effort in obedience to what he ought to do.

Idealists believe in evaluating pupils to do the following:

1. Expressing subject matter acquired clearly and accurately.
2. Putting forth *much* effort in learning.
3. Being able to use reason and logic effectively.
4. Using quality ideas saliently in speaking and in writing.
5. Placing high worth on eternal values (apriori) such as goodness, beauty, and truth. With adequate mental development, the individual may reach out to achieve these ideas and ideals.

Perennialism is a philosophy of education directly related to idealism. Perennialists believe in students studying the Great Books of the western world. These books contain the writings of great minds of the past and their ideas have stood the test of time and place. Recent writings do not contain the worth as do the classics. They have not, as yet, been determined as remaining important as the years have gone by. The writings of William Shakespeare, Robert Louis Stevenson, Nathaniel Hawthorne, Henry Wadsworth Longfellow, among others, tower above those of recent endeavors in literature. Perennialism spokesperson, Mortimer Adler (1902-1998), developed his philosophy in *The Paideia* of which Tanner and Tanner (1990) wrote the following:

> The perennialists refusal to consider the nature of the learner in developing the curriculum is reflected in the Paideia Proposal. Instead of seeing childhood and youth as distinct phases of human development requiring uniquely appropriately learning experiences for effective growth, childhood and youth are seen as being obstacles to be overcome as quickly as possible. "Youth itself is the most serious impediment in fact, youth is an insuperable obstacle to being an educated person," declares the Proposal. The proposal goes on to call for twelve years of basic schooling for all,

capped by the Socratic study of great literary works and other works of art. This kind of learning "aims at raising the mind up from a lesser or weaker understanding to a stronger and fuller one," declares Adler, and the "art of the teacher depends on the teacher's understanding of how the mind learns by the exercise of its own power," declares Adler, as though the mind exists as a separate entity.

Perennialism believes in assessing student achievement in the following ways:

1. Achievement in acquiring ideas from classical writings.
2. Active involvement of students in discussions pertaining to the *classics* by using the Socratic method of inquiry.
3. Use of the mind or mental powers through the exercise of their own powers, such as in heavy student involvement in inductive learning. A questioning approach by the teacher needs to be used as an art, not a science, of teaching.

## References

Atkinson, Carroll, and Eugene T. Maleska (1965), *The Story of Education*. New York: Chilton Books, pp. 87-88.

Brubacher, John S., *A History of the Problems of Education*. New York: McGraw-Hill Book Company, pp 128-129.

Dewey, John (1916), *Democracy and Education*. New York: The Macmillan Company.

Harper, Ralph (1955), "Significance of Existence and Recognition for Education," *Modern Philosophies of Education*. Chicago: The University of Chicago Press, p. 215.

Harris, Albert J., and Edward R. Sipay (1985), *How to Increase Reading Ability*. White Plains, New York: Longmans, Inc., p. 71.

Tanner, Daniel, and Laurel Tanner (1990), *History of the School Curriculum*. New York: The Macmillan Company, p. 333.

Thayer, V. T. (1970), *Formative Ideas in American Education*, New York: Dodd, Mead and Company, p. 224.

# Statewide Testing and the Innovative Mind

There have been a plethora of recommended innovations which have been advocated and/or implemented. These innovative ideas come from within the school district, the school, and/or the teacher. State mandated testing stresses innovation from without or from personnel external to the local school system as compared to those which are more closely home based including those innovative ideas which may come from the individual teacher. The question which arises here is the following: How do external rules and regulations such as state mandated testing influence local development of the curriculum?

### Characteristics of State Mandated Testing

State mandated testing emphasizes selected philosophical beliefs which differ from locally determined efforts in working toward curriculum improvement. Thus, state mandated objectives stress the following:

- Objectives developed and written on the state level make for a core of learnings which all pupils are to achieve in their states and on their respective grade levels.
- Salient subject matter can be measured and reported in numerical terms.
- Comparisons can be made among states, schools and teachers when reporting pupil achievement.

- Report cards may be included in the media to indicate measured comparisons among states, school districts, and schools.
- Failing schools may be identified which did not meet average yearly progress (ayp) standards.
- Pupils may transfer to a different school if their school is determined to be failing two years in a row, as determined by measurable state mandated test results.
- Reading and mathematics are the two leading curriculum areas in which pupils need to be tested. These two curriculum areas represent the basics for learner mastery.
- Pupils are to be tested in grades three through eight; a pupil may be held back from promotion if he/she does not pass a grade level state mandated test.

State mandated tests are standardised in that the time limits for test taking are the same for all pupils regardless of ability levels or handicaps involved. The test items, too, are the same for all test takers. When test results are reported, separate categories are shown for majority groups as well as minority students be they African, Americans, Hispanics, Native Americans, and English as a Second Language students. The purpose here is to narrow or eliminate achievement gaps among all categories. This indeed is a worthy goal!

- Reading and mathematics are the only two academic areas in which students take state mandated tests. This tends to minimize other academic areas such as science, social studies, and the fine arts. Those areas tested do receive major attention in the school curriculum. What is to be tested is what will be taught.
- Much time is spent by teachers in drilling pupils on possible content on the state mandated test. Drill is rote learning and de-emphasizes higher levels of cognition such as critical and creative thinking as well as problem solving.

- Considerable time is taken in classroom instruction for students to learn the art of test taking. Students then are taught skills to take multiple choice test items, adhere to time limits in test taking, and use the same format as is stressed on state mandated tests. Test taking is not a lifelong skill.
- A single test score determines pupil achievement and promotion.

## Innovations in the Curriculum

There are specific curricular plans which have received much attention in educational journal articles as well as in oral presentations given at state and national teacher education conventions. These will be mentioned briefly and how each does not fit into a state mandated curriculum.

- Local efforts to improve the curriculum. The locally developed curriculum may not harmonize with state mandated testing. Thus, if creativity is stressed locally, state mandated tests stress conformity of pupils to drill in memorizing subject matter which might be on a test.
- Multiage instruction whereby younger and older pupils are taught together in purposeful lessons and units of study. State mandated tests stress learnings for separate grade levels such as grades three through eight.
- Multicultural instruction. This is not emphasised in mandated tests. The separate subjects of reading and mathematics, presently, receive priority and are tested upon only. Multicultural education is a social science discipline largely and at the preset time, social studies has not been discussed for inclusion, at this point in time, for state mandated testing.
- Portfolio development as an alternative or supplement to testing. Portfolios stress each pupil collecting a random selection of daily classroom work which indicates progress of pupil products; state mandated

testing ignores every day work of each learner, completely. Rather, a single test score indicates pupil achievement.

- Community service projects do not count in determining pupil achievement since this does not involve academic course work such as in reading and mathematics. It is true that reading and mathematics may be used in degrees in community service, but they do not zero in on these two curriculum areas. However, a good citizen does assist in community service.
- Drug abuse education is not inherent in state mandated testing. Unless there is time for drug abuse education, reading and mathematics, as basics in the curriculum, will be focused upon largely by teachers. Drug abuse is rampant in the societal arena and is a major concern in terms of health of individuals and related crimes committed to support the negative habit.
- The fine arts of music, drama, and art education are important in a well rounded personality. There is, however, no thinking about testing in these three curriculum areas.
- Social development is not measured in state mandated tests. However, social development in getting along well with others is of utmost importance to all, in the here and the now.
- Moral education certainly is a worthy area of concern for educators. Immorality can be very costly for the individual and for society. Each person needs to have a clear vision of moral standards in every day living. Moral education could be taught as a separate unit of study or woven in to each curriculum area. Modeling proper moral standards, also, is indeed salient.
- Peer mediation gives pupils opportunities to be actively involved in governing the self. It takes time for individuals to be proficient in peer mediation. Here,

pupils involved need to be good listeners to both sides in a disagreement and then come up with a solution which is fair to the opponents. State mandated objectives has no room for peer mediated instruction and does not test pupils in this area. And yet, it is important for pupils to be able to govern themselves.

- Citizenship education is completely omitted in state mandated objectives and testing. The role of the individual in a lawful society needs adequate attention. To be a contributing societal member is relevant when there is rampant or considerable crime in society. Citizenship education is vital for all in society and be contributing members in state or nation. It is very costly to society for any individual to be a prison inmate.

**Recommendations for Improving Assessment Procedures**

There are numerous ways to change assessment practices from what is to what should be. First, state mandated tests need to be tried out in pilot studies more so than what has been done. It does not make sense for 25% or more of high school graduates to fail the high stakes test and not receive a diploma. Item analysis needs to be done to sort out good from bad test items which are vague and hazy. Clearly written test items need to be in the offing. Test items need to be valid and cover what pupils have had chances to learn. Thus, objectives should be available to all teachers and these objectives need to provide guidance as to what should be taught. The objectives should possess clarity to teachers so that benchmarks are available as to what needs to be taught. Adequate time needs to be spent on writing relevant objectives which truly reflect worthwhile subject matter for pupil acquisition. Validity and reliability data on state mandated tests need to be available to schools. This information, in part, will say something about the quality of the state mandated tests. Test sores should be used to analyze difficulties faced by pupils and remediate that which is unacceptable.

Second, a single test should not be used, solely, to determine if a pupil passes or fails the state's standard for promotion. A good second evaluation device might well be the portfolio whereby a pupil may indicate how well he/she did in the classroom on a daily basis. With a portfolio of randomised selection of a pupil's products may be assessed with a quality rubric. Here, the evaluator of the rubric may actually see work completed by the pupil. This is quite different than looking at a single test score which is to tell it all about a pupil's achievement.

Third, development of tests to appraise learner achievement and objectives for teachers to use in teaching takes much time and effort. The entire process of state mandated testing needs to be thought through carefully. It seems as if state mandated testing has been rushed through the senate and the house and signed by the governor. When many are failing because of low test scores, is that the way to go? What happens to the learner's self concept in the process? Is it a good procedure to set the bar so high that many fail the state mandated test in grades three though eight as well as on the exit exam for high school graduation? Before NCLB, there were a plethora of articles written on the harmful affects of flunking students on any grade level. Research was then quoted on how detrimental this practice was on pupils. Presently then, there are attempts to flunk a certain number of pupils through state mandated testing.

Fourth, results from state mandated tests should provide information to teachers on which test items a pupil missed and what is recommended to assist these pupils to achieve more optimally. Helpful information is needed, not punitive results for pupils. The No Child Left Behind (NCLB) Act of 2001 punishes schools for not meeting annual yearly progress (ayp) goals. The ayp was established by each state in the union and is merely an estimate, not an absolute of what pupils should achieve yearly. When pupils lack ayp standards in a school for two consecutive school years, they may opt out and attend a different school. The poorly performing schools generally are in low income areas. Research does substantiate this with no exceptions. Perhaps it would be better to improve services within the "poorly" performing schools with the following assistance:

- An adequate number of good tutors to work one on one with selected pupils who need individual assistance.
- Ample materials of instruction to use in assisting each pupil to achieve optimally.
- Qualified teacher aides to help the regular classroom teacher to meet needs of learners in a classroom.
- Have enough of manipulative materials for pupil use in learning.
- Use of adequate audio-visual materials to guide pupils to understand learnings stressed in ongoing lessons and units of study.
- State of the art computer services for all pupils in school.

Fifth, positive approaches should be emphasised in assisting pupil achievement. The NCLB stresses punitive procedures such as the following which need to be eliminated:

- Report cards in the media which make comparisons among states, schools, and school districts of pupil achievement based on state mandated test scores.
- Pupils opting out of a school due to two consecutive school years of that school not having met annual yearly progress scores.
- Failing of pupils due to not having passed a state mandated test.
- Passing of an exit test in order to receive a high school diploma. More evidence of failure is needed than the single test only.

**Quality Criteria Needed in Instruction**

The classroom teacher needs to experience inservice education which helps pupils to achieve optimally. He/she needs to use criteria from educational psychology in teaching and learning situations. First, the teacher needs to capture pupil attention when teaching. Thus, this teaching strategy involves obtaining the interests of learners. Otherwise pupils will not be attending to what is being taught. Interest is a powerful factor in learning. After the teacher has taught a given set of pupils for a period of time, he/she will know what it is that captures pupil attention. Relating the subject matter taught to the pupil's very own experiences will generally help to secure pupil interest.

Second, assisting the pupil to attach meaning to and in ongoing experiences will help learner achievement. Meaningful learning is at the heart of optimal pupil achievement. If pupils do not understand that which is being taught, the chances are subject matter being acquired will soon be forgotten. Before reading the subject matter, pupils need to have background information which relates directly to the ongoing lesson. This will assist pupils to integrate the new with the familiar knowledge. What is learned must make sense.

Third, pupils need to perceive purpose in learning. Sensing purpose assists pupils to strengthen felt needs to learn new subject mater. There is a reason then for learning. It takes a short amount of time for the teacher to state a purpose for pupils to acquire new subject matter. The purpose must have inherent the reason or reasons for achieving the new facts, concepts, and generalisations. If a new skill is to be acquired by pupils, the teacher may say the skill or ability when stating the purpose or reasons for learning.

Fourth, the goals of instruction always need to be kept in mind by the teacher in teaching and learning situations. These goals or objectives help to maintain a vision for what needs to accomplished by pupils and keeps learning on track.

# Psychology in Teaching Mathematics

Mathematics teachers need to study diverse psychologies of learning so that individual learners may be guided to attain as optimally as possible. With a thorough knowledge of the psychology of learning, teachers may do a better job of teaching mathematics to pupils of all ability levels. Individual differences among learners must be provided for in order that each pupil may learn as much mathematics as possible. A quality mathematics teacher emphasises objectives, learning opportunities, and appraisal procedures that assist pupils individually to perceive meaning in the mathematics curriculum.

## Meaning Theory in Teaching Mathematics

Mathematics teachers need to be certain that each pupil attaches meaning to facts, concepts, and generalisations acquired in the curriculum. With meaningful subject matter, pupils may understand that which was taught. Understanding content presented in mathematics assists the pupil to clarify information. Clarity of understanding stresses that pupils comprehend subject matter presented. In deductive teaching, the teacher explains each fact, concept, and generalisation so that meaningful learning may accrue. When induction as a method of instruction is used, the mathematics teachers asks numerous questions of pupils to receive feedback if they understand what was taught. We believe that teachers must spend adequate time in guiding pupils to perceive meaning, deductively and inductively, through the use of concrete, semiconcrete, and abstract materials of instruction in terms of content taught.

Directly related to pupils attaching meaning to ongoing content presented, learner must be able to use subject matter acquired. If subject matter acquired is used, the chances are it will be retained better than if it were not used. The teacher should assist pupils to apply facts, concepts, and generalisations acquired. Thus, information can be used in solving word problems from the basal textbook used in the classroom. Pupils may also use previously acquired content when solving life-like problems in mathematics. The teacher might write problems and photocopy them for learners to respond to. These problems are directly related to what has been taught in ongoing lessons and units in mathematics. Learners too may write problems and exchange papers with others to solve each problem so that application can be made of what has been learned previously. Discussions led by the teacher can also get pupils wholeheartedly involved in making use of subject matter learned.

The mathematics teacher needs to guide learners to engage in higher levels of cognition when using meaningful materials for learners. Thus, pupils need to have opportunities to engage in critical thinking. In separating the relevant from the irrelevant in working to secure answers to a word problem in mathematics involves critical thought. A separation then of what is salient as compared to that which is not important is necessary in critical thinking. That which is significant is then used to obtain an answer to a word problem contained in the basal or written by the teacher or a learner. Life in society demands that pupils become proficient now and in the future as an adult in the area of critical thought. Separating reality from fantasy and the real from that which is imaginary are necessary ingredients in critical thinking.

Novel solutions are needed to solve numerous problems. Creative thinking then needs adequate emphasis in the mathematics curriculum. For example, to solve a word problem, several algorithms may be used to arrive at a answer. Each algorithm might well provide the correct answer. Learners should become familiar with diversity involved here so that the algorithm that works best for the pupil may be used. Unique solutions to word problems should assist pupils to explore different options to each problem in the societal arena. Hopefully, this transfer from the mathematics curriculum to the real world of society will be in evidence. In society, individuals meet up with unique situations in which solutions are needed that are different from any solution used in the past.

Life-like problems actually faced by learners in mathematics need adequate emphasis in the curriculum. These problems involve buying and selling items, how to stay within one's own budget, as well as an increased use of mathematics in society emphasize problem solving involving reality. A creative mind may be necessary presently for the pupil as well as in the future to solve these problems involving mathematics. Creative thinking must be a definite goal in the mathematics curriculum. Critical thought is also necessary for pupils in solving life-like problems in mathematics. Comparing solutions in answer to a problem certainly stresses critical thought. Further situations involving critical thought emphasizes analyzing a problem in mathematics to study component parts. After comparing and analyzing possible solutions in dealing with problems in mathematics in the real world, a synthesis is needed. To synthesize, creative thinking again is in evidence. Synthesizing emphasizes securing wholeness in coming up with a solution to a problem area. Steps inherent in solving life-like problems (or word problems) in mathematics include the following:

1. Defining the problem whereby clarity is in evidence.
2. Gathering information in arriving at a tentative solution.
3. Developing a hypothesis based on the acquired information.
4. Testing the hypothesis in step three above.
5. Revising the hypothesis, if needed.

In addition to pupils attaching meaning to what has been learned, applying that which has been learned, and engaging in higher levels of cognition, pupils also need to perceive purpose in learning in ongoing lessons and units of study in mathematics. There are selected approaches which can be used by the mathematics teacher to guide pupils to perceive purpose for achieving. A deductive procedure might be used. With deduction, the mathematics teacher explains to learners why the subject matter to be studied is relevant. We believe that the small amount of time needed to explain to learners why the subject matter to be acquired is salient in time well spent in teaching and learning situations. Instead of a deductive approach in guiding pupils to perceive purpose or reasons for learning, there are teachers who prefer in inductive approach. Here, the mathematics teacher asks questions of pupils as to why they believe the content to be studied is relevant to learn. Inductive procedures are more time consuming as compared to deduction since responses must come from learners when determining the relevance in studying vital facts, concepts, and generalisations in mathematics.

A third approach in guiding pupils to perceive purpose in learning is to use extrinsic rewards. Here, the mathematics teacher needs to announce prior to instruction what pupils are to learn as well as the reward that will accrue to learners if they achieve this goal. Rewards to be given might be inexpensive prizes. Tokens to be exchanged for prizes, time given for a self selected activity, or extra recess time. The reward must motivate pupils to achieve more optimally in mathematics. It is given to pupils only if they have attained a goal announced by the teacher prior to lesson presentation. The amount of learning that must be acquired before the pupil secures the reward is determined by the teacher. The working for the reward is a motivator for the learner. Receiving the reward for goal attainment is a reinforcer to encourage similar future behaviour.

Interest is a powerful factor in learning. The mathematics teacher needs to obtain the attention of all learners during teaching-learning situations. To demand attention of pupils does not capture learner interest in mathematics. Rather, the teacher needs to use a variety of materials in teaching mathematics to obtain intrinsic interests of learners. These activities include lifelike problems which need solution, textbook and workbook assignments, films, slides, video tapes, video disks, illustrations, teaching aids, technology, integrated learning systems, teaching units, as well as resource units of study in mathematics. In using a variety of learning activities, the mathematics teacher has a better chance in securing learner interest as compared to a single type of material. The tone of the teacher's voice must have appropriate voice inflection, pitch and juncture. A monotonous tone of voice will not tend to obtain learner interest and attention. Quality eye contact with pupils should aid in obtaining pupils attention and promote learning in mathematics. Interest of pupils in ongoing lessons and units of study develops effort for achieving.

## Theories of Learning in Mathematics

Selected theories of learning in educational psychology used by the teacher should assist pupils to attain at a more optimal level. Operant conditioning, as developed by B.F. Skinner (1904-1988), has done much as a theory of learning to guide learner progress. Dr. Skinner stressed the use of programmed learning in emphasizing behaviorism as a psychology of learning. Here, a qualified programmer would determine what pupils are to learn in any unit of study in mathematics. The body of knowledge within the unit is broken down into component parts. The steps of attainment are very small when working on a programme in mathematics, be it in textbook or software form. The pupil, here, generally reads a sentence or two, depending on the maturity level of the involved learner. He/she then views a related illustration, responds to a test item, and checks the response. If correct, the pupil is rewarded. If incorrect, the pupil now knows the correct answer and is also ready for the next sequential programmed item. The programme has been tried out previously in pilot studies with needed modifications made. The content to follow in each programme moves from the simple to the increasingly more complex. The same procedure, or a slight modification, may follow in each step of learning such as read a sentence or more, view an illustration, respond to a test item, and check the correctness of the response as provided by the programmer. Answers given by the learner are either correct or incorrect. By being correct approximately 90 per cent of the time in responding, the pupil can make continuous progress with increasingly complex items in programmed learning. A positive self concept could be an end result for pupils if they respond with an approximate 90 per cent correct in terms of accuracy. Tutorial programmes using computers tend to stress tenets of programmed instruction. Simulation in computer use may also stress programmed learning, providing it is not too open ended in its subject matter presentation. B.F. Skinner believed strongly in answers being either right or wrong when learners make responses. Shankaranarayana wrote:

For Skinner (1969), "teaching is an arrangement of contingencies of reinforcement which expedite learning." Skinner believes that promotion of learning is possible by giving attention to the following factors—the behaviour that is to be learned, the reinforcers that may be used, and the scheduling of reinforces.

Skinner recommends the use of programmed instruction which provides for individual differences by allowing students to achieve at their own rate of speed. In terms of Skinner' operant behaviorism, "a programme can be seen as an arrangement of material that will lead students to emit correct responses and will also provide reinforcement for that response... The essential elements of programmed instruction... are (1) an ordered sequence of stimuli, (2) specific student response, (3) immediate knowledge of results, (4) small steps, (5) minimum errors, (6) gradual shaping of terminal bahavior and (7) self pacing.

B.F. Skinner has a well known and popular name in education. His experiments in teaching and education have indeed been numerous. Morris and Pai (1976) wrote the following:

> As Skinner has pointed out several times, the most important task of the teacher is to arrange conditions under which desired learning can occur. Considering the fact that teachers are to bring about changes in extremely complex behavior, they should be specialists in human behaviour. Effective and efficient manipulation of the multitude of variables effecting children's intellectual and social bahaviours cannot be accomplished by trial and error alone, nor should such work be based solely on the personal experiences of the teacher, since this covers only a limited range of circumstances. Consequently, a scientific study of human behaviour is vital in the improvement of teaching, because it provides us with accurate and reliable knowledge about learning and leads to the development of new instructional materials, methods, and techniques. Similarly, an empirical analysis of the teaching process is essential, for it clarifies the teacher's responsibility through a series of small and progressive approximations. This approach makes teaching practices more specific, thereby facilitating a more effective evaluation.

## James Popham and Behaviorism

James Popham from the University of California is a strong advocate of behaviorism. Dr. Popham (1970, see bibliography entries) developed a series of filmstrips and related cassette tapes proposing behaviorism as a needed central theme of teaching and learning. Behaviorists believe strongly in the use of measurably stated objectives in teaching pupils. These precise objectives are written prior to teaching learners. Ideally, there is no leeway in determining what will be taught when viewing the written statement of objectives. The teacher then is certain as to what will be taught. He/she may announce to pupils that which will be taught before teaching and learning. Pupils then know what is required of them in terms of subject matter to be acquired. Learners need not out guess the teacher to realize what is expected as to precise objectives to be achieved.

According to Popham, the learning opportunities chosen by the teacher must contain only that which is in the stated objective(s), no more and no less. Evaluation of pupil attainment in mathematics needs to be done in terms of the measurably stated objectives. Thus, a very close alignment indeed is in the offing among the objectives, the learning opportunities, and the evaluation procedures. Validity, a measurement term, is in evidence if the evaluation techniques harmonize with the stated objectives in mathematics.

James Popham with his stress placed upon behaviorism as a psychology of instruction in teaching mathematics advocates the following:

1. Vague hazy objectives need to be eliminated or rewritten so that a sharp focus exists in terms of what will be taught.

2. Learning opportunities must be very carefully chosen since each needs to guide pupils to attain that which is in the stated objective.

3. Evaluation procedures should ascertain if each pupil has attained the precise objectives.

4. A different teaching strategy needs to be used if a learner did not achieve an objective.

5. Sequence of objectives is arranged by the mathematics teacher.

Dr. Popham places extremely strong emphasis upon choosing precise, measurable stated objectives for instruction. He places little stress upon choosing learning opportunities, except that they should match up very precisely with the stated objectives. Evaluation is done strictly in terms of what is mentioned specifically in each objective for pupil attainment.

## Robert Gagne' and Task Analysis of Objectives

Robert Gagne (1984) is a leading psychologist in education who recommends a behaviorist approach in teaching; however, his thinking is more open-ended as compared to Drs. Skinner and Popham. Gagne's eight sequential steps of hierarchical learning for pupils may be of considerable help to teachers in planning the mathematics curriculum. The eight steps of sequential learning for pupils are the following—signal learning, stimulus-response, chaining, verbal association learning, multiple discrimination, concept learning, rule learning, and problem solving as being the most complex form of achievement. Gagne was a former mathematics instructor and found task analysis as being a very appropriate way of determining sequence for pupils. We will comment on a few of the levels we believe to be especially relevant in teaching. Stimulus-response psychology is very relevant for mathematics teachers to consider. For example, once pupils attach meaning through the use of manipulative materials that 7 + 6 and 6+ 7 = 13, this addition fact may be committed to memory. Thus, on a flash card or computer programme the *stimulus* is 7 + 6 or 6 + 7 = .... If correct, pupils should respond with the answer being 13. Drill and practice should not be used prior to meaningful learning by pupils. But, once meaning is there, pupils may need to associate the stimulus and the response in a somewhat rote manner. Gagne's step of chaining might involve pupils using a series of concrete and semiconcrete materials to indicate and show that 7 + 6 and 6 + 7 = 13. Which materials might these be? Sticks, corn and bean seeds, paper squares, and buttons, among other items, may be used by the learner in sequence to show a set of seven and a set of six and by joining the two sets together obtain a set of thirteen markers. The commutative property may also be shown by a leaner. Chaining is involved in that the pupil used diverse materials to show the value of two addends. Multiple discrimination, in the Gagne's hierarchy of objectives stresses pupils noticing differences and likenesses in ongoing lessons and units of study. Analysis is involved here in that pupils separate the relevant from the irrelevant such as in seeking solutions to story or word problems. To do so indicated the need to make separations from what is needed to what is unnecessary. We believe the last three terms used by Gagne are very significant in planning the mathematics curriculum. Thus, concept learning is very relevant. It takes a variety of learning opportunities using different materials of instruction for pupils to understand concepts such as addition, subtraction, multiplication, division, inverse operations, radius, radius squared, radius cubed, and exponents. Understanding concepts are needed on the pupil's part in order that sequential achievement is possible in mathematics.

Gagne's principle or rule learning indicates that learners relate concepts so they become usable. A rule or principle such as "to find the area of a circle, square the radius and multiple by the value of pi" is necessary in a specific situation; otherwise pupils could not ascertain the area of a circle. The last idea in Gagne's hierarchy is problem solving. Thus, principles or rules are needed to understand how to solve the problem of determining the area of a square, triangle, or parallelogram.

A strong point in Gagne's hierarchy of objectives is that the teacher needs to go back a step or level if a pupil does not understand what is to be done. For example, if a pupils cannot solve a problem, perhaps he/she does not attach meaning to the involved rule or principle. If the rule or principle is a stumbling block to the pupils progress, he/she may need to go back to learning the meaning of the inherent concepts within the rule or principle.

## Jerome Brouner and the Structure of Knowledge in Mathematics

Jerome Bruner, professor from Harvard University, advocate a structure of knowledge approach in teaching mathematics. The structural ideas in mathematics would be identified by professional mathematicians in their academic area of specialty. These professional mathematicians then choose key or main ideas for pupil attainment. The structural ideas may be used again and again by learners as they proceed to more complex learnings on sequential grade levels. In mathematics then pupils may attain the following in increased levels of complexity:

1. Commutative and associative properties of addition and multiplication.
2. Distributive property of multiplication over addition.
3. Property of closure.
4. Subtraction as the inverse operation of addition.
5. Division as the inverse operation of multiplication.

The above examples of structural ideas can be emphasised on sequential grade levels at increasing levels of complexity. For example, first grade pupils may learn that 4 + 3 = 7 and 3 + 4 = 7; this stresses the commutative property of addition. At a higher grade level, fifth grade pupils may learn meaningfully that 18, 996 + 38, 649 = 38, 649 = 18, 996.

Jerome Bruner stressed the use of three kinds of materials in teaching mathematics to pupils. In sequence, these would be enactive, iconic, and symbolic. Enactive materials emphasize the use of concrete materials and other objects for learner manipulation in a hands on approach in learning. Second, pupils learn through the use of iconic materials which include pictures, illustrations, video tapes, video discs, slides, filmstrips, and other audio visual aids. Third, Bruner stresses the use of symbolic materials, such as printed content in textbooks, library books, and other abstract content. This sequence in pupil learning then emphasizes the teacher using concrete, semiconcrete, and abstract materials in teaching.

Jerome Bruner advocates the use of inductive methods of instruction in which pupils discover structural or major academic ideas of a discipline. To emphasize Bruner's approach in teaching, the teacher should attend to the following:

1. The teacher needs to have an excellent knowledge of the structure since these key ideas become objectives for learner attainment.
2. To achieve objectives on the pupils' part, the teacher needs to sequence learning opportunities in that individuals experience the enactive, the iconic, and the symbolic in that order.
3. The teacher must appraise pupils to ascertain how many of structural knowledge objectives are being attained by pupils in a spiral curriculum. With a spiral curriculum, pupils meet up again in increasing levels of complexity the structural ideas which serve as objectives of instruction.
4. The teacher needs to become a quality asker of questions involving the ongoing mathematics lessons so that pupils can truly learn in an inductive manner. Inductive teaching then assists pupils to achieve the structural ideas.
5. Inductive teaching in mathematics must be used together with the enactive, iconic, and symbolic materials of instruction.

## Jean Piaget and Developmental Psychology in Mathematics

Jean Piaget studied pupils in clinical settings for over forty years in Switzerland. He identified different stages that pupils go through in the maturation process. The first stage called the Sensorimotor Stage occurs from birth to two years in the infant's life. Here, parents need to have objects for the young child to manipulate and experience in a friendly environment. The child then experiences and perceives objects such as toys in the real environment. He/she may touch, smell, and see the objects. Listening to sounds made by these objects is also salient in sensorimotor learning.

The preoperational stage of development of the child roughly occurs from ages two to seven years. Here, the young child perceives one variable largely. Thus, the preoperational child when viewing two tumblers of the same brand name and size as having an equal amount of water in each, if this is the case. Now, in front of the child, one of the two tumblers of water is poured into a taller thinner tumbler. The child is asked which has more water inside the tumbler. The preoperational pupil will answer the taller thinner tumbler does. The child perceives one variable in that one tumbler is taller than the other and therefore contains more water. If two spheres of clay are held infront of the preoperational child and both are identical in amount, the child will say neither has more clay in it than the other. But, if the experimenter flattens one sphere infront of the child, he/she will say that the flattened clay has more in it than does the sphere of clay. Again, the preoperational child perceives one variable only and that being the flattened piece of clay is longer than the spherical lump of clay. Teachers of kindergarten and first grade pupils need to be aware that preoperational pupils lack maturation to notice that there is more than one variable to objects being observed. Preoperational pupils are perceptional-oriented. How something looks to the child is the correct perception or view. They tend to center on one variable such as the larger the area that one of two sets of marbles is placed in, even though both sets have an equal number of marbles, the larger the number of members of that set in the enlarged area. Thus, if a set of six marbles is placed in a larger area, it will have more marbles than a set of six placed in a smaller region.

From ages seven through eleven, Piaget, in his research, found that these learners still needed concrete objects to learn from. Piaget called this the stage of concrete operations. Here, the learner has matured to emphasize reversibility. Thus, the pupil may notice that the order of addends can be changed and yet the sum stays the same. Or, the concrete operations pupil learns that there are number families such as 7 + 5 = 12 and 5 + 7 = 12, which can be undone through subtraction within that number family such as 12 – 5 = 7 and 12 – 7 = 5. Reversibility also indicates that one can go back to an earlier stage of working on a project or activity and come back to the original starting point. One may go back (reversibility) to an earlier stage in unit teaching to further analyze what was done. One can also reverse to the original stage prior to emphasizing reversibility. Thus, the concrete operations development pupils may perceive several variables when reversibility is in evidence.

Additive composition is also a part of the learner's stage of concrete operations. With additive composition, the pupil in perceiving numerous variables, may define, for example, what the identity elements are for addition and multiplication. There are numerous descriptions which can be given in the definition indicating again the pupil's ability to focus on several items at one time. All the definitions possible add up to a sum pertaining to the identity elements for addition and multiplication.

The principle of associativity is also a part of the concept the stage of concrete operations. With associativity, the pupil can add there or more numbers in any order. Or three or more factors may be multiplied in any order and the product is the same. Many tasks may also be taken up in any order and the results are the same or similar. In all facets of the pupil being in the stage of concrete operations, the teacher still needs to refer to and use concrete materials along with the abstract being emphasised.

At about twelve years of age, pupils enter the stage of formal operations. At the stage of formal operations, learners might be able to think abstractly in mathematics without reference to concrete materials of instruction. Learners in all stages of development need to operate or focus on what is being learned for learning to really take place.

There are numerous implications for teaching mathematics when using Piaget's research in teaching-learning situations. These include the following:

1. The teacher must study the maturational levels of pupils in order to know what and how to teach these learners.

2. There can be much wasting of time in teaching what the maturational level of the involved pupil is not ready for. Then too, the teacher must teach what the maturational level of the pupil is ready for in mathematics. Otherwise time slips by without the learner attaining as much as possible.

3. Hastening the readiness of pupil for learning mathematics does not work. The maturational level will indicate what can/cannot be taught.

4. There needs to be an adequate amount of concrete materials available for teaching since through the age of eleven, the stage of concrete operations is still in the offing.

5. Securing attention for learning is salient since learners do not achieve unless they mentally operate upon the content being presented.

According to Piaget and Imhelder (1969), there are definite factors that the impinge upon pupils as they progress in intellectual development. These are biological maturation; interaction with experiences in the natural environment; social activities; and homeostasis, a balance between the self and experiences in the physical environment.

Biological maturation stresses pupils going through the stages of sensorimotor, preoperational, concrete operations, and formal thought. However, there are factors that influence these stages of biological maturation. One factor is pupils interacting with the natural environment. The richness of experiences here has much to do with learners developing biologically. Thus, a stimulating environment in mathematics definitely affects progression in biological development. Working with other or being in groups that stress collegiality and its influence on both biological and the affects of the natural environment. Certainly, pupils learn much from each other pertaining to the world of mathematics. In supervising student teachers and cooperating teachers, we notice how pupils might affect each other very positively in ongoing lessons and units in mathematics. For example, in one class it was difficult for a pupil to understand and attach meaning to why the divisor is inverted and multiplication is stressed in the division of fractions. When this pupil and three others worked together in cooperative learning, one pupil made it very clear as to why the divisor is inverted and then multiplication occurs in the division of fractions.

Homeostasis emphasizes feelings of satisfaction that a solution has been found to a problem. Thus, there is balance between the individual and his/her environment. Equilibration has then occurred. In the previous example, when a learner understood what is involved when fractions are divided with the "invert the divisor and multiply" rule, the pupil also has reached a state of homeostasis at that point. Homeostasis may be followed again by a desire to know a new fact, concept, and/or generalisation. A good teacher will guide pupils to reach a state of disequilibrium so that an inward desire to learn is involved to seek new information and subject matter.

Piaget emphasizes that what is learned is grouped together in schems. These schemes provide key ideas upon which future learning of the pupil is based. Schems are also called structural ideas. Structural ideas or schemas are patterns of behavior of the individual. The pupil who has been actively involved in learning that 6 + 4 = 10, may now use these learnings to achieve the new to be stressed such as 6 + 5= .... And 5 + 6 = ... New content might then fit into the older preexisting structures. In other words, previous content acquired in mathematics now sets the stage to learn more of higher decade addition. The involved process is called assimilation. There had to be accommodation so that the old and the new content might be blended.

Piaget (1971) continually emphasizes active involvement of the learner in the mathematics curriculum when writing the following:

> If we desire... to form individuals capable of inventive thought and of helping the society of tomorrow to achieve progress, then it is clear that an education which is an active discovery of reality is superior to one that consists merely in providing the young with ready made wills to will with and ready made truths to know with.

## John Dewey and Problem Solving in Utilitarian Situations

John Dewey (1859-1952) advocated a utilitarian mathematics curriculum in which school and society would be related. Thus, what is useful in society should provide the basis for the school curriculum. Thus, in mathematics, pupils with teacher assistance identify a problem area. The problem is significant to the learner. He/she feels a definite need to find needed solutions. The problem then must be adequately delimited so that an answer can be found. Data or information is acquired in answer to the identified problem. The answer is tentative and subject to change due to further testing of the results. John Dewey did not consider textbook problems as being lifelike and reality based. Predetermined questions raised by the teacher and objectives written prior to instruction for pupils to attain do not stress problem solving. Rather within context in an ongoing unit of study preferably, the learner or a committee of pupils choose a problem in mathematics which is vital to solve. This is a practical problem to solve which emphasizes being useful and stresses application of content/skills acquired.

Problem solving then emphasizes the useful and the utilitarian in the pupil's life in the school setting. Mathematics is a curriculum area that can truly emphasize that which is functional. Thus, situations such as the following may stress a practical mathematics curriculum with problem solving involved:

1. Measuring ingredients for a representative food dish of a foreign nation being studied in social studies.

2. Planning and preparing a holiday meal in school whereby each pupil brings a certain amount of a food item.

3. Averaging scores of the number of words spelled correctly by a pupil from six sequential weeks of spelling test scores.

4. Developing a line graph from pupils individual birth dates in a calendar year.

5. Operating a simulated supermarket in the classroom using real or toy money.

The above are merely suggestions for a reality based mathematics curriculum. One needs to remember that John Dewey advocated that problems come from pupils and not from an extrinsic source. The teacher guides learners in selecting and solving problems. John Dewey believed that pupils liked to work on committees rather than individually in solving problems. Learners, too, desired to find out on their own instead of being told how to locate an answer. Pupils were to be active, not passive recipients of knowledge. Creative behavior is preferred much more so as compared to conformity endeavors.

In summarizing John Dewey's problem solving approach in teaching pupils, the following are salient points:

1. Activity centered approaches are emphasised in teaching in that pupils are the focal point of the curriculum.

2. Mathematics stresses that pupils with teacher guidance select relevant lifelike problems which need solving.

3. A learning by dong, not passivity on the part of pupils, is a must for learning to accrue in mathematics.

4. Purpose and interest on the learner's part make for learner effort and perseverance in solving problems.

5. The role of the teacher is to encourage, help, and assist pupils in attaining solutions to problems.

**In Summary**

There are numerous psychologists who may provide teachers with guidance in teaching mathematics. B.F. Skinner advocated a highly structured curriculum in which pupils would make few errors when achieving objectives arranged in a ascending order of difficulty. The programmer arranges the frames of learning in mathematic by using a sequence of read, view an illustration, respond, and check order. A psychology of behaviorism is emphasised here. Responses are either correct or incorrect as given by pupils individually.

James Popham believes in using measurement driven instruction (MDI) with the objectives stated behaviorally. The stated objectives leave no leeway for interpretation. The mathematics teacher then provides learning opportunities which contain only that which is in the stated objective. Appraisal is done in terms of the stated objective to determine if learners individually have been successful achievers.

Robert Gagne emphasizes a hierarchical arrangement to teacher written objectives whereby the learner attains each in ascending order or complexity. Should an objective in mathematics be too difficult to achieve, the teacher needs to assist pupils individually to go back to a previous goal so that background information may have been attained. Then, the pupil should be ready sequentially to achieve the original objective. We will review the last three objectives Gagne stressed in curriculum development. These are in sequence: concept development, attaining generalisations, and solving a problem, by the learner. The mathematics teacher writes the objectives for pupil achievement. Dr. Gagne, a former mathematics teacher, found that the teacher needed to go back to an earlier level of achievement if a pupil could not attain the preset objective being stressed in the curriculum. Thus, if a learner did not understand how to solve a mathematics problem, he/she might need to go back to studying the related generalisation that is inherent in the problem. Should the learner not understand the generalisation, he/she may need to study the related concept(s). Once the concept(s) are understood, the pupil is ready to be taught the related generalisation. If the generalisation is meaningful, the involved pupil might then be ready to solve the problem. Robert Gagne emphasised going back to an earlier level of achievement if the pupil did not attach meaning to what is presently being taught. Sequence in learning mathematics is very important to Robert Gagne. All good teachers of mathematics prize highly if content, skills, and attitudes are learned sequentially by learners. This may mean reversing to an earlier level of attainment if a pupil does not understand or comprehend that which is being taught presently. The sequence may also pertain to a learner being taught more complex subject matter in mathematics if presently the objectives have been achieved.

Robert Gagne' advocated a hierarchy of objectives for pupils to attain in mathematics which meet the following standards:

1. The objectives are arranged so that each pupil may attain an appropriately ordered set of goals which move from the easier to those increasingly more complex.

2. The teacher may place another objective between two others if a pupil makes an error at that point.

3. The problems to be solved tend to be more abstract than those advocated by John Dewey.

4. The objectives are determined prior to instruction.

5. Quality sequence in mathematics makes for fewer learner errors when being engaged in a lesson or unit of study. The teacher sequences or orders the objectives for learner attainment.

Jerome Bruner emphasised that pupils on any grade level attain structural ideas in mathematics. Mathematicians at the university level select and agree upon these ideas.

The structural ideas are available to teachers who teach pupils. Inductively, pupils are to achieve these structural ideas on an increasingly difficult level as they progress through sequential levels of attainment.

Jean Piaget stressed the importance of pupils going through specific maturational levels such as the sensorimotor, preoperational, concrete, and abstract levels. Biological maturation is salient when teachers ascertain what should be taught to pupils. The stage of concrete operations, for example, has associatively as one of its subcategories. The associative properties of addtion and multiplication, using concrete materials, should be taught at this stage (ages seven to eleven) of learner development).

John Dewey advocated a problem solving approach in which pupils identify and solve problems. The problems are lifelike and practical. The useful and the utilitarian are emphasised. Dewey placed strong emphasizes upon democracy as a way of life. Democracy then is more than a political system or a way of governing individuals. Democracy is a way of associating with others and a means of communication. It is a means of involving all who will be affected by a given decision (Dewey, 1916). Democratic means are needed to identify and solve problems. These problems need to be reality based and practical in the societal arenas. Pupils then need guidance to select and solve life-like problems in mathematics. To stress democracy in the school and classroom settings, learners should work cooperatively in problem solving endeavors in mathematics.

The teacher of mathematics needs to use a psychology of teaching which will guide the learner to achieve as optimally as possible. There are diverse psychologies available to provide guidance in helping pupils achieve, grow, and learn in mathematics. Pupils need to be able to use with has been acquired. Meaning is then attached to facts, concepts, and generalisations achieved in mathematics. The National Council Teacher of Mathematics in 1989 developed excellent criteria, goals, and objectives for pupils to achieve. These are listed in their book curriculum and Evaluation Standards for School Mathematics. The psychologies discussed above may well be used to guide pupils in goal attainment from those listed in Curriculum and Evaluation Standards for School Mathematics.

## References

Dewey, John (1916). *Democracy and Education*. New York: The Macmillan Company.

Gagne', Robert (19, 1996-102, 84). *The Conditions of Learning*. New York: Holt, Rinehart and Winston.

Morris, Van Cleve (1976). *Philosophy and the American School*. Boston: Houghton Mifflin Company, 340.

Piaget, Jean (1971). *Science of Education and the Psychology of the Child.* New York: Viking Press, 26.

Popham, James (1970). *Alternative Avenues to Educational Accountability: Appropriate Practice: Educational Objectives; Establishing Performance Levels; Modern Measurement Method; Opening classroom structures; Selecting Appropriate Objectives; and Teaching Units and Lessons Plans.* (These are filmstrips and related tapes on behaviorism as it applies to teaching and learning).

Shankaranarayana, B.L. (1990). *Achievement in Mathematics Under Guidance Discovery Learning and Reception Learning Conditions.* D thesis. Mysore, India: University of Mysore, 6-7.

# Quality and Quantity in the Mathematics Curriculum

Mathematics, a basic in the curriculum, is heavily emphasised, along with reading, in state mandated testing. To have a good mathematics curriculum, carefully chosen objectives need to be in the offing and implemented in the instructional arena. These objectives need to stress a balance among cognitive, affective, and psychomotor ends. Teaching and learning contain a plethora of specifics which are necessary to adhere to. Thus, to do the best possible, the pupil needs adequate nutrition, sleep, and decent living facilities. Then too, the pupil must feel safe in school and in the home setting as well as experience en route safety between home and school. A school needs to be a place where pupils feel they belong and are accepted by others. Feelings of rejection are highly negative. The entire school system needs to work in the direction of pupils and school personnel being highly accepting of others in a multicultural environment. Also, a pupil desires to be known for something done well. The school and classroom setting need to provide opportunities for pupils individually to be successful learners and thus receive praise for achievement and progress. Self confidence in mathematics is a must in the curriculum (See Maslow, 1954).

## Cognitive Objectives in Mathematics

Each cognitive objective needs to be chosen carefully in mathematics. Quality sequence of objectives begins in the preschool years and goes throughout higher education. Thinking skills are vital in mathematics. Too many teachers stress rote learning and memorisation of mathematics content. This is not adequate. Pupils need to understand what is being learned. To understand means to attach meaning to ongoing lessons and units of study. Any number pair, for example, such as 8 + 7 may have a memorised answer but this is survey, not depth learning. Learners need to attach meaning to "8" representing a quantity of objects which can be counted as a set. This is true no matter how large the addends are. The foundation for meaningful mathematics learnings must begin early in the child's life.

Logical thing needs adequate emphasis in mathematics. The commutative, associative, and distributive properties then should sequentially be stressed. A child may learn the logic in that 8 + 7 = 15, a swell as 7 + 8 = 15. At any age level, this commutative property of addition saves much time in learning in that it cuts in half the number of addition facts to be learned. Logical thinking transfers in sequence to all branches of mathematics.

Critical thinking is salient in that pupils need to be able to analyze mathematical subject matter. For example, any value then such as 5123 might be analysed in terms of thousands, hundreds, tens, and ones. Column addition stresses that the ones need to be added to ones, tens to tens, hundreds to hundreds, and thousands to thousands with the possibilities of regrouping and renaming. Later on, increasingly complex numerical values and reasoning will be involved.

Inherent in critical thinking is creative thought. Here, the pupil needs to be flexible in terms of using a variety of algorithms. There are diverse algorithms which might be used in coming up with answers in problem solving. Then too, problem solving requires identifying a problematic situation, gathering information, developing an hypothesis, and testing the hypothesis in a life-like situation. Deliberations is involved. It takes time and effort to solve relevant problems. Within the framework of critical and creative thinking, problem solving is vital as well as useful. Subject matter is used creatively as needed to solve problems.

Being able to estimate well and check the estimation correctly is a vital skill. Estimating in mathematics is a highly useful and important skill in everyday life. Mentally in being able to estimate well in specific situations is emphasised in terms of time, distance, volume, and area. A practical use of estimation must be stressed in the curriculum.

Being able to interpret graphic information correctly is necessary when gleaning information from the media. Thus line, bar, picture, and circle graphs, need interpretation as to what is being conveyed. Knowledge of correct interval size and statistical procedures such as in using the mean, median, mode, quartile as well as standard deviation, among others, need to be taught developmentally. Meanings need to be attached to grouped and ungraded numerical data as well as descriptive and inferential statistics. Inferences need to be made of carefully collected and organised statistical data.

A rich mathematics vocabulary needs to be in the offing and integrated into each mathematical lesson and unit of study. Subject matter needs to be taught developmentally and sequentially in order to provide learners with background information to master each new objective. No pupil should be left behind without a well defined scope and sequence programme of mathematics (Ediger and Rao, 2000, Chapter One).

**Affective Objectives in Mathematics**

Too frequently, affective objectives are minimised in teaching due to the inability to accurately measure if these kinds of objectives have been achieved by pupils. The teacher, through daily observation, may notice the quality of attitudes possessed by pupils. Growth in a desire to achieve more optimally in mathematics, as an attitude, provides opportunities for pupils to attain vital facts, concepts, and generalisations in mathematics. These learnings need to be reflected upon and communicated to others in an atmosphere of respect. Accepting others makes committee endeavors more enriching and pleasant. Rudeness and a lack of tolerance toward others has no place in situations where pupils interact with each other.

Neat, legible and accurate writing is necessary when communicating mathematical ideas in writing. Communication skills are important in mathematics, including the ability and desire to convey ideas orally. Processes and procedures in mathematics need to be conveyed which are meaningful to other pupils, the teacher, and parents in the home setting. Wanting to communicate clearly and accurately provides opportunities to develop thinking abilities. Each learning obtained provides a foundation for achieving increasingly more complex ideas. It takes understanding and quality attitudes to attach meaning to vital subject matter such as fundamental operations on number, linear measurement, area, volume, weight, ratio and proportion, among others salient learnings. The pupil needs to have an inward desire to learn and achieve. Quality attitudes then in the affective dimension aid pupils to achieve and accomplish. Having good attitudes go a long way in doing well in a developmental mathematics curriculum (See New, 2003).

**Psychomotor Objectives in Mathematics**

Ample and meticulous attention must be given to psychomotor objectives in the mathematics curriculum. These kinds of objectives emphasize pupils applying what has been learned. When application is made, pupils practice what has been learned previously. Retention of learnings is improved upon when facts, concepts, and generalisations are used by pupils. Using that which has been learned also makes it possible for review and practice to take place in a meaningful way.

However, in applying learnings, meaningless drills are minimised. Making application may mean using what has been learned in a new process, skill, or practical situation. There are a plethora of situations in which previously achieved ideas in mathematics may be used. The following are several suggested learning opportunities:

1. Making mathematical models.
2. Constructing items where mathematics is used in an ongoing unit of study.
3. Dramatizing a mathematical situation.
4. Drawing diverse geometrical figures to show design and spatial relations.
5. Modeling a process or procedure to share with others.

Then too in every day life, pupils need to use what has been learned in mathematics applied to practical situations. When items are purchased or sold, mathematics is needed in making these transactions (See National Council Teachers of Mathematics, 1989).

In all kinds of psychomotor, affective, and cognitive objectives being emphasised in teaching mathematics, the teacher needs to follow principles of learning from the psychology of education, including the following:

1. Learning activities need to actively engage pupils. Pupils need to be wholeheartedly involved in ongoing lessons and units of study. The chances are a passive child will not learn much in mathematics.
2. Pupils need to make sense of subject matter taught and learned. It wastes learner time if a lack of understanding results from the facts, concepts, and generalisations being taught.
3. Motivation is a powerful factor in learning. With quality learning opportunities, pupils should feel energised to learn, to do, and to accomplish. Adequate motivation

provides an inward desire for pupils to acquire mathematical learnings.

4. Learning styles need to be stressed in teaching pupils. Thus, selected pupils like to learn in collective situations whereas others prefer individual endeavors.

5. The teacher needs to select interesting activities to achieve objectives. This is important in order to secure pupil attention in the lesson presentation.

6. Individual differences need adequate provision since pupils differ from each other in talents and abilities. Each pupil needs to achieve as optimally as possible in the curriculum.

7. A variety of appraisal procedures need to be used to ascertain pupil achievement. Achievement in cognitive, affective, and psychomotor objectives need to be evaluated in terms of quality criteria (See Peressini, 1997).

**Appraisal Procedures in Mathematics**

There are diverse evaluative procedures available to measure mathematical achievement. State mandated testing is one procedure to ascertain what pupils have learned. One kind is norm referenced whereby each pupil may be compared on a grade level with others in the nation. Thus, a local pupil's score may pertain to being on the 34th percentile, for example. This means that out of every 100 pupils having taken the test, 66 pupils are higher and 34 are lower in making the comparison. There are no accompanying objectives for the teacher to use in teaching when norm referenced tests are used. From pupil test results on the norm referenced test, there will be a spread of scores from the 99th down to the first percentile. Criterion referenced tests (CRTs), developed state wide, do have accompanying objectives for the teacher to use in teaching. The subject matter taught then is valid in terms of what will be covered, in general, on the test. The spread of scores from high to low will be much less from CRT results as compared to norm referenced testing. Norm referenced test writers plan for a spread of test results from the 99th to the first percentile whereas CRTs emphasize, if possible, that all pupils be successful in learning. The objectives furnished to the teacher harmonize with the CRT so that is a better chance for pupils to score higher on the CRT as compared to the norm referenced test (Ediger, 1995, 7- 10).

Second, teacher observation may be used continuously. Here, the teacher may notice the kinds of errors made by pupils and assist in remediation. The teacher may record the common kinds of errors made by pupils in class and then remedy these in small group or large group instruction. Errors made may be due to a lack of knowledge, carelessness, haste, incorrect copying of numerals to perform mathematical operations, a lack of legibility in writing numerals, and/or neatness, among others.

Third, teacher written tests may help ascertain what pupils have learned in mathematics. These might be multiple choice, true/false, matching, short answer, completion, and/or essay. Each kind of test has a different purpose for its use as compared to the others. For example, multiple choice test items may largely measure salient facts learned by children whereas essay tests may stress problem solving, emphasizing higher levels of cognition.

Fourth, a test may emphasize multiple languages to reveal information acquired in mathematics. Thus, a young child may show that 4 + 5 = 9 by using beads with a set of four yellow and five read beads, totaling nine beads whereas a different child may show the same addition fact with four white tally marks and five red tally marks on the chalkboard to indicate a sum of nine. The four basic operations on number may be shown in a plethora of ways including blocks, strips of paper, pencils, chalk, buttons, among others.

Fifth, daily discussions might well reveal what a pupil has learned in a lesson or unit of study. The pupil may indicate learnings acquired in a discussion by participating actively, showing a learning asked for with a drawing on paper or use of every body show cards whereby a child may answer a question by holding up the correct card such as "five" in answer to an addition, subtraction, multiplication, or division number pair, i.e. 9 × 8 =, shown on a card.

Sixth, teacher made materials can be excellent to use in teaching. For example, two pupils may use flash cards in drill and practice. One person then shows a card and the other provides the answer. The flash cards are stacked face down on a pile. The roles of pupils may reversed after the first pupil is through responding to the face down pile of cards.

Selected teachers have also made excellent game boards with a pupil moving forward one space if he/she answers correctly to a number pair on a card, originally turned face down. The first child who comes to the end of the race track, by moving forward one space at a time for each item answered correctly wins the game.

Seventh, workbook exercises completed by pupils in meaningful activities may provide the teacher with much information about a pupil's achievement in mathematics. Working pages in a workbook for the sake of doing so has little value. Rather, there must be a clear pupil purpose for working an exercise.

Eighth, software programmes may well provide challenges to pupils in mathematics achievement. Tutorials provide new learnings to pupils. Each programme is sequenced by the programmer and each answer given provides immediate feedback to the learner. Continuous evaluation based on each response provided by a learner gives the teacher necessary information on a pupil's progress. Drill and practice programmes give the learner opportunities to practice skills in mathematics in which weaknesses have been exhibited previously. Pupils should experience drill and practice based on need and not for the sake of doing so. Simulation programmes emphasize life-like situations in mathematics in which pupils solve realistic problems. Continuous feedback is provided to pupils in problem solving. Gaming programmes provide the learner chances to use a game like approach in achieving new concepts and generalisations in mathematics. The game may be played individually or within a small group or committee. The computer monitor shows what the pupil has learned and which learnings are presenting difficulties (Ediger, 1989, 20-23).

## Closing

Pupils need to have challenge, yet an achievable mathematics curriculum. Each pupil needs to learn as much mathematics as possible for use in school and in society. The objectives of instruction need to be chosen carefully by involved persons. The learning opportunities to achieve objectives need to assist in providing for individual differences among learners. Assessment must be ongoing and sequential to provide appropriate order of mathematical experiences for pupils.

## References

Ediger, Marlow, and D. Bhaskara Rao (2000), *Teaching Mathematics Successfully*. New Delhi, India: Discovery Publishing House, Chapter One.

Ediger, Marlow (1995), *"Current Concepts in Teaching Mathematics,"* Philippine Education Quarterly, 7-10.

Ediger, Marlow (1989), "Psychology in Teaching Mathematics," *Delta K*, Vol. 27, No. 4, 20-23.

Maslow, Abraham (1954), *Motivation and Personality*. New York: Harper and Row.

National Council Teachers of Mathematics (1989), *Curriculum and Evaluation Standards for School Mathematics*. Reston, Virginia: NCTM.

New, Rebecca S. (2003), "Reggio Emilia; Nw Ways to Think About Schooling," *Educational Leadership*. 60 (7), 34-39.

Peressini, Dominic (1997), "Parental Reform of Mathematics Education," *The Mathematics Teacher*, 90 (6), 423-427.

# Trends in the Mathematics Curriculum

There are definite trends which need to be emphasised in the mathematics curriculum. These trends are relatively stable, but may be subject to modification in time. Trends do not stress what is here today but gone relatively quickly. Teachers and school administrators need to study, analyze, and think about which trends are salient to emphasize. By reading recent literature in educational journals and university level teacher education textbooks, observing quality instruction in the classroom, observing video tapes on teaching excellence, among others, the mathematics curriculum may be updated. Each trend needs to be studied indepth, and those deemed worthwhile when using recommended criteria might well be implemented in the classroom. Which trends might then be implemented in the school mathematics curriculum?

## The Mathematics Curriculum

The mathematics teacher needs to follow important tenets from the psychology of education in teaching and learning situations. Thus, the teacher needs to:

- Provide engaging activities for pupils so that an inward desire to learn is in evidence. Instead of passive learners, pupils need to be enthused and interested in ongoing experiences in mathematics. Intrinsic motivation to learn has long been an ideal in the curriculum. Motivated pupils pursue and achieve in mathematics. They are able to attain challenging developmental objectives within the framework of appropriate learning opportunities.

- Assist pupils to attach meaning to ongoing experiences in mathematics. Concrete and semiconcrete activities help pupils to attach meaning to vocabulary terms directly related to ongoing units of study. With meaning, pupils understand what is being taught. Vagueness and guess work is eliminated from the curriculum. Then too, meaning attached to facts, concepts, and generalisations being emphasised in teaching and learning situations provides a foundation for achieving more complex learnings, which meaningless learnings do not provide.

- Assist pupils to perceive purpose in learning. Unless the pupil sees reasons for achieving in mathematics lessons and units of study, the chances are he/she may not attain as much as would otherwise be the case. There are a plethora of purposes for achieving relevant ideas in mathematics. A few talented pupils may believe that it is valuable to learn mathematics for its very own sake. Others might be guided to learn for the sake of its use in daily life, and still others find it difficult to determine any purpose for its study. The mathematics teacher needs to assist pupils inductively or deductively to find values in accomplishing as optimally as possible. He/she may ask questions of pupils pertaining to the values of learning selected facts, concepts, and generalisations in an ongoing lesson. An inductive procedure of learning is then in evidence. Or, the teacher may state the reason(s) for pupils achieving the objectives of instruction. This is a deductive approach (Ediger, 1999, Chapter Ten).

- Guide pupils to use their individual strengths in learning. Multiple Intelligences theory lists eight different intelligences which individuals possess. Thus, the strongest intelligence needs to be used as possessed by any individual student. *Verbal intelligence* may provide well for those who gain much from school mathematics through reading. A well chosen basal textbook might then provide learning opportunities which involve word problems, computation, and written work. A second intelligence, namely *logical thinking* or reasoning, may be used much in all facets of mathematics. Reasoning logically is used in obtaining structural ideas in mathematics. The commutative, associative, and distributive properties, as examples, stress much logic. Pertaining to the commutative property in addition and multiplication, $a + b = b + a$; $a \times b = b \times a$. *Interpersonal intelligence* may emphasize pupils working in committees for those possessing this intelligence. *Interpersonal Intelligence* involves working Individually in ongoing mathematics lessons. Knowledge of multiple intelligences theory assists the mathematics teacher to study children carefully and use relevant theories to make decisions in the instructional arena. Using multiple intelligences theory helps children in using their own unique personal strengths to do mathematics (See, Gardner, 1993).

- Use classroom management approaches which assist pupils to achieve more optimally. There are pupils who do better in a very quiet learning environment whereas others prefer a more busy-like atmosphere in the classroom to achieve more optimally. Those who like a very quiet environment may be seated in divided study carrels whereas others who like a more business-like humming noise may then work collaboratively in groups.

Selected pupils like to have a more formal learning environment than others in the classroom. These pupils may like a structured teaching and learning situation such as direct explanations and directions pertaining to the new lesson in mathematics before proceeding with assigned work. Others may like a more open ended approach such as having a voice in decision-making including teacher pupil planning of the curriculum.

There is also a dichotomy in selected pupils liking a step by step procedure of instruction to achieve a generalisation(s), as compared to those who prefer to begin with holism and then proceed to the parts in mathematics instruction. These factors in classroom management involve learning styles possessed by individual pupils (See, Searson and Dunn, 2001).

- Integrate computers and technology into the mathematics curriculum. There are developmentally appropriate software packages which need to be brought into ongoing lessons and units of study in mathematics. These software programmes assist pupils to achieve vital objectives more effectively. The following kinds of computer programmes need to be used when it benefits pupils sequentially:

    1. Tutorial whereby new learnings are developed by pupils to achieve objectives.

    2. Simulation in which pupils respond to specific ordered items in order to solve a problem. Continuous feedback is provided each pupil in terms of being successful in problem solving.

    3. Drill and practice whereby a pupil practices on certain basic number pairs. Where a pupil is weak, he/she receives additional practice in those specific areas of mathematics.

    4. Games whereby pupils may learn mathematics knowledge and skills through a gaming situation. Two or more may be on each side. In providing the most correct answers, each side attempts to win the game as math items are answered correctly when presented on the monitor.

Multimedia approaches need to be used to provide for a variety of individual differences among pupils. Each material of instruction used should assist pupils to achieve as optimally as possible (See, Watts-Taffe, et al., 2003).

**Objectives of Instruction**

Each objective needs to be determined carefully in mathematics lessons and units of study. The objectives should be challenging, but achievable. Knowledge objectives, as one of three categories, should consist of subject matter which is relevant for pupils to learn. Here, viable facts, concepts, and generalisations should be in the offing for learner attainment. Pupils need to comprehend what is taught so that application may be made of these learnings. What is of use in classrooms and in practical learnings must be analysed in order to separate that which is accurately done as contrasted with the inaccurate. Diagnostic procedures then must be used. After inaccuracies have been diagnosed, then a synthesis of knowledge needs to accrue. The synthesised ideas might then be applied in problem solving. Evaluation of the solutions to a problem needs to be assessed so that weaknesses in thinking and in solutions may be noticed.

A second category of math objectives pertains to skills for pupils to attain. Skills emphasize a doing procedure by using the knowledge acquired. There are a plethora of valuable skills for pupil achievement. These include the following:

- Reading math content accurately in order to improve necessary skills. There are two dimensions here, the first is word recognition. Pupils may need assistance in word recognition. Assistance to be given here include

1. **Use of phonic clues.** Where there is consistency between symbol (grapheme) and sound (phoneme), the pupil needs it learn to use a sounding out method of word recognition.

2. **Use of context clues.** The unrecognised word needs to be replaced with one which makes sense in relationship to the surrounding words in that sentence or paragraph. Meaning theory is in operation here in

that the word used for the unknown one must make for meaningful subject matter.

3. **Syllabication.** A pupil may recognize a word by removing either a familiar prefix or suffix. After the remaining word is recognised, then the prefix and/or suffix may be replaced so that pupils recognize what was initially an unknown word.

4. **Use of picture clues.** For young children, especially, there may be selected illustrations on a page which may be referred to in identifying an unknown word.

To comprehend ideas effectively when reading, pupils need guidance and practice to:

1. Reason and use logic in mathematical sentences and statements.
2. Do analytic thinking in order to appraise what is salient from the non-salient in math problem solving.
3. Do creative thinking to come up with novel ideas in how to solve problems effectively.
4. Apply learnings acquired in mathematics.
5. Attach meaning to important vocabulary terms (Ediger, 1998, Chapter Fourteen).

A third category of math objectives for pupils to achieve are attitudes. Thus, to achieve optimally, the pupil needs to:

1. Develop a positive attitude toward mathematics in school and in society.
2. Have a desire to increase knowledge and skills in mathematics.
3. Achieve a positive attitude toward problem solving.
4. Assist others to attain as optimally as possible with equity being a key concern.

5. Be able to stay on task in ongoing math lessons and units of study (See Kennedy and Tripp, 1991).

State mandated objectives In mathematics exist in all fifty states in the union. There is much pressure placed upon pupils to achieve satisfactorily on these tests. Equally much pressure is being placed upon mathematics teachers to secure adequate, annual yearly progress (AYP), achievement results from pupils. Pupils are tested annually in grades three through eight in mathematics and reading. A pupil may be held back in promotion if he/she fails the state mandated test in any of these grade levels, three through eight. Also, a pupil does not receive a high school diploma in many states unless the mandated mathematics and reading tests have been passed. A failure to comply with the criteria may well make it that a state does not receive federal moneys from the No Child Left Behind (NCLB) Act, Cavanagh (2003) wrote the following:

"Tree rural Vermont school systems are making an unusual attempt to avoid the penalties their schools face under the No Child Left Behind Act, through a deft shifting of the federal funding they receive under the Title One program.

Officials of the three districts believe the move will allow them to put off, at least temporarily the consequences provided under the federal law for schools that fail to make 'adequate yearly progress' on student test scores.

District administrators say they are not trying to shirk the federal mandate to improve their schools, nor are they rejecting the Title One money outright. They say they want to surely avoid what they view as overly harsh federal penalties that would prevent them from making academic strides on their own. By shifting federal Title One money, the school system hopes to fall under the potentially less serious consequences specified under Vermont's accountability programme for non-Title One schools. Vermont, along with every other state, submitted such a plan to the US Department of Education earlier this year to demonstrate how it would comply with the testing and accountability requirements of the No Child Left Behind law."

In addition to required state mandated testing, voluntarily the teacher needs to assist each pupil in developing a portfolio showing daily work performed by pupils in the classroom. A random sampling of representative pupil work should be included in the portfolio. Thus, the following may become a part of a pupil's products in a portfolio:

1. Evaluated daily pupil written work in mathematics.
2. Diagrams, charts, graphs, and listed formulas for finding area and volume, completed by the pupil.
3. Teaching and learning aids made by the pupil including a place value chart, a fraction and a decimal chart, and a mathematics vocabulary chart, among others.
4. Snapshots of teaching aids made which otherwise would be too large to place inside a port folio.
5. A video tape showing the quality of the pupil's interaction in cooperative learning experiences.
6. Cassette recordings of oral book reports given in class. These should be library books written on mathematical content.
7. Self evaluation device used to assess the learner's perception of his/her own achievement.
8. Teacher written test results (Ediger, 2002; 7-10).

The teacher may write quality tests to ascertain pupil achievement in mathematics. Proper standards need to be used with clarity in writing test items to use in determining what pupils have learned. Written by teachers, multiple choice tests are generally used to measure progress of learners. With four distractors, it is more difficult for pupils to guess the correct answer when responding to multiple choice items as compared to true/false tests. True/false can minimize the guessing facet by having pupils write the correction within a 'false' test item. Matching, completion, and short answer tests may also be written to determine if pupils have acquired salient facts.

Essay tests provide opportunities for pupils to use writing skills as well as higher levels of cognitive knowledge acquired. These tests need to have each test item adequately delimited so that only the important ideas are incorporated. Otherwise, the content written to answer an essay test question may become voluminous. However, enough needs to be written for each essay question so that it truly is a response which indicates a pupil's knowledge and writing skills. There is this problem whereby an essay test question may become too broad in scope as compared to being too narrow. When an essay question becomes too narrow, it may be better to write it in short answer or completion test item form.

All teacher written tests should be aligned with the objectives of the unit title or course being taught. There is qualify help available for teachers in selecting relevant objectives in the mathematics curriculum. The National Council Teachers of Mathematics (NCTM, 1989) gave much attention in choosing vital objectives for pupils to achieve. They presented NCTM standards for elementary education with the following topics, as an example:

**K- 4**

- Estimation
- Number sense and Numeration
- Concepts of Whole Number Operations
- Whole Number Computation
- Geometry and Spatial Sense
- Measurement

- Statistics and Probability
- Fractions and Decimals
- Patterns and Relationships

**Grades 5-8**

- Number and Number Relationships
- Number Systems and Number Theory
- Computation and Estimation
- Patterns and Functions
- Algebra
- Statistics
- Probability
- Geometry
- Measurement

Pupils should have ample opportunities to experience a high quality mathematics curriculum. The chosen objectives, learning opportunities, and assessment procedures need careful selection and be aligned with each other.

## References

Cavanagh, Sean (2003), "Vermont Districts Seek To Avoid Federal Consequences," *Education Week*, 23 (5), 1,15.

Ediger, Marlow (1999), *Improving the Teaching of Elementary School Mathematics*. Kirksville, Missouri: Simpson Publishing Company, Chapter Ten

Ediger, Marlow (1998), *Teaching Reading Successfully in the Elementary School*. Kirksville, Missouri: Simpson Publishing Company, Chapter Fourteen.

Ediger, Marlow (2002), Measurement Theory Versus Constructivism," *Journal of Research in Education*, 1 (1), 7-10.

Gardner, Howard (1993), *Multiple Intelligences: Theory Into Practice*. New York: Basic Books.

Kennedy, Leonard M., and Steve Tipps (1991), *Guiding Children's Learning of Mathematics.* Belmont, California: Wadsworth Publishing Company.

National Council Teachers of Mathematics (1989), *Curriculum and Evaluation Standards for School Mathematics.* Reston, Reston, Virginia: NCTM.

Searson, Robert, and Rita Dunn (2001), "The Learning Style Teaching Model," *Science and Children,* 38 (5), 33- 36.

Watts-Taffe, et. al. (2003), "Preparing Inservice Teachers To Integrate Technology with the Elementary Literacy Program," *The Reading Teacher,* 57 (2), 130- 138.

# Issues/Design in the Reading Curriculum

It is vital to pay careful attention to designing the reading curriculum. The design provides the framework for the teacher in the instructional arena. There is a structure when paying much attention to designing the curriculum in reading. This structure provides parents, school administrators, and pupils the essentials of what needs to go into a quality reading curriculum. The design should be of major significance to all interested in developing good readers. Within a carefully developed design, there are issues which need identification and attempts made at resolution.

## Objectives in the Curriculum

Which objectives should pupils attain in reading instruction? There are a plethora of possible ends for pupil attainment. Questions which arise pertaining to objectives include the following

- Should the objectives be stated in terms of being performance goals, measurably stated objectives, or general objectives?
- Should there be balance among knowledge, skills, and attitudinal objectives, or should one kind of objective receive preference over the others?
- Who should sequence objectives—the teacher, the pupil(s), pupils with teacher guidance, or a combination of individuals?

**Learning Activities**

There are learning activities which are more formal and direct as compared to others. Thus, an issue in reading pertains to how tightly knit a learning activity should be in terms of rigidity. Toward the other end of the continuum is how open-ended the activity is for pupil choice and interaction. Which learning activities should then be chosen for pupils to achieve the desired ends?

- Basal textbooks, workbooks, library books, and other types of print discourse.
- Visual aids including illustrations, study prints, pictures, drawings.
- Audio visual aids including video disks, video tapes, films, filmstrips, slides.
- Audio tapes including radio, cassette recordings, book reports.
- Pupil constructed items including dioramas, models, murals, bulletin board displays, games.
- Dramatisations including informal, formal, socio-dramas, dramatic play.
- Teacher directed experiences including discussions, panel reports, debates.
- Computerised instruction including tutorial, diagnosis and remediation, simulation, drill and practice.
- Chalkboard and overhead projector use in teaching reading (Ediger and Rao, 2003).

**Methods of Teaching**

The teacher must be an effective evaluator of pupil achievement to notice under which methods of teaching a pupil does best. Thus, the teacher needs to have much knowledge about each pupil in terms of cognitive, affective, and psychomotor development. A good teacher then notices where a pupil is achieving presently and provides the learner with learning opportunities to promote sequential progress. An issue then in determining which methods of teaching to use in the classroom pertains to direct versus indirect means in teaching and learning situations. Which methods of teaching should then be used in reading instruction?

- Teacher use of the basal reader manual in determining objectives, learning activities, and appraisal procedures.
- Lecture, deduction, induction, pupil selection of objectives, teacher/pupil planning of the curriculum.
- Peer teaching, peer mediated instruction, interactive peer learning, debates, pupil lead discussions, individualised reading, sustained silent reading, excursions, reciprocal teaching and learning, problem solving approaches, project methods, and experience charts.
- Programmed reading, individually guided education (IGE), teacher guided reading instruction, Big Book approaches used in teaching, linguistic procedures (Charles Fries and Leonard Bloomfield), Reading Recovery, Success for All (Robert Slavin), Distar, Stimulus/Response theory of learning.
- Learning Styles Theory (Dunn and Dunn, 1979), Multiple Intelligences Theory (Gardner, 1993).

Methods of teaching used must meet personal needs of pupils. Each pupil needs to achieve as well as possible in reading instruction.

### Assessment of Pupil Achievement

A quality programme of assessment of pupil achievement needs to be in evidence. The evaluation must determine how well pupils are doing in reading as well as provide feedback on which areas the learner needs to improve upon to become better reader. Assessment procedures need to be valid and reliable. Both formal and informal methods of assessment need to be used. Informal methods include

- Teacher observation, rating scales, check lists, teacher and pupil journal writing, pupil self evaluation, anecdotal records, paper pencil test items written by the teacher (true/false, essay, matching, multiple choice short answer and completion), pupil developed portfolios,
- Evaluation of pupil products and processes, such as ar projects, construction items, creative and forma dramatisations, discussion groups, committees at work written work, oral presentations by pupils evaluated in terms of desired criteria.

A salient and critical task of the classroom teacher is to be a good evaluator. Based on evaluation of each pupil's achievement, the teacher may then remedy pupil deficiencies and provide for sequential progress. Popham (2003) suggests teachers ask themselves the following questions when developing classroom evaluation devices:

- Do my classroom assessments measure genuinely worthwhile skills and knowledge?
- Will I be able to promote my student's mastery of what's measured in my classroom assessment?
- Can I describe what skills and knowledge my classroom tests measure in language sufficiently clear for my own instructional planning?
- Do my classroom assessments yield results that allow me to tell which parts of my instruction were effective or ineffective?
- Do my classroom tests take up too much time away from my instruction?

Summative evaluation include the following tests to ascertain learner progress:

- State and district mandated tests, standardised tests, and criterion tests used as formal evaluation devices
- Personality tests, readiness tests.

There are salient principles of assessment which are important to use when designing evaluative devices to ascertain pupil achievement. These include the following:

- Use assessment is an integral part of curriculum and instruction.
- Devote time to essential learnings.
- Set high standards for teaching and learning
- Clarify targets early (pupils should understand what they are to know and do if they achieve the objective).
- Aim for more authentic assessments (assessments should be geared to finding out student's ability to apply knowledge and skills successfully in meaningful tasks).
- Collect multiple indicators of learning—an array of evidence (Parker, 2001).

**Supervision in the Reading Curriculum**

The reading supervisor should work continually in the direction of having classroom teachers update their teaching skills. There are a multiplicity of demands placed upon the reading supervisor to assist teachers to guide pupils to achieve optimally. The following are ways to aide teachers to do a good job of teaching; thus the reading supervisor may help

1. Children who are discipline problems in the classroom to have their energies channeled in a positive direction to improve reading skills and attitudes. Assisting teachers in reading and implementing research results on disciplining pupils may help redirect energy channels of learners.

2. Classroom teachers by being a good listener to the formers' teaching of reading problems, by assisting with diagnosis and remediation of pupil difficulties.

3. By being approachable. Teachers then might realize they can go to the supervisor with problems in reading instruction.

4. Classroom teachers to have high, but reasonable, expectations for pupils in reading Pupil expectations to achieve can be raised by the regular teacher as well as by the supervisor.

5. In developing inservice programmes in reading instruction for teachers. He/she determines what assistance teachers and pupils need to use phonics and to comprehend reading subject matter (Ediger and Rao, 200).

**Philosophy of Evaluation**

Measurement Driven Instruction (MDI) advocates believe in teachers setting predetermined objectives for pupils to achieve. These objectives are

- Highly specific and their meaning is clear to all involved in their use in teaching.
- Specific in that a pupil has/has not achieved each objective as a result of instruction.
- Sequentially arranged, starting with the easiest and gradually moving toward those increasingly more complex.
- Aligned with the related learning activities. Thus, the learning activities assist pupils to attain the desired objectives.
- Written so that teachers receive feedback on each pupil's achievement from having taken the test.

As compared to MDI, problem solving instruction emphasizes pupils identifying problems, contextually, within ongoing units of study. Once a problem has been clearly identified, then viable answers need to be sought. Answers are tentative and subject to revision. Each possible answer needs to be evaluated with study and thought. Modifications and corrections might then well be made.

Problem solving does not stress predetermined objectives for pupils to use in studying reading. Rather, pupils identify problems within a given situation or contextually. The pupil owns the problem. The teacher is there to assist, help, and encourage.

Pupils individually do learn under different conditions and situations (Dunn and Dunn, 1979).

## References

Dunn, Rita, and Kenneth Dunn (1979), "Teaching Styles/Learning Styles, *Educational Leadership,* 36 (4), 238-244.

Ediger, Marlow, and D. Bhaskara Rao (2000), *Teaching Reading Successfully.* New Delhi, India: Discovery Publishing House, 304-308.

Ediger, Marlow, and D. Bhaskara Rao (2003), *Improving School Administration.* New Delhi, India: Discovery Publishing House, Chapter Seven.

Gardner, Howard (1993), *Multiple Intelligences; Theory into Practice.* New York: Basic Books.

Parker, Walter S. (2001), *Social Studies in Elementary Education.* Upper Saddle River, New Jersey: Prentice-Hall, Inc., Chapter Ten.

Popham, W. James (2003), "The Seductive Allure of Data," *Educational Leadership,* 60 (5), 51.

# Meaning in Reading Symbols Across the Curriculum

Symbols abound in each curriculum area. These symbols need to be understood by pupils within the context of reading. Generally, reading is perceived as consisting of identifying words and increasing comprehension skills. But, there are a plethora of additional symbols which pupils need to read and comprehend meaningfully.

Reading across the curriculum, emphasizing abstract words, will be discussed first, followed by symbols peculiar to diverse academic disciplines.

## Reading Abstract Words

When reading abstract words, the following words recognition techniques become important and are developed individually by pupils as optimal achievement permits:

- Context clues whereby the reader attempts to identify an unknown word by having it fit in as it relates to other words in the sentence.
- Phonics in which the pupil attempts to identify an unknown word by associating a sound with one or more letters of the alphabet.
- Syllabication skills in which an unknown word is divided into selected syllables and then recognised.
- Onset and rhymes where a word not identified is divided into an initial consonant followed by the rest

of the word, e.g. s.. elf," "p ... ayment," "d ... ogmatic." To divide an unknown word into these parts aids in identifying the unknown.

- context clues whereby the learner perceives the shape of the word for identification purposes. Unknown words then can provide clues with longer as compared to shorter words, as well as taller letters versus shorter letters (Ediger, 2003, 71- 76).

Hopefully the above named approaches will assist the pupil to have an increased number of words become sight words and to be recognised immediately in fluent sequential reading of subject matter.

## Reading Map and Globe Symbols

In ongoing social studies lessons and units of study, pupils are asked to read abstract map and globe symbols. A legend will provide the meaning of each symbol on the map/ globe. Thus, a pupil sequentially will need to learn to read the abstract symbols for rivers, highways, lakes, political boundaries, seas, mountains, plains, plateaus, and time zones. A river, for example, will be represented with a wavy line.

Pupils also need to be able to read different colors on a map/globe to understand elevation features. When looking at a region on a map/globe, the pupil will attach related meanings by looking at the legend. For example, a blue color will indicate a body of water such as the Atlantic or Pacific Ocean.

There are salient words in geography which pupils need to learn to read. These include the following:

1. Meridians, parallels, degrees, Tropic of Cancer and Tropic of Capricorn, latitude and longitude.
2. Cardinal and intermediate directions, North Pole and South Pole, sea level, desert, rain forest, regions, place location,
3. Tornados, hurricanes, earthquakes, and floods.

The geography teacher needs to establish vital objectives of instruction as to which map and globe symbols pupils should learn to read. These objectives need to be arranged sequentially for teaching purposes. It is easy to omit relevant objectives in reading unless they are written down and then implemented (See Parker, 2001).

Salient concepts in history, political science, economics, and anthropology/sociology should also be identified and taught in a manner which provides for individual differences in the classroom.

## Reading Symbols in Mathematics

Salient mathematical abstract concepts need to be taught in context. These concepts should provide relevant learnings for pupils in order to understand the language of mathematics. The teacher needs to observe that pupils individually find the mathematical concepts to make sense. A variety of concrete, semi-concrete, and abstract materials must be used as learning opportunities for pupils to achieve objectives. Diverse assessment procedures need to be used to appraise learner achievement and progress.

The following symbols/words, among others, need to be read by pupils and taught inductively/deductively, in a sequential manner as pupils achieve in a developmental mathematics curriculum:

1. Greater than (>), less than (<), +, –, ×, %.
2. Sum, factors, product, addends, minuend, subtrahend, difference, quotient, dividend, divisor.
3. Length, width, area, parallelogram, square, triangle, rectangle, solid, cube, sphere, hemisphere, weight, metric system (liter, kilogram, meter, centimeter).

Each of the above need to be taught in a manner whereby pupils may establish meaning to what is being taught. Depth teaching needs of be emphasised. Applying each concept in functional settings increases the retention rate of learning for pupils (Ediger and Rao, 2001, Chapter Six).

Weiker wrote the following:

> Teachers must be empowered with confidence, knowledge and skills to present mathematics and science education effectively to all pupils. Teacher training programmes should strive to provide teachers with a solid knowledge base and an understanding of how pupils learn mathematics and science as well as appropriate instruction methods and skills to apply their knowledge. School districts must be required to employ qualified mathematics and science teachers to ensure a background of content knowledge and scientific understanding. Professional development should be encouraged throughout a teacher's career. Teachers should continually expand their content knowledge, become familiar with research based teaching methods and apply best teaching practices within their classrooms.

**Science Concepts and the Learner**

Science concepts for the learner need to be salient for pupils to learn. Careful selection of these concepts is vital. Proper order of contextual teaching of each will assist pupils to inculcate their meanings.

Earth sciences will stress the following concepts, among others, which pupils needs to identify in reading and understand their meanings:

1. Classification and content of rock formations
2. Minerals in the earth's crust
3. Resources of energy and its categories
4. Plate tectonics, earthquakes, and volcanoes
5. Weathering and formation of the soil
5. Erosion, deposition, and fresh water
8. Oceanography and water movement
9. Weather, climate, the atmosphere
9. The planets, gravity, and the solar system

10. Exploration of space (See Holt Science and Technology, 2002).

For each of the above numbered phrases, pupils need to learn to read and attach meaning to these vocabulary terms. In number one, for example, the vocabulary terms of igneous, metamorphic, and sedimentary (rock) will be read with related explanations of each.

Life science concepts provide challenge for pupils to expand their knowledge base as well as to read increasingly complex ideas. The following are examples of vital concepts:

1. Cells, monera, viruses, protists, fungi, invertebrates, life-cycle of vertebrates,
2. Fish, amphibians, reptiles, birds, mammals.
3. Nutrition, digestion, respiration, circulation, excretion, heredity (Bough and Schwartz, 1994).

The above are selected life science concepts which pupils will meet in print to read meaningfully. If pupils, for example, in number one above read about "viruses," they will read about the many kinds and mutations which cause new and recurring kinds of sicknesses and respiratory diseases such as SARS, West Nile, and New Castle.

Physical science concepts taught within the framework of experiments and demonstrations assist pupils to use what has been learned. The following taught sequentially, through a variety of learning opportunities, should assist pupils to find physical science practical as well as fascinating:

1. The elements, molecules and atoms
2. Heat energy, effects of heating, insulation
3. Evaporation, refrigeration, solar energy
4. Simple and complex machines, friction
5. Magnetism, static electricity, current electricity, electro magnets

6. Sound, speed of sound, vibrations
7. Light, shadows, rainbows, shadows, mirrors
8. Lenses, the eye' retina (See McLaughlin and Thompson, 1999).

Formulas in chemistry might provide difficulties for pupils in reading such as $C_6 H_{12} O_6$. The Periodic Table of Elements contains abbreviations for each element found on the planet earth. Thus "C" stands for carbon, H stands for hydrogen, and O stands for oxygen. The subscripts 6, 12, and 6, stand for atoms of each chemical involved in the formula, representing sugar. These learnings provide highly complex understandings for pupils. (See Fredericks, 2003 for approaches to use in science reading instruction).

## References

Blough, Glenn, and Julius Schwartz (1994), *Elementary School Science and How to Teach It*. New York: Holt Rinehart and Winston.

Ediger, Marlow (2003), "Ten Major Problems in Reading Instruction," *Experiments in Education,* 61(4), 71-76.

Ediger, Marlow, and D. Bhaskara Rao (2001), *Teaching Mathematics Successfully*. New Delhi, India: Discovery Publishing House, Chapter Six.

Fredericks, Anthony D. (2003), "The Ins and Outs of Guided Reading," *Science and Children*, 40(6), 22-27

Holt Science and Technology (2002), *Earth Science*. New York: Holt Rinehart and Winston.

McLaughlin, Charles W., and Marilyn Thompson (1999), *Physical Science*. Columbus, Ohio: McGraw Hill Book Companies, Inc.

Parker, Walter (2001), *Social Studies in Elementary Education,* Eleventh Edition. Upper Saddle River, New Jersey: Prentice Hall, Inc., Chapter Five.

Weaker, Patricia M. (2003), "A New Century—A New Vision for Math and Science Education," *The Delta Kappa Gamma Bulletin,* 69(3), 39-41.

# Reading Instruction and the Struggling Reader

There are a plethora of quality reading activities for pupils who have difficulties in learning to read. These pupils, as do all learners, need to experience the best possible objectives of instruction. Learning opportunities need to be developmental so the struggling reader may do the best possible to achieve the desired ends of instruction. Evaluation techniques need to be chosen carefully and aligned with the stated objectives so that the teacher may ascertain what pupils have/have not mastered. Additional learning activities may then be provided which assist struggling readers to be successful in reading. Which are possibilities to help struggling readers achieve as optimally as possible?

## Learning Activities in Reading Instruction

Learning activities which are chosen need to assist pupils to achieve the objectives of instruction. Relevant objectives, carefully selected, need to be in the offing. A listing of learning activities follows which assists struggling readers to achieve as optimally as possible. Readiness for each plan of reading instruction needs to be in the offing.

1. Sustained Silent Reading (SSR) is generally emphasised during the school day whereby each pupil in a classroom as well as the reading teacher read to themselves silently. The allotted time here may be flexible, usually 15 to 20 minutes in duration, once or

twice a week. The teacher must read also so that pupils may see a role model who serves as a person to emulate. Each person chooses their very own reading materials, generally from the classroom or school library. These library books need to be readily available for pupil use. Struggling readers do better if they can choose what to read instead of having assignments made continuously. Children tend to choose topics of personal interest as well as those having an appropriate level of reading difficulty.

2. Individualised reading also stresses a plan whereby each pupil checks out a library book to read. The allotted time for each person reading a library book silently of his/her own choosing may be approximately 45 minutes daily if Individualised reading substitutes for a basal reading approach. If the individualised reading programme is used alongside the basal reader, then

   - It might alternate in daily use.
   - It might be integrated/correlated in subject matter. After a pupil has completed the reading of a library book, he/she may have a conference with the teacher to evaluate the quality of oral reading as well as comprehension skills. Diagnosis may be followed by remediation. After the conference has been completed, the teacher needs to record the results for future use. The pupil may then select another library book to read.

3. Personalised reading stresses the importance of pupils in a small group viewing selected objects, placed by the reading teacher, on a learning station. Pupils need to view each object carefully. This is followed by pupils saying what they saw when looking at these objects. The teacher records each idea on the chalk board as it is given. Only one pupil is to respond at a time as well as give the teacher adequate time to record each pupil's contribution. After the experiences of pupils have been

recorded, the teacher reads aloud the contents by pointing to each word read. Pupils need to be very attentive in looking at the words as they are being pointed to in the oral reading activity. Next, pupils read the content aloud together with the teacher. Again, the teacher points to each word as it is being read aloud. Later, pupils may read the content independently. This approach may be used as often as needed to help pupils individually develop their very own sight vocabulary.

4. Predictable stories or poems may be read aloud together with the teacher. The teacher may read aloud the content first as pupils follow along in their book. The predictable content makes it so that pupils 'know' what comes next in sequence. Selected stories and poems may have a refrain whereby pupils join in as they point to the words being read. Later on, pupils may read independently that which was read together.

5. Tape recordings of library book content may be used by pupils as they read the related subject matter. The pupil may then follow along in the library book as the tape plays the content. Pupils have opportunities here to develop their individual sight vocabularies for reading. The struggling reader is not hindered in word recognition and can enjoy content read.

6. A peer may read aloud subject mater from a basal textbook as the struggling reader follows along in his/her own text.

7. Retired teachers may volunteer to listen to a set of pupils read aloud from the basal and assist in word recognition problems. They might assist in helping these pupils in different kinds of word recognition procedures such as phonics and context clues.

8. Programmed reading, either computer based or book form, might present content for pupils to respond to in a step by step procedure. The content is broken down into specific bits of information such as a sentence or

two for pupils to read at a time, as given on a monitor when computer based. After reading the short sentence(s), the pupil responds to a completion test item to check comprehension. If correct in given the response, the learner moves on to the next small bit of information with the same sequence of read, respond, and check. The pupil is generally highly successful in working by the self on programmed learning since the content is carefully sequenced into small bits of information. He/she can work at the optimal rate of personal speed desired involving programmed reading.

9. Reciprocal reading involves the pupil and the teacher in reading aloud or silently. The teacher reads aloud a given short selection followed by asking the pupil a related comprehension question. Next, the pupil reads aloud a short selection to the teacher followed by asking a comprehension question covering content read orally. This procedure of reciprocal reading may be continued as long as desired.

10. The reading teacher may choose library books on a topic which interests the struggling reader. If the reader likes books on zoo animals, for example, the child should be encouraged to read as many developmentally appropriate library books possible on this topic.

11. A controlled vocabulary reader may be used in teaching pupils. There is considerable repetition of words used in a controlled vocabulary story. New words are brought in rather sparingly so that a pupil rehearses words read in story content. For many pupils, the controlled vocabulary may seem monotonous, but for struggling readers the repetition is necessary so that appropriate practice on controlled words is in evidence.

12. New words to be read may be printed neatly on the chalkboard for the struggling reader. The pupil should practice saying the words aloud as the teacher points to each. Being able to identify, these new words prior

to the reading activity, helps the pupil to read the selection successfully as a result.

13. Words not identified correctly in a developmentally appropriate reading activity, may each be printed neatly and clearly on a three by four inch card. From a set, a partner may hold up a card and have the struggling reader identify the word. Sequential cards, each with a word printed thereon, may follow in assisting the reader to be increasingly successful in reading.

14. A game board with spaces marked thereon from beginning to finish may be attractively made. A set of cards with incorrectly identified words may be placed adjacent to the game board. The cards should be face down. Two pupils may play in the game. One pupil holds up a card for the other learner to see and identify correctly. If correct, the pupil advances the number of spaces as indicated when a spinner was spun. If incorrect in identifying a word on the card, the pupil waits until the other child has had a turn by looking at a card face up. The spun spinner will indicate how many spaces to advance forward if the observed word is identified correctly.

15. Library books which have a heavy endowment of pictures may be used in reading instruction. The pictures with a small amount of print provide situations whereby picture clues might be used to identify unknown words. If a child does not recognize a word, the chances are by looking at the illustrations on the same page, the learner will correctly identify the unknown word. Vocabulary development is also being emphasised when pupils study the sequential illustrations in the picture book.

16. The teacher may choose a reading selection and delete every third major word, much like the cloze approach in determining the reading level of a pupil. The

approach used by the teacher in deleting every third word is to have pupils fill in correct words in the proper blank spaces which are appropriate when using context cues. With one of three words omitted in a reading selection, the context clues are indeed heavy and the pupil may practice reading content which has a challenge attached. The challenge being to ascertain the correct word when one of three words is omitted.

17. It is rather common for pupils to select and take home library books to read. Parents who take much interest in their children may assist in word recognition when pupils read at home. Both pupils and parents may read sequential library books and discuss their contents. This should spur on interests to read on the part of the struggling reader.

18. There are homes which have and own library books in the home setting. There needs to be a way of communicating to the teacher which books pupils have read in the home setting.

19. Reading Recovery is based on a one on one relationship involving the teacher and a pupil. After readiness has been provided for the pupil, the teacher may read a selection once and then together with a pupil read the same content. Rereading may be done as often as desired, before moving on to new content.

## Closing

The struggling reader has usually met up with a considerable amount of previous failure in reading. Rather, the teacher needs to guide each pupil to be successful in reading. To counteract feelings of defeat in reading, the struggling reader needs to experience the following tenets which come from the psychology of learning:

1. Reading materials need to be interesting so that careful attention is given to each learning activity involving reading. When the pupil does the choosing, he/she tends to select what is of interest.

2. Reading materials should have perceived purpose. The learner's purpose may vary from one time to the next. On one occasion, the pupil may wish to select stories on farm animals. The next time, the pupil may choose stories of other lands. Thus, reasons for choosing a library book to read vary from time to time. There are a few pupils, however, who would like to read on one topic only, such as dinosaurs. The pupil is the chooser when selecting library books to read.

3. Reading materials need to emphasize meaning. With meaning, pupils understand that which is read. It certainly is frustrating if reading is being done and it is not comprehended. If pupils become increasingly independent in the use of phonics to identify consistently spelled words and the use of context clues for identification of unknown words, they will tend to become independent in identifying words and attach meaning to what is being read.

4. Reading materials should foster pupil curiosity. The teacher needs to encourage and reward curiosity. Never should it be stifled. Curiosity on the learner's part will foster a desire to read to find out more of what exists in the natural and social environment.

5. Reading materials should be on diverse topics and genres in order to meet individual needs of learners. Meeting needs of individuals assists pupils to achieve more optimally.

## References

Brown, Kathleen J. (2003), "What Do I Say When They Get Stuck On A Word? Aligning Teacher Prompts With Student's Development," *The Reading Teacher,* 56 (8), 720-733.

Dewey, John (1916), *Democracy and Education.* New York: The MacMillan Company.

Douillard, Kim (2002), "Going Past Done: Creating Time for Reflection in the Classroom," *The Language Arts,* 80 (2), 92-99.

Ediger, Marlow (1997), *Teaching Reading and the Language Arts.* Kirksville, Missouri: Simpson Publishing Company, Chapter Five.

Ediger, Marlow (2002), "Measurement Theory Versus Constructivism," *Journal of Research in Education,* 1 (1), 7-10.

Ediger, Marlow (1998), *Teaching Reading Successfully in the Elementary School.* Kirksville, Missouri: Simpson Publishing Company, Chapter Eight.

Ediger, Marlow, and D. Bhaskara Rao (2003), *Elementary Curriculum.* New Delhi, India: Discovery Publishing House, Chapter Eight.

Hoff, David (September 3, 2003), "Large Scale Study Finds Poor Math, Science Instruction," *Education Week,* 23 (1), 3.

Gardner, Howard (1993), *Multiple Intelligences: Theory Into Practice.* New York: Basic Books.

Searson, Robert, and Dunn, Rita (2001), "The Learning Styles Teaching Model," *Science and Children,* 38 (5), 22-26.

Slavin, R.L., and N.I. Karweit (1984), "Mastery Learning and Student Teams: A Factorial Experiment in Urban General Mathematics Classes," *American Educational Research Journal,* 21: 725-736.

Symonds, W.C. (2000, September 25), "A Technology Revolution is About to Sweep America's Classrooms," *Business Week,* 116-128.

# Computers, Technology, and the Reading Curriculum

The debate continues on the pros and cons of educational technology in reading instruction. It is one approach, among others, to assist pupils to increase reading sills. There are a plethora of reasons for advocating technology use. Certainly, technology is in rampant use around all in society. Supermarkets, banks, department stores, and very small places of business use computers and other technology to help in conducting business efficiently and effectively. In the educational arena, there has been some hesitancy in using instructional technology, but in most schools, it is there and can be readied for use in teaching reading. Ritchie (1996) wrote the following as to why technology is not increasingly used in the school setting:

- A lack of administrative support.
- Inadequate staff development and technological support.
- Low quantity, quality and access of technologies in the classroom.
- Non-existent of cursory plans for adopting and implementing technology in the classroom.
- The failure to allocate a technology coordinator to help train teachers and coordinate the technologies.
- A lack of funds and personnel to maintain equipment.

- Continual assessment of content acquisition through traditional methods.

## Computer Assisted Reading Instruction

Computer assisted reading instruction is a mode which has helped selected pupils to increase skills in reading. Pupils differ from each other in many ways and computerised instruction is an approach which is individualised. The learner may pace his/her rate of instruction. Thus, a single frame in computer use may be attended to as long as desired and needed. Once a computerised programme has begun, a pupil may work independently. There are several modes which may be used here. Tutorial is a mode which provides reading instruction in guiding pupils to meet new objectives of instruction. The methods used may be quite repetitions but has interesting built-in reward devices to motivate pupils to learn. The methodology tends to emphasize read a small amount of content on a frame, respond to a question covering content read such as a multiple choice test item, and notice the correct answer as given by the programmer. If the pupil is correct, he/she is rewarded. If incorrect, the learner is still ready to go on to the next programmed item of read, respond, and check. Interesting drawings, such as a large smiley face may appear on the monitor to indicate reward for each correct response made by a pupil.

A second kind of computer programme is drill and practice. There may be selected words which pupils need to develop as their basic sight vocabulary. These may well be developed through a drill and practice approach. When the words become a part of the pupil's sight vocabulary, they can increasingly become independent readers. Drill and practice of selected words in reading has always be important, maybe through the flash card method. These cards soon became tainted and smudged. Pupils might then recall a word through these markings, rather that through the configuration of the word, as should be the case.

Diagnosis and remediation as a third method of computerised reading instruction may be used wisely to help pupils overcome problems in print materials. Diagnosis and remediation programmes attempt to find out what pupils specifically are doing incorrectly. Formerly, the teacher attempted to ascertain why pupils were reading content incorrectly. With computerised instruction, the teacher is released from helping that child to assisting another depending upon specific needs. Each learner is to be given the kind of assistance needed to achieve as optimally as possible. Reading is an individual matter and computerised instruction might well assist pupils to do as well as possible in reading, by remedying difficulties faced in the instructional arena. With common problems which readers reveal, selected needs of pupils may be met through collaborative endeavors. Thus, by learning collectively, these pupils can achieve more optimally based on their learning style.

Fourth, simulation can be an interesting and exciting way for pupils to achieve more optimally in reading. Here, pupils might work individually or collaboratively in devising an answer to a problematic situation. The programmed problem presented on the monitor is developed as realistically as possible. A life-like dilemma is presented, followed by choices for consideration. Generally, the choices are provided in multiple choice form. The pupil(s) are to select one of the four. They are then provided feedback on the monitor, based on their choice. An additional problem is given on the monitor, followed by four possible decisions as to what to do next. One choice from the four is made, followed again by feedback. The problems are presented sequentially, followed by feedback for each decision. In sequence, another problem is given whereby pupils need to respond with an answer. The methodology is the same continuously; however, the content in the problem changes much as well as the decisions to be made involving one of the four multiple choice items. A considerable amount of reading is done within a realistic context. The fascination and interest of the problem challenges pupils to choose and make choices.

Fifth, a gaming model in computerised instruction can generate much enthusiasm among learners. A game may involve four words on a screen with a pupil selecting the one which is spelled incorrectly. If the pupil responded correctly, he/she is ready for the next sequential frame of four words. A reward motto may then appear on the frame such as, "Good luck!" If a pupil responded incorrectly, he/she sees the correct answer on the screen and is still ready for the next set of four words.

Two sides may challenge each other in a computerised game. Fair rules need to be developed. Healthy competition, not dog eat dog, need to be in evidence between the opposing sides to determine the winning side in the correct spelling of words (Ediger and Rao, 2000, Chapter Nineteen).

There are then a plethora of possibilities in using computer software in reading instruction. Software used should assist pupils to achieve objectives of instruction in reading. It must provide for individual differences and meet personal needs of learners. Each programme needs to capture pupil interest and develop purpose for improving reading skills. The programme being used needs to contain sequential content for readers. Motivation should increase with programmed instruction in reading. Pupils are then challenged to achieve increasingly complex objectives. Motivated learners are necessary to achieve as much as possible, individually, in reading.

Teachers and administrators need to select those computerised programmes in teaching reading which are truly beneficial to the learner and do not represent busy work or the mundane.

**Formative and Summative Reading Programs**

In units of instruction or within the framework of state mandated objectives, computerised programmes may well be used as formative measurement devices. They can then help to determine

- A change in course of action within the ongoing unit of study.
- An improved order of presenting content so that the pupil benefits increasingly so, from the instructional unit.
- New ways of increasing energy levels for pupil learning.
- Ways of varying learning activities in the curriculum to maintain and increase interest in reading instruction.
- Approaches to guide pupils to perceive reasons for learning.
- Means of remedying that which was done incorrectly.
- The entire design of determining the reading curriculum (Ediger and Rao, 2001, Chapter Twelve).

In contrast to formative evaluation, summative assessment stresses the end of unit or course modifications which need to be made. Certainly, at the end of the unit or course, summative evaluation needs to be used to ascertain changes which need to be made before the unit or course is taught again.

These changes/modifications might well include the following:

- Develop and use criteria to help decide which facet of computerised reading instruction should be kept and which omitted when using the unit of instruction again for next year's group of pupils.
- Study and think through carefully how computerised instruction can be used more effectively.
- Assess new computer and technology strategies to strengthen the reading curriculum.
- Talk to teachers and school administrators about new programmes of instruction which might well improve the teaching of reading.

- Implement a multi-media strategy which may challenge pupils to achieve more optimally in reading.

Pertaining to technology use in the schools, Edwards (1994) wrote:

> Schools not preparing students for the evolving world do them and society a disservice. The global information network is here. The basics have changed. Education must change to keep the US competitive in a world where the information exchange is the driving force. Solve problems—don't buy toys. This is the most overlooked aspect of planning. Talking about chips and harddisk size is not what planning is. Decide what problems you need to solve; then shop for technology to solve them. This part of the strategic plan will be your guide to the endless possibilities on the market.

Identifying problems means focusing upon what your goals are now and in the future. (If not, back up several steps.) You will need to cross-reference school system needs so every piece of technology fits into the total plan and expensive duplication is avoided. Do lots of research before plunking down money. It's a buyers market, so talk to all the vendors you can, asking where to see the technology in action, and asking those using it what they like and don't like. If a piece seems almost right, an alternative will be just right. School buyers do well to shop around. Many who do not jump into technology early feel overwhelmed by catching up. If you are among them, you have plenty of company. There is a lot to learn, but numerous resources are available. If you have a lot of catching up to do, remind yourself you'll never start any sooner and jump in. You'll soon be taking megabytes with the rest of them.

### Planning a Quality Technology Curriculum

A key factor in developing a quality technology curriculum is the amount of planning therein. Computer programmes need to assist in pupils in achieving objectives. They should not be purchased and used for the sake of doing so, but rather pupils are definitely helped in reading instruction. Technology needs to be integrated and become an integral part of the curriculum. The teacher needs to ask the personal question, "How might specific programmes or technology in general guide pupils to achieve optimally. Active learning needs to be stressed. It is the pupil who will be interacting with each programme or presentation. Optimal use must be made of each computer in the classroom so that each learner can benefit from these approaches in learning. Pupils from low income homes, in particular, need to have their fair share of compute instructional time. They tend to lack computers in the home setting and technology is widely used in society. School and society should not be separated from each other, but be integrated entities. How to integrate harmoniously computer programmes and technology with the rest of the curriculum will be a continual challenge to teachers. Integrate seamlessly will and is a problem for teachers. Inservice education needs to be available to teachers to make this blend.

Teachers need to have a knowledge of the psychology of learning and of research to manage the successful use of computer technology in the reading curriculum. The teacher's skillful use of the computer will assist to maximize and encourage its use. He/she may use computer services, also, to involve pupils individually in productive achievement when not being taught directly. Managing the classroom makes it so that those who are being taught directly by the teacher as well as those working on their own without instructional direction are achieving as much as possible. While a teacher is working with a given group in reading instruction, the others also need quality learning activities to benefit fully from the curriculum. To increase the effectiveness of instruction, a multimedia approach may be used; this adds sound, video, pictures, and music to the printed script within the framework of programmed materials of instruction. There is a much better chance of pupils retaining what has been learned if a multimedia approach is used in the reading curriculum. An increased number of senses are then used by pupils such as sight and sound. Thus, hypertext, sound, animation, still images and video become an inherent part of computer and technology use.

**Inservice Education**

Ample opportunities should be provided for teachers and school administrators to continually grow in technology use. Workshops may be planned and implemented; however, needs of participants may not be met here due to teachers and administrators operating at different levels of achievement in technology use. The author suggests the following approach in which the needed technology is available in a suitable room. Participants may sign up in groups to come to the room for instruction by a person well versed in school technology use. That person needs to be able to provide help and information to these who ask for it. An approach which should be avoided is where there are too many teachers and administrators working on technology problems at a given time. The number should be low, perhaps five participants for one technology specialist. Participants should feel very free to ask questions and receive assistance without feeling minimised. The technology specialist must take adequate time to answer questions and provide help without being biased against anyone. Each participant should have questions answered about problems in technology use. In fact, the specialist should encourage questions rather than being abrupt with queries from teachers and school administrators.

Ample opportunities should be given to assessing the worth of the specialist to improving the school curriculum. A ten point scale may be used in the assessment process with ratings continued from excellent to poor being on the graduated markings. Each of the ten items needs to be defined such as excellent meaning—the specialist was readily available, helpful, and took time to explain the assistance given. Poor—the lowest rating—the specialist was too preoccupied with other things to provide help, did not seem to understand my questions, and was unable to supply needed information.

When a small group of five are receiving instruction from the specialist, they should be able to receive the one on one training necessary. A large group of participants makes a situation whereby the one attempting to help participants finds the range very wide in guidance needed. There are too many needing help and it is impossible to meet anyone's needs in general. Participants in small groups may have a wide variety of kinds of assistance needed, for example, as in multimedia computing, including:

- How to do desk top publishing with image affects including scanned photographs of charts, maps, live art, and graphs, as well as drawings.
- How to convey information through sound effects. Sound cards, with built in amplifiers, will possess the quality of a stereo in the home setting. These sound cards make CD ROMS sound loud enough to be played back on the speaker. Trainees feel more involved and interested with quality sound effects.
- How to show information in several formats in book form. The computerised book form allows the participant to secure information with the help of hypertext. Hypertext is important in multimedia computing.
- How to do animation as in moving graphic images. Computer generated moving images, as in the movement of a reptile, assists pupils to understand essential involved features, being discussed by the teacher.
- How to use videos in teleconferencing and in teaching complex tutorials.

There are a plethora of advantages in using multimedia including the following:

- The graphs and diagrams aid in attaching meaning to content presented and are integrated in context.

- Sophisticated ideas/skills can be presented through multiple approaches.
- The pupil may learn at his/her own pace.
- A learner might well learn on his/her own since multimedia is relatively easy to operate.
- Live situations may be viewed at the desired speed and repeated as frequently as desired.
- Ample opportunities are available for collaborative work (See Premila, 2001).

Using computer assisted instruction can certainly help pupils to achieve more optimally. It needs to assist pupil achievement when traditional materials used in teaching/learning do not suffice or when computer assisted instruction can teach subject matter/skills more meaningfully. Technology is widely used in the societal arenas and will continue to make rapid inroads in the education process.

Finally, technology will have greater intelligence. This intelligence will be displayed in several ways. First, the technology will have more features and greater capacity.

Second, it will have capability to learn from the user, so that it can customize its services to fit the user's learning and interest. Future technology will not only provide data bases but also knowledge bases. And technology will be able to stay abreast of that information most valued to the user and alert him or her to its availability. Integration, interaction, and intelligence. These are the three features we can expect of technology in the future. And they will change the way technology is employed in the schools (Mehlinger, 1996).

## References

Edwards, Jack L. (1994), "Getting Started on Technology," *Education Digest,* 59 (5), 47.

Ediger, Marlow, and D. Bhaskara Rao (2000), *Teaching Reading Successfully.* New Delhi, India: Discovery Publishing House. Chapter Nineteen.

Ediger, Marlow, and D. Bhaskara Rao (2001), *Teaching Social Studies Successfully*. New Delhi, India: Discovery Publishing House, Chapter Twelve.

Mehlinger, Howard (1996), "School Reform in the Information Age," *Phi Delta Kappan,* 77 (60), 405- 406.

Premila, K. S. (2001), Effect of Computer Assisted Instruction and Assessment (Drill and Prentice), in Learning Mathematics Among High School Students—Gender Perspective. Ph D thesis evaluated by the author for Mother Teresa Women's University, Kodaikanal, India.

Ritchie, Don (1996), "The Administrative Role in Integration of Technology," *Bulletin of the National Association of Secondary School Principals,* 80 (8), 43.

# 21

# Increasing Reading Comprehension

It is indeed difficult for high school teachers to provide for individual differences among students when the gap in reading achievement is large in a classroom. With 25 students in a high school sophomore class, there may be a range of student reading achievement from a low of third grade reading level to a high of grade fourteen. The teacher then must attempt to meet achievement levels of all students in this classroom. How is this to be done? The teacher may print legibly the new words in the next lesson on the chalkboard. The teacher may then pronounce each word clearly as the student looks at it carefully. The textbook meaning needs to be provided for each new word. It is good to use the related illustrations as each new word is being defined or used contextually. Good readers may be reading other subject matter rather than following the preceding plan of providing readiness for reading for the next day's lesson (See Beach, 1993).

**Understanding Indepth What has been Read**

Quality comprehension of what has been read by the student needs to be stressed by the teacher. Too often, shallow thinking has been an end result of student reading. Instead, there are a variety of comprehension skills which need to be emphasised.

Students may need considerable assistance in reading factual information. Every fact read need not be remembered. In reality, it is impossible to do so. There needs to be a yardstick for student use to ascertain which are salient and which facts are of lesser value. This needs to be taught to students. By looking at the topical heading, the student may determine which facts are of major value to retain. The important facts will relate directly to the topical heading and thus increase their meaning. Students need direct practice to analyze which are major and which are minor facts. Then too, finding specific details which answer a question may well provide more security as to the worthwhileness of some as compared to other facts.

Reading for a sequence of ideas does aid in providing meaning to subject matter read. Sometimes, the content does not possess the best order and thus hinders student understanding. When writing is connected to reading, students may fail to communicate well in written work due to inappropriate sequence written by the author. The author must present a model to students. When communicated orally during a discussion what an author said, the student may well be a more effective communicator when providing ideas which are sequential.

History, as an academic discipline, emphasizes chronological order of information. If the chronology is incorrect, the subject matter is erroneous. Adequate time needs to be spent in assisting students to read, write and speak in a sequential manner (See Durkin, 1993).

As students mature in the language arts and as it cuts across the curriculum, they will meet up with two or more points of view in a reading selection. In contrasting the multiple points of view, the student needs to comprehend each thoroughly. Meaning theory is very important. He/she needs to draw upon background experiences in order to achieve richer and fuller understandings. Literal and figurative language needs to be weighed in terms of involved meanings. Vocabulary terms used also change meanings, since a synonym may make for shades of difference in understanding the author's purpose. The author's purposes when making these comparisons need to be adjudicated to ascertain what the intended learnings are.

Analyzing also becomes an important interpretation skill. When analyzing, the student thinks critically in terms of indicating if a statement is accurate versus inaccurate, fact or fiction, and/or realistic versus fantasy. Reflection by the student is salient here in that the learner needs to think upon thinking. Thus, the learner needs to determine what is known and what is left to know. Then too, the student must determine how something is known. Sometimes analytic thinking is called critical thinking.

Students need to experience making contrasts and comparisons. In contrasting, one notices how two or more ideas are alike. Careful thinking is necessary here. There may be very slight differences. At other times, the differences are more obvious (See Norton, 1992).

Logical thought is involved in making the contrasts. Mathematics makes heavy use of logical thinking. For example, if "a" is greater than "b", and "b" is greater than "c", then "a" is greater than "c." In much of life, logical thinking is done such as—if this worked in that situation, then it also should work here in the new situation; this is done frequently in ongoing activities. In making comparisons, the student wants to know the differences between two or more ideas. For example, how is the formula for finding the area of a square different from that of finding the area of a rectangle?

The student needs to determine how the subject matter read relates to his/her own life. A student may perceive very little or no relationship of what was read to his/her own personal life. Subject matter becomes more meaningful if the student relates what is read to his/her personal life. This is something which must be taught and be reflected upon. Ideas become more useful if they become a part of the personal self. Frequently with the development of background information, the reader tends to be able to integrate the self with the contents read. Familiarity with the subject matter contents assists the reader to integrate the self with the script more thoroughly. Thinking abilities and skills also assist the student to develop indepth learning and increase the fund of ideas to be used.

Cause and effect thinking skills are highly useful. Too frequently, the student fails to realize there are reasons for a certain happening. It is easy to think of the cause for eating and that is one is usually hungry. However, the writer has noticed frequently that students do not think of historical events being caused. It seems that events to many persons seem to occur in a vacuum. There may be multiple causes for events such as for a conflict, e.g. World War II. In the natural sciences, students may think of natural disasters, including earthquakes, to seemingly have just happened. Rather, indepth study depending upon the developmental level of the student, requires serious intensity study be given to the many causes of this and other natural phenomena of mudslides, avalanches, erosion, volcanic eruptions, among others. Explanations are indeed complex for indepth reading!

To read and study intelligently, the reader needs to be able to make predictions. This is true not only in word recognition but also in terms of what might happen in a narrative account. A good recognizer of words uses the context to ascertain what the next words will be and thus read more rapidly than otherwise would be the case. A fluent reader who reads at an understanding optimal rate of speed tends to comprehend much better than those who read more slowly. A slow reader is definitely handicapped in grasping sequential ideas. He/she struggles much over word identification and then loses out on comprehension and higher levels of thinking. High school students need to develop word recognition and comprehension skills which in return permit diverse kinds of complex thinking. When making predictions of future events in a novel, the student needs to be a good predictor of ideas to be read. As he/she reads, checking on the accuracy of the original prediction is made. The prediction may well be modified if need be. Being able to predict well is salient in society, also. Very frequently, an individual makes predictions or speculates on the near future or even on events which may occur in space and time. By making predictions, the individual attempts to orientate himself/herself better in terms of what will be read. As the act of reading continues, the reader makes needed adjustments in ideas adhered to, with modifications forthcoming (Ediger, 1998).

Drawing conclusions is a highly worthwhile skill for students to develop. Not only must the student relate ideas to draw conclusions but also read between the lines. In other words, the conclusions contain what was read literally figuratively, and inferentially. Literal interpretation contains content the way ideas are written. The reader then attempts to obtain a duplicate of written subject matter. Realism as a philosophy of education emphasizes that the observer may secure reality as it truly is. One then can know what is real in its entirety. Here, the reader obtains subject matter as it is written with no alterations. A minimum of creative ideas are added as possible in securing subject matter read in a literal manner. Figurative interpretation stresses the use of words in a creative manner and novel interpretations made by the reader. The following phrases cannot be taken literally:

- He/she finished the work in a blink of the eye.
- He/she rolled up the sleeves and used elbow grease to get the work done.
- They discussed the topic until it was like beating a dead horse.
- He saw the handwriting on the wall.
- I felt like walking on water when giving my report.
- She was a good Samaritan.
- It will take a loaves and fishes miracle to earn enough money.

- That person had the patience of Job.
- She was a Dorcas.

In comparison, inferential reading emphasizes reading between the lines and intelligent guessing about ideas. With inferential reading, not everything is said by the author in the printed script. Something is left unsaid, but can be gleaned in creatively in meaning. Creativity is necessary on the part of the student to read inferentially.

Thus, to draw conclusions, there is a fusion of ideas such as in combining literal, figurative, and inferential interpretations. Summarizing ideas is sometimes confused with drawing conclusions. However, in a summary, the major ideas read are joined together in a main idea. The summary is broad and contains specific ideas joined together to form a whole (See Rosenblatt, 1993).

Reading and thinking may indeed be quite complex when mental operations are involved. High levels of cognition are involved in thinking. Thinking skills are always useful, presently as well as in the future. Many people have made decisions based on inadequate information and have made minimum or little progress in life. This is regretful! It behooves the teacher to assist students to do well in diverse kinds of thinking skills. Students, too, need to put forth much effort to become the quality of person desired. Motivation is required. Reading is involved when thinking skills are developed. It becomes complex in the thinking arena when word recognition and comprehension of script are also inherent (Ediger and Rao, 2003).

## References

Beach, R. (1993), *A Teacher's Introduction to Reader Response Theories.* Urbana, Illinois: National Council Teachers of English (NCTE).

Durkin, Deloris (1993), *Teaching Them to Read, sixth edition.* Boston: Allyn and Bacon.

Ediger, Marlow (1998), *Reading and the Language Arts in the Elementary School.* Kirksville, Missouri: Simpson Publishing Company.

Ediger, Marlow and D. Bhaskara Rao (2003), *Teaching Language Arts Successfully.* New Delhi: Discovery Publishing House.

Norton, D. (1992), *The Impact of Literature Based Reading.* New York: Merrill Publishing Company.

Rosenblatt, Louise (1983), *Literature as Exploration, fourth edition.* New York: Modern Language Association.

# Assessing Reading in the Science Curriculum

Reading, as one learning activity in science lessons and units of study, needs to be assessed to notice needs of pupils. The science teacher needs to be thoroughly grounded in science content and methodology and yet also needs to be an instructor of reading. For pupils to do well in reading science subject matter, there needs to be continuous appraisal of how well a pupil is doing and of what is left to be done. A variety of procedures need to be used to evaluate pupil achicvement in order to provide data on achieved and unachieved objectives.

Science emphasizes a hands on approach in learning. This is an important way of learning. Reading is another method to acquire scientific information in knowledge and skills.

## Using Basal Science Textbooks and Library Books

One problem in the science curriculum is to integrate reading with pupils doing related science experiments and demonstrations. First, pupils do need to be able to read from the basal/library books in the curriculum. Important ways of assisting pupils to read well and comprehend science content need to be in the offing. When pupils are to read a given selection from the basal/library book, there need to be approaches in helping pupils in word recognition. The teacher or a pupil may pronounce an unknown word to learners without further assistance. The argument given for this approach is that a pupil may continue to read without interruption if the unknown word is pronounced at once. The pupil needs to raise his/her hand at once to let the helper know that a word is not recognised.

In contrast, the argument given against immediately pronouncing an unknown word to the reader is that this does not emphasize a future time to identify an unknown word independently. Thus, context clues may be stressed. Help is then given to the reader in using a technique to identify an unknown word. The teacher assists the pupil to notice surrounding words and guides the reader to put in place a word which makes sense. Sometimes while reading science content pupils will substitute a meaningless word for the unknown. By substituting a meaningful word for the unknown word, the pupil is more likely to zero in on a rightful word. If the word given is still not correct, the teacher might assist the pupil to look carefully at the initial consonant of the unknown word. Most words begin with consonants and they are quite consistent between symbol and sound. Being able to sound out the initial consonant plus context clue use should do it for the pupil. However, in doing these word recognition techniques, the reader may lose out momentarily on the trend of sequential thought.

Much phonics may be emphasised in reading science content. These learnings would be stressed for those who might benefit from phonics instruction, but only to comprehend science subject matter better. Rightfully, phonics, if taught, belong in the reading curriculum, but is taught in science when stressing reading across the curriculum. There are graphemes (symbols) which relate directly to their corresponding phonemes (sounds). The question then arises, "How much phonics should be taught in reading science subject matter?" In addition to emphasizing initial consonants along with context clues for the pupil to identify unknown words, the pupil may also benefit from looking at ending letters of unknown words to assist in word recognition. As in initial consonants, the ending consonants must be equally consistent to emphasize phonics instruction. Vowel letters individually can vary much in sound such as the long "a", the short "a", and the "a" governed by the letter "r". If words or word parts are not spelled consistently between symbol and sound, they should be taught as basic sight words in science.

It is up to the teacher if he/she wishes to teach syllabication skills in reading science content. There are valuable syllabication skills to teach such as the prefix "un", which is used very commonly in writing science subject matter. The science teacher needs to determine how much time is available for teaching word recognition and comprehension skills.

Being able to identify words is important only if it helps pupils to read fluently and thereby comprehend what is printed. One kind of comprehension is to read for facts. These facts must be meaningful and are useful for higher levels of cognition. Facts should be useful in school and in society. Sometimes a pupil, on his/her own, desires to remember facts for the sake of doing so and this is commendable.

Second, reading to develop concepts is very valuable in terms of comprehension. A concept is a single word or phrase. Igneous, sedimentary, and metamorphic, are concepts. Inside of any concept are valuable facts. For example pertaining to sedimentary rocks, pupils should learn how they are formed, what kind of materials make for this kind of rock, and how it is used.

Third, pupils need to learn to read to develop generalisations. A generalisation relates concepts, such as "Rocks may be classified as being sedimentary, igneous, and metamorphic."

Fourth, pupils need to read for the main idea. Here, pupils may be helped by having them provide in one sentence what a chapter is about. The sentence must be comprehensive enough to cover the contents read.

Fifth, pupils need to read for a sequence of ideas. The order of presenting these ideas is salient when reading for a sequence of ideas. Too frequently, something is false due to an incorrect order given of events, dates, ideas, and subject matter (See Holt Science and Technology, 2002).

Sixth, cause and effect reading is important in science. There are causes for volcanic eruptions, erosion, hurricanes, tornados, floods, and folding/faulting. These concepts are frequently studied by pupils in units on "The Changing Surface of the Earth."

Seventh, reading to solve problems is salient. Pupils then with teacher guidance identify a problem, gather information for a possible solution, develop a tentative hypothesis, and then assess the hypothesis in a life like situation.

Eighth, pupils need to skim subject matter in order to locate that which is important. Thus, skimming may be done when seeking the right entry in a dictionary, the table of contents or in the index.

Ninth, pupils need to be flexible in word identification and use the approach that is most appropriate in word recognition, be it in using phonics, context clues, picture clues, and/or structural analysis.

Tenth, pupils need to evaluate the self by using meta-analysis skills. Thus thinking about thinking is vital when using meta-analysis in appraising the self in achievement or lack thereof (Ediger, 1996, 45-53).

**Exemplary Science Teachers**

Exemplary science teachers have thought through the entire areas of teaching methods and science content when the instruction process takes place. Varied strategies are used in teaching. Concrete, semi-concrete, and abstract materials are used in instruction. Why? Pupils differ from each other in a plethora of ways and the teacher needs to design instruction which meets the needs of each learner. Methods of grouping then need to be flexible. There needs to be whole group, small group/committee endeavors, and individual study. How pupils are grouped depends upon the involved purpose. If a science experiment is to be performed, the size of the group needs to be such that all can see clearly and ask vital involved questions. These groups may be homogenous or heterogeneous. The groups may also be based on interest factors or what is purposeful to a group. Whatever the case, the teacher needs to have high expectations for each to achieve and yet be successful at the same time.

Pupils need to be given feedback to indicate how well they are doing on a specific activity or on a group project. With the feedback, pupils may build on what has been learned. Scaffolding can be done based on where a pupil is presently in achievement. Proper rules of conduct helps pupils to achieve more optimally. These rules are to assist and not hinder pupil achievement. An orderly classroom helps each to achieve as optimally as possible. All pupils should be actively involved in the task at hand and not be disrupted by pupil misbehavior.

The teacher needs to encourage quality attitudes among learners. Negative attitudes hinder pupil achievement. Positive feelings toward pupils assists the latter to feel wanted in the classroom. Learners then should be increasingly involved productively in the classroom. Being a good manager of the science curriculum is important. Positive approaches in management makes for a good learning environment. To group pupils flexibly, for example, takes a good manager of learners in the classroom. The curriculum too needs to be effectively implemented. If there is inappropriate sequence between and among classes, pupil disruptions may occur and learning goes downhill (See Morrow, 2003).

There are key methods of instruction to emphasize the size curriculum. Vital concepts to stress in the teaching of science include the following:

1. Inductive and discovery learning for pupils to arrive at answers to questions.

2. Problem solving and project methods of learning.
3. Experimentation and demonstrations. This is the heart of the science curriculum.
4. Key concepts and generalisations to emphasize in teaching and learning (See National Research Council, 1996).
5. Science equipment to do experiments and demonstrations.
6. Portfolios, journaling, and criterion referenced tests to evaluate pupil achievement.
7. Basal textbooks, library books, magazines, and science encyclopedias.
8. Variety of learning activities to provide for individual differences.
9. Various informal assessment techniques including teacher observation of pupil achievement as well as teacher written tests.
10. Inservice education such as conducting faculty meetings, implementing computer use workshops, and housing a professional library (including Science and Children, and the Science Teacher which are National Science Teacher Association publications (See Mehlinger, 1996).

## Scope and Sequence in Science

Subject matter chosen for pupils to acquire needs to be:

1. Significant for learners. Trivia and the unimportant must be weeded out since there is much salient content for pupils to learn.
2. Useful in dealing with problems in society, such as attempting to solve environmental dilemmas—saving the natural environment versus exploiting it to seek more jobs for people.

3. Important for an educated person to know such as current events dealing with natural phenomenon, e.g. earthquakes and tornados, among others.

4. Attainable for pupils in ongoing activities and experiences.

A lack of success is detrimental to a pupil's achievement and progress.

5. Challenging to motivate pupils. High expectations for a pupil is a must. Low achievement needs to be substituted with rigor in the science curriculum (See Blough and Schwartz, 1995).

6. Planned to provide opportunities for pupils to organize and classify content obtained.

7. Flexible to encourage pupil input into each science lesson, including questions raised by learners, as well as emphasize pupil/teacher planning.

8. Vital in stressing key structural ideas in ongoing units of study.

9. Evaluated in using voluntary national standards and objectives and mandated state objectives of instruction.

10. Appraised rather continuously to keep abreast with current trends in teaching science (Ediger and Rao, 2001).

## Conclusion

Pupils need to experience a quality science curriculum. The planned curriculum needs to include salient objectives for pupil attainment. The learning opportunities to achieve objectives need to provide for each child's interests, purposes, and achievement level. A good programme of appraisal assesses how much pupils have learned and how much is left to learn. Optimizing pupil achievement is a necessity. Carefully designing each science lesson and unit of study should be a requirement.

## References

Blough, Glenn O., and Julius Schwartz (1995), *Elementary School Science and How to Teach It.* New York: Holt, Rinehart and Winston.

Ediger, Marlow, and D. Bhaskara Rao (2001), *Teaching Science Successfully.* New Delhi, India: Discovery Publishing House, Chapter Two.

Ediger, Marlow (1996), "Evaluation of Pupil Achievement," *Education Magazine,* 45-53.

Holt Science and Technology (2002), *Earth Science.* New York: Holt, Rinehart and Winston.

Mehlinger, Howard D, (1996), "School Reform in the Information Age," *Phi Delta Kappan,* 77 (6), 405- 406

Morrow, Lesley Mandel (2003), "President's Message," *Reading Today,* 20 (6), 6.

National Research Council (1996), *National Science Education Standards.* Washington, DC: National Academy Press.

# Reading in Technical Education

Tech-Prep has received much attention in career education. Dutton (1995) lists the following characteristics of career paths for secondary school students:

1. Career paths are for all students. They provide an academic foundation and special areas of concentration so that all students are prepared to articulate to a two year or a four year college program, even if they choose to go directly into a job or military service immediately after high school graduation.

2. All secondary curricula are organised into four to six career clusters.

3. All students in eighth or ninth grade are counseled to select a career focus and develop a four or five year plan (reviewed each year).

4. All students are required to select a career cluster and take a concentration of at least three courses in one subject area.

5. Contextual learning environments and materials are encouraged/supported in all courses.

6. Integration across subject matter areas and team teaching are encouraged/supported

7. Special mentoring and tutorial services as well as other support services are provided for all students, as needed.

8. Flexible schedules and block time schedules are being reviewed or used to accommodate various learning/ teaching methodologies and student learning rates.

Tech prep/school to work characteristics also are retained. Each school has:

1. A core of applied courses in mathematics, science and communications.
2. Local partnerships of representatives from education, business community, other community organisations, and parents.
3. School to work transitional activities, including work-site experiences.
4. Seamless and progressive curriculum articulation from elementary school through middle level and high school to postsecondary education and/or career employment.

The purpose of public education is to prepare students with the knowledge, skills, and competencies they need to be successful. Schools must change, and principals carry the primary responsibilities for restructuring our schools and transforming educational processes so that all students are prepared for a continuously changing technological/ information society. Many principals are taking advantage of the evolving tech prep/school-to-work efforts to restructure and transform their schools to meet these needs (Dutton 1995, page three).

Reading is a skill that is important to all individuals, be it in the workplace or in recreational endeavors. The technical education student must become a proficient reader so that optimal achievement is possible in the workplace. Reading skills need to be upgraded continuously due to higher expectations presently from each person on the work-force. It is quite obvious that what was considered to be a proficient reader ten years ago is no longer adequate. New knowledge is developed continuously by specialists in the field. Within the framework of increased available knowledge, there are new vocabulary terms, concepts, and ideas that must be understood. Thus, reading skills should be developed throughout one's lifespan. Achievement in reading is ongoing and never complete. Low motivation (Wallace, 1995) in reading needs to be overcome with students perceiving a need for relevance in becoming good readers. Quality reading skills are necessary in technical education and in society.

## Reading and Technical Education

We have spoken to many high school instructors over the last two decades and approximately 30 per cent mention that the textbooks used in different courses are too complex for students to comprehend. Learners lose out on much information when not being able to read and understand content in basal textbooks. Generally, each high school course taken by students requires a considerable amount of reading. Reading can, of course, be an excellent way of learning. It is one way of learning much subject matter in technical education. Reading can be a rather rapid procedure of attaching meaning to that which is and must be experienced in problem solving in the workplace. Technical education instructors must be certain that students have mastered the basics in becoming good readers. The basics include higher levels of cognition that are involved in the processes of reading in the technical education arena. No student should be allowed to fall through the cracks due to inadequate reading skills. Diagnosis and remediation may be necessary to lift a student from where he/she is presently to a level of achievement and accomplishment in reading salient materials (Olson, 1995).

Technical education instructors need to be certain that each student can read well enough to comprehend content necessary in the workplace. To comprehend means to be able to state orally in one's own words what has been read. If students cannot do this, diagnosis must occur to determine the causes of difficulties in reading. This may mean providing assistance to these students in word analysis skills such as phonics, syllabication, context skills, and structural analysis. Hopefully, the technical education instructor will be able to sequence reading skills for students beyond that of word analysis. However, the technical education instructor needs to ascertain where each student is achieving in reading at the present time and then provide sequential experiences in reading technical education materials.

Which skills in reading then does the technical education student need to acquire beyond that of word analysis? First, each student needs to be able to read directions accurately and understand the contents. Written directions that are not understood may mean faulty ways of doing and proceeding in a given operation. If the student lacks proficiency in reading directions, assistance must be given in this category. The learner needs much practice in reading to understand directions so that increased success in the workplace will be in evidence. To comprehend content adequately in reading, the technical education student should be able pronounce 95-98 per cent of sequential words correctly that were read in a given selection. If the rate of word identification goes increasingly below the 95 per cent level, the student will have difficulties in understanding what has been read.

There is a second dimension in reading, other than identifying words correctly, and that being to attach meaning to what has been read, such as the learner being able say orally what the directions emphasise need to be done. Generally, if a student can answer three out of four questions correctly covering content read, he/she is able to comprehend subject matter adequately in technical education. Should comprehension go below this level, the technical education student may not function well in the workplace. This is an informal method of determining reading comprehension levels. The percents given above for word recognition and for comprehension are not absolutes, but do indicate what is necessary to read proficiently in job performance. Students should not have had prior experience in reading the technical education content using this informal method of ascertaining if the textbook(s) used are on the reading level of the involved student. The instructor could also use the cloze procedure to determine if the technical education textbook is on the reading level of the student, or if it is too difficult or too easy for the student. The cloze method, an additional approach to determine reading proficiency of learners, stresses that every fifth word be omitted from the content in the technical education reading selection. The student then orally reads the content, without previous practice, to the instructor. The student must read correctly the omitted words as well as the rest with a fifty-five per cent accuracy rate for the book to be on his/her reading and understanding level. If the per cent of correctly pronounced words continues to go below the fifty five per cent level, the learner will need increased assistance in reading subject matter content. Meaning and understanding of technical education content are musts (Ediger, 1994). A variation of the cloze method is the maze method to ascertain reading levels of individual students. With the maze method, every fifth word is also omitted in the selection which the student has not had a chance to read previously. Nor has the reader listened in to others who have read the content orally in all the informal means of determining reading levels that have been discussed above. For each omitted word in the maze method, there are three multiple choice items from which the reader may select the correct one. If the technical education student obtains ninety per cent or higher in the number of correct responses, the textbook(s) are on his or her reading levels (Harris and Sipay, 1985). I would recommend using these informal approaches in determining reading levels of students if they are having perceived difficulties in obtaining ideas through the use of symbolic materials. Adequate diagnosis must be in evidence with remedial assistance provided so that each technical education student achieves optimally. No learner should fall through the cracks. Each needs guidance and assistance to do well in technical education and be successful in the workplace.

The National Assessment of Educational Progress (NAEP) administers tests each year to students of ages 9, 13, and 17. Results from testing students in reading indicate a definite lack of achievement in higher levels of thinking. Thus, it behooves teachers to make certain that students can achieve well in critical thinking. To think critically, the learner must be able to separate facts from opinions. Much knowledge is needed to do this. Too frequently, readers accept as fact those opinions that have been read. All people have opinions on diverse topics and this certainly can be excellent. However, what is fact can be verified; opinions cannot and tend to represent that which is based on inadequate data or information. Critically thinking also stresses being skillful to separate accurate from inaccurate subject matter. Again, this is a complex skill since one has need to know what is correct and what is incorrect as far as ideas in reading are concerned. Appraising the worth of information read is vital to technical education students. Technical education students, as do all people in society, need to be life-long learners to be able to read critically and continuously refine reading skills.

A further skill in higher levels of cognition in reading is to read creatively. With creative reading, one anticipates what will appear next in printed content. Feedback is secured rather frequently when making these predictions since sequential content in reading will indicate if one is on the right track. The technical education instructor can assist learners in making these predictions by having the student read up to a certain point. The student then indicates what might come next in ideas read even though the print is covered up. The reader may then uncover the printed materials to check prediction accuracy. Speed in reading may also increase when these predictions are made since a more holistic procedure is being stressed as compared to reading very analytically, such as being a word caller in identifying slowly each word met. A fluent reader uses a variety of word recognition techniques to identify unknown words and reads to comprehend. Word recognition techniques are tools that the technical education student should possess to read fluently. A creative reader reads in a fluent manner due to using word recognition techniques judiciously to identify the unknown. He/she can also predict well what will come next in sequence in terms of ideas presented in symbolical form. Creative thinkers are needed in society since quality ideas, techniques, and innovations accrue due to unique, novel, and original content identified by any person in the workplace. The creative being attempts to find better ways of doing things and desires improved products in the societal arena.

There is so much to read for each person that one needs to read as rapidly as possible and yet compression does not suffer in the process. Instructors should not under estimate the importance of guiding students to become the best readers possible in order to increase employability skills. In times of higher unemployment in society, it becomes increasingly salient for students to read well in the work place.

Students and workers should also read for self-enrichment and wise use of leisure time. Too many persons in society are passive individuals when viewing television programs, especially those programmes of dubious educational value and moral worth. With appropriate skills in reading, the workers can truly enjoy reading content on diverse topics as well as to develop and maintain skills in a continually changing workplace. Change in needed skills and knowledge certainly is in evidence and the wise individual upgrades the self continually on what is necessary to be a valued worker in society. Thus, reading to solve problems becomes salient. Workers face problems in the workplace to complete tasks and responsibilities. Reading relevant materials may be one way to solve a problem. Technical education students presently and in the workplace must first of all clearly identify the problem. One reason that individuals are not able to secure answers to dilemma situations is that clarity is lacking in problem identification. A creative person should be able to select a relevant problem that needs a solution. Next, a hypothesis or answer to the problem needs to be developed. Too frequently, hypotheses are hastily attained and do not possess the quality necessary to solve a problem. Any hypothesis is tentative, and information must be secured that relates to testing the hypothesis. Here the technical education student must have ideas on where to obtain content needed to test the hypothesis. There are times when the student must recall past experiences and achieve a conclusion rather quickly on testing the hypothesis. At other times, the learner may have a considerable amount of time to adequately test a hypothesis. Osterroth (1994) stresses the importance of students understanding vital concepts that will be used in the solving of problems. Selected hypotheses may be discarded due to their not holding up to quality standards under the testing. In technical education, the best solutions possible to problems encountered are needed to solve dilemma situations. Creativity is necessary in solving vital problems. At the workplace, individuals are needed to identify and solve relevant problems.

## Conclusion

Workers in technical education need to be good readers to comprehend content read in a meaningful manner. Standards keep going up in terms of what society expects in the workplace. One must continually upgrade skills in reading and use these skills to be a productive individual in school and in society. Managers and owners expect individuals to read well and achieve optimally in the world of work. Continual progress in reading is a must. Quality sequence in reading experiences should guide the technical education student to become the kind of reader which benefits the workplace as well as enriches the self. Bowden and Merritt (1995) emphasise four factors in the adult education curriculum. These are to consider age, needs, desires, and goals of the student. Certainly, instructors in technical education need to provide for individual differences among learners so that success presently and in the workplace will be in evidence.

## References

Bowden, Randall, and Richard Merritt, Jr (1995). The Adult Learner Challenge: Instructionally and Administratively, *Education*, 115: 426-431.

Dutton, Maurice (1995, pages 11 and 12). The Evolution of Tech Prep/ School-to-Work: Career Paths for all Students. *Bulletin of the National Association of Secondary School Principals.*

Dutton, Maurice (1995, page three.

Ediger, Marlow (1994). Meaning in the Reading Curriculum, *Reading Improvement*, 31: 49-52.

Harris, Albert J., and Edward Sipay. *How to Increase Reading Ability.* New York: Longmans Inc., 1985.

Olson, Judith (1995). Course-Based Reading Remediation: A Collaborative Experiment, *Reading Improvement* 32: 53-56.

Osterroth, Peter (1994). Variations in Problem solving Ability and Levels of Conceptual Development, *Journal of Instructional Psychology,* 21: 265-266.

Wallace, James (1995). Improving the Reading Skills of Poor Achieving Students, *Reading Improvement*, 32: 102-104.

# Challenging all Students in the Social Studies

Social studies as a curriculum area lacks challenge for selected students. Boredom or a lack of meaning in the social studies seems to be in the offing for these students. The social studies teacher, in many cases, appears to lack a repertoire of learning opportunities to challenge all students in class. These teachers need to experience motivation and renewal through inservice education.

Social studies is a major curriculum area and necessary to stress quality citizenship. Students need to have opportunities to learn, achieve, and grow in the social studies curriculum as a separate subject as well as in an integrated curriculum area. These learnings across the curriculum will assist students to realize the relationship of content rather than each having a divided component part.

## Challenge in the Social Studies

To feel challenge, each student needs to have learning opportunities which harmonize with his/her present level of achievement. If learnings are too difficult, students may not feel it is worth it to pursue and achieve. If the activities are too easy, then students may feel bored and lack interest. The teacher truly has a difficult task to determine present achievement levels of each student as well as ascertain possible of optimal achievement. The student too must accept responsibility for putting forth as much effort as possible. Together, the student and the teacher with parental support may experience quality in the social studies. There needs to be encouragement for individuals to strive, do, engage in, and grow in understandings, wisdom, moral devilment, and ethical behavior. Also, the social studies may have not only general education purposes but also vocational and a vocational interests. What are selected procedures which may be used to develop a challenging social studies programme for all students?

First, the teacher needs to know the approximate reading level of each student. When a student reads aloud a significant paragraph to classmates at the beginning of a new school year, the teacher may obtain a working knowledge of reading achievement of that pupil. This procedure may be carried over for the first two weeks of school. The teacher may notice if the learner can read approximately 95 per cent of the running words correctly without previous practice. The book is generally considered to be on his/her reading level if this is done. A second component for a book to be on the reading level of a student is when three out of four questions may be answered correctly covering subject matter read. The teacher may obtain a gauge by raising a few questions covering what has been read. The teacher may determine reading levels by having a student or two each day read aloud a paragraph to classmates and then answer questions covering the content. Classmates hear the subject matter read aloud pertaining to the unit taught. Never should students feel embarrassment when reading aloud or when answering questions orally in the classroom. Respect for others is a key concept when teaching citizenship and democratic living. The results from the assessment of reading achievement are to be used in making adjustments in the social studies curriculum. A variety of learning opportunities may challenge and yet be used to provide for diverse achievement levels (Ediger and Rao, 2003, Chapter Seven).

Second, students need to experiences a variety of library books which supplement the social studies curriculum. These library books need to be about diverse genera and reading levels to provide for individual differences. Students need encouragement to read a plethora of library books which assist in clarifying meanings in the social studies. These books may also be read during sustained silent reading (SSR) and in the individualised reading programme (See Dahl, et. al. 2003).

Third, students need develop breadth and indepth study by making graphs (picture, line, bar, and circle), tables, and charts (vocabulary, narrative, organisational, time lines) in ongoing units of study. These devices assist students to understand and attach meaning to what is being studied. Students may work in committees and collaboratively develop graphs, tables, and charts. There needs to be a reason for their development and not merely for the sake of doing so. For example, by developing and viewing a picture graph, students may see at a glance how corn, wheat, and oats production differ among the leading agricultural states in the nation. The picture graph needs to be made neatly, have a title, show effort in its making, and be accurate.

Fourth, adequate emphasis needs to be given to multicultural units of study. Students need to have opportunities to learn about diverse cultures in society. A major goal here is to respect and accept diverse cultures being studied. An appreciation of diverse cultures needs to be stressed. Each culture has contributions to make in the areas of music, dance, foods, games and recreational activities, architecture, work and jobs, transportation, level of technology, and communication means. Learning activities need to be varied in order to provide for students of different abilities (See Parker, 2001, Chapter Five). Fifth, students do possess different intelligences. Students do show more strengths in one intelligence as compared to another. They might also show abilities in several or even in all intelligences such as in verbal/linguistic, scientific, logical/ mathematical, visual/spatial, musical, bodily/kinesthetic, interpersonal, inteapersonal, and existential. Social studies teachers need to be aware of these different intelligences and integrate them into each unit of study. Strengths and interests of students must be considered when developing the curriculum (see Gardner, 1993).

Sixth, good human relations and classroom climate need adequate emphasis. A classroom needs to posses characteristics which assist students to achieve as optimally as possible. A tense, highly competitive, rigid, formal environment will not assist students to learn optimally. Nor does a disruptive school climate help students to achieve. Rather, a learning environment must be conducive to help students achieve. Standards need to be developed and enforced pertaining to a wholesome learning environment.

Seventh, a variety of learning opportunities need to be in the offing to help students use their individual learning style to achieve, grow and develop. Thus, concrete materials (objects, items, excursions, realia, and models), semiconcrete materials (films, filmstrips, slides, illustrations, CDs, DVDs, use of transparencies and the overhead, internet, software and the computer, and video tapes), as well as abstract materials (textbooks, library books, encyclopedías, pamphlets, and scripted materials) should be used in teaching and learning situations. With the use of a variety of activities, the social studies teacher needs to involve learners in becoming motivated students, not passive recipients of knowledge and skills (Ediger, 1995, Chapters Six and Seven.

Eighth, a quality evaluation programme needs to be in the offing. Teacher written tests, student self evaluation, objective and subjective assessment must be in the offing. Objective evaluations provide numerical results pertaining to student work whereas subjective evaluation involves judgments made to assess the following student made products: dioramas, murals, models, puppets, and bulletin board displays.

Portfolios developed by each student, with teacher guidance, make it possible for observers to see the actual work of students. The following are possibilities for a student portfolio:

- Written summaries, conclusions, outlines, essays, and reports.
- Cassette recordings of oral book reports and read alouds given in class and within committees.
- Art work including pencil sketches, murals, water color work, and picture photos as they relate to ongoing units of study.
- Construction work including the making of games played in other regions; model urban, village, and rural scenes; as they help to clarify that which was studied.
- Paper/pencil test taken and the results discussed in class.
- Assessment of the self in terms of criteria developed by students with teacher assistance (Ediger and Rao, 2003, Chapter Eight).

Ninth, there needs to be proper balance among social science disciplines for unit teaching in the social studies. Thus, the following need to be in emphasis:

- History with its relevant stress upon events of the past as they illuminate what is being studied in ongoing units. Primary and secondary sources need to be used in data gathering by students.
- Geography with its salient regions and geographical phenomena directly related to relevant subject matter in the curriculum.
- Economics with its goods and services needed by people in society.
- Anthropology and sociology with emphasis placed upon culture in the social studies.
- Political science and its stress placed upon rules, regulations, as well as laws (local, state, federal, and international) as they affect human behavior (National Council for the Social Studies, 1994).

Tenth, appropriate methods of teaching must be used. Inservice and continuous education of the teacher is necessary. The teacher needs to select the objectives, learning opportunities to achieve the chosen objectives, and evaluation procedures to assess student achievement.

Methods of teaching to be used in implementing the social studies curriculum need to follow relevant principles of learning from educational psychology:

- Learning activities for students should be interesting and engaging.
- Learning activities for students should be sequential so that students experience proper order of facts, concepts, and generalisations.
- Learning activities should be purposeful in that students need to perceive reasons and justification for learning what is relevant in social studies.
- Learning activities should provide for different ability levels of students in the classroom.
- Learning activities should be meaningful so that knowledge and skills are understood by learners.
- Learning activities should motivate students to learn.
- Learning activities should challenge students to achieve higher, but reasonable expectations.
- Learning activities should emphasize life-long student learning.

The above principles of learning should assist students to achieve optimally. Each student needs to learn as much as possible to be successful, presently as well as the future.

**Philosophy of Instruction**

There are vital philosophies of instruction which the teacher needs to have adequate knowledge of. The most important philosophy to emphasize in teaching social studies is experimentalism. Experimentalists believe in the use of problem solving strategies. Why? They believe that change is a key factor in life. Society is constantly changing. With change, new problems arise which need to be solved. One cannot know the real world as it truly exists; only approximations of the real world may be known. The person in wishing to solve problems desires to know reality as it truly is and move closer to this reality with problem solving.

The student then identifies a problem. The problem needs to be clarified so it may be tentatively resolved. Information needs to be obtained so that an hypothesis may be developed. The hypothesis is tentative and subject to change with its assessment. These are not rigid steps, but rather they are flexible and open-ended. Problem solving is practical for use in school and in society (See Dewey, 1916).

There is also room for idealism as a philosophy in teaching social studies. Idealism is an idea centered school of thought. Idealists believe that one cannot know the real world as it truly exists, but a person may receive ideas of it only. Subject matter, being idea centered, then becomes salient for students to learn. Carefully selected knowledge ends must be chosen. There is much content for students to learn and each generalisation and its supporting facts must be relevant. Student motivation for subject matter attainment is vital. Subject matter may be chosen for the solving of problems, but not necessarily so. It has its values for students to use in school and in society. Abstract learnings are then salient for student achievement. A good background of subject matter will be useful for students as they become adults in the societal arena.

Behaviorism as a third philosophy has its origin in believing that everything which exists can be measured. Thus, what students are to learn must be stated with the use of measurable objectives. These objectives are precise and students may reveal through testing if an objective has/has not been achieved. Only that which can be measured as an outcome is stated as an objective. The objective to be achieved by students is stated prior to experiencing leaning activities. Test items are aligned with the measurably stated objectives. Much emphasis is then placed upon testing to notice if the objectives have been achieved by students. State mandated objectives are based upon the philosophy of behaviorism.

A fourth philosophy and somewhat opposite of behaviorism is constructivism. Constructivism is based upon the student developing his/her own knowledge or his/her own truths. With Constructivism, students do more of selecting of what to learn as compared to behaviorism. Then too, the objectives of instruction are generally not stated prior to learning but rather emerge as the learning activity for students progresses. Students sequence their very own learning with teacher guidance. The teacher motivates, encourages, and helps students in learning. Competition among and between students is not stressed, nor emphasised. Portfolio development harmonizes well with Constructivism. This is an opportune way to reveal student achievement and not by state mandated test scores. There certainly is room for constructivism in the social studies in which students may volunteer to do art and construction experiences. Written work of different kinds such as prose, poetry, and subject matter may be written as they relate to ongoing units of study in the social studies. Student input into the curriculum is very important with teacher/pupil planning of the curriculum (See Stumpf, 1971).

The social studies curriculum must be built upon using vital strands of unit teaching. Students should develop high qualities in citizenship development. This must be done through teaching and learning situations in a carefully developed social studies curriculum and implementing relevant philosophies of education.

## References

Dahl, Karen, et. al. (2003), The *Reading Teacher,* 57 (4), 310-319.

Dewey, John (1916), *Democracy and Education.* New York: The Macmillan Company.

Ediger, Marlow and D. Bhaskara Rao (2003), *Psychology and the Curriculum*. New Delhi, India: Discovery Publishing House, Chapter Seven.

Ediger, Marlow and D. Bhaskara Rao 2003), *Teaching Social Studies Successfully*. New Delhi, India: Discovery Publishing House, Chapter Fourteen.

Ediger, Marlow (1995), *Philosophy in Curriculum Development*. Kirksville, Missouri: Simpson Publishing Company, Chapter Nine.

Gardner, Howard (1993), *Multiple Intelligences: Theory Into Practice*. New York: Basic Books.

National Council for the Social Studies (1994), *Curriculum Standards for the Social Studies*. Washington, DC: NCSS.

Parker, Walter C. (2001), *Social Studies in Elementary Education*. Upper Saddle River, New Jersey: Prentice-Hall, Inc., Chapter Five

Stumpf, Samuel Enoch (1971), *Philosophy, History and Problems*. New York: McGraw—Hill Book Company.

# The Curriculum and Adult Education

Adults generally tend to seek knowledge, skills, and attitudes which assist in enriching the self or guide in retraining for a new position or job. In the societal arena, there is an explosion of knowledge with change being in evidence. Seemingly, new ideas, technology, and beliefs abound in a nation and world that is subject to modification, revision, and reconstruction. A stable society that is unchangeable, eternal, and the same does not exist. Therefore, it is imperative for all persons to engage in continuous education.

The adult world provides ample opportunities to each individual to learn grow, and develop. Each person must take advantages of the numerous chances to achieve at a higher level than what is presently in evidence. The adult must perceive life as being positive and good with its many opportunities. Each opportunity may flee and not return unless one accepts that which is in the offing. A high school diploma or its equivalent must be the very minimum of formal education course work that an adult should attain. It becomes increasingly more difficult to secure a job in society with less than these minimal requirements for a diploma.

## Adults and the Educational Arena

Adults individually need to view course offerings at nearby colleges and universities to determine that which might be beneficial. If an adult perceives purpose for taking one or more classes, reasons for learning might well be in evidence. Purpose can provide the motivation to pursue, achieve, and develop. Intrinsically, the adult views education then as being worthwhile. Trusting one's own judgment to make decisions and choices makes for a better self-concept. Values for learning may be perceived more clearly when purpose is involved in completing course requirements. General education or vocational courses may be taken to enrich the self or be better prepared for competence in the vocational arena.

Interest is a powerful factor in learning. All things being equal, a person possessing interest in ongoing learning opportunities should attain more optimally as compared to the one lacking interest.

Instructors of adult education classes need to secure the interests of learners. This can be done in the following ways:

1. Being well prepared for each lesson taught.
2. Emphasizing stimulating questions during class time.
3. Using voice inflection such as proper stress, pitch, and juncture in onging units of study.
4. Having good eye contact with learners.
5. Inviting all to participate in discussions.

Using a variety of teaching methods should also aid students to attend better to ongoing lessons and presentations. Thus, discussions, explanations, committee endeavors, audio-visual presentations, as well as reading activities aid in securing learner interests and attention. A challenging environment which promotes curiosity and extends learning needs to be in the offing. The instructor needs to develop and maintain student interests in content presented.

In addition to purpose and interest in adult education, the instructor must provide meaningful subject matter and skills to students. With meaning, the student understands that which has been taught. The student through comprehension is able to use what has been learned. If a student does not attach meaning to content and skills presented, he/she will not understand what has been taught. Quality sequence within the learner will also be lacking. New objectives to be achieved should be built upon that which has previously been acquired by the learner. Thus, the learner perceives relationship of knowledge and skills. Related knowledge and skills are understood better as compared to isolated items and bits. Educational psychologists have long recognised the importance of instructors guiding students to understand relationships and meanings when attaining objectives in adult education.

Quality attitudes need to be developed by adult learners. Good attitudes assists students to achieve more optimally in knowledge and skills ends. To develop positive attitudes, the learner must feel successful in ongoing activities and experiences. Success in learning emphasizes that adults on an individual basis are reaching upward in realizing optimal attainment. Goals stress challenge and yet students are able to achieve continually at a higher level as much as individual abilities permit. With positive attitudes, each student enjoys learning and wishes to grow continually in knowledge, skills and attitudes.

Quality attitudes stresses that adults are willing to work with others so that group and committee endeavors are sequential and relevant in goal attainment. Being able to work harmoniously with others in informal situations as well as in the world of work emphasizes situations in life which are pleasant and self-fulfilling. Negative human relations are detrimental to human growth and achievement. Adults individually desire to attain the optimal self when participating in general education and/or vocational education programs.

## Philosophy of Adult Education

Instructors in adult education need to use diverse methods of teaching to guide student learning. Vital to all learning is solving problems in course work and in society. Problem solving activities can be readily implemented in the adult education curriculum. The instructor needs too emphasise opportunities that will stress objectives of instruction in problem solving. In an ongoing lesson, students should be encouraged to raise questions. These questions readily become problems whereby an answer or a hypothesis must be developed. Each hypothesis is tentative and subject to testing, using reputable sources of information. An adequate number of references should be used in testing each hypothesis. If need be, the hypothesis may be revised.

With a problem solving philosophy, the student is heavily involved in course work taken. Active involvement, not passive reception, in each flexible step of problem solving is necessary on the part of the adult learner. Stimulating teaching might well activate the adult to identify problems. Reference sources to check hypotheses must be ample in number. They definitely must relate directly to the hypotheses being evaluated. Knowledge and skills are only tentative in problem solving, never absolutes.

A second philosophy that may be used in adult education instruction is measurement driven instruction (MDI). With MDI, the instructor writes precise objectives prior to instruction for the student to achieve. Each objective must be written in measurable terms. No leeway basically exists in determining what will be taught when viewing the precise ends of instruction. The instructor aims toward the ends of objectives when teaching students. Learning activities are selected on the basis of guiding students to achieve the specific objectives. Either the adult does or does not attain anyone objective as a result of instruction. The instructor may measure how many objectives the adult learner achieves. Feedback from the learner to the instructor provides the latter with information on the success of his or her teaching adult learners. Quantitative results from each student accrue from the taking of tests. These measurable results of testing can then be given in per cent of items correct, percentile ranks, standard deviations, and quartile deviations. Objective results are then available to the instructor when using MDI as a philosophy of instructor.

With MDI, adult learners could attain the precise objectives at different rates of speed on an individual basis. The instructor then monitors instruction to notice student achievement. He/she stimulates, encourages, and motivates learners. Students may also notice how well they are doing by viewing changes in sequential test results. If improvement is in the offing, the learner should receive better test results as revealed numerically. When the instructor announces prior to instruction what each student is to attain, the student can know with much certainty which facts, concepts, and generalisations are to be achieved when the precise objectives are communicated.

A third philosophy stresses students being heavily involved in decision-making in terms of what to learn (the objectives), as well as the means of learning (activities and experiences). Stations of learning may be set up in the classroom by the instructor or through student-instructor planning. Each task at a station is challenging and provides for individual differences. The adult learner selects, from among alternatives, which tasks to complete and which to omit. More tasks are available for students to complete than what is possible so that choices are truly in evidence. If selected tasks do not meet learner needs, he/she may plan with the instructor alternative tasks. The adult education instructor monitors and evaluates learner progress.

The student should be able to choose individual tasks as well as those which involve committee endeavors. Materials of instruction are located at each center for students to seek answers to questions or to receive more information on a given topic, inside and outside the framework of problem solving. Students then may select tasks which do or do not stress problem solving. The individual is the chooser of tasks to pursue, not the teacher not within a framework of predetermined objective.

A contract system may also be used to promote choice in that the adult learner with instructor guidance determines what the former is to learn. The choices are written up in contract form and signed by both student and the instructor. The due date for the project is written on the contract. The contract agreement must relate to the objectives of the course. Otherwise, it is quite open-ended in terms of what students may achieve.

Informal educational opportunities also stress the student choosing which activities to participate in. Thus, visiting museums, traveling to scenic and historic places, checking books out from the public library for reading during one's leisure time, and viewing video-tapes, among other experiences, emphasise the student choosing from among alternatives as to which learning opportunities to pursue.

A subject centered adult education class may also be stressed as a philosophy of teaching. Here, the abstract is prised above the concrete in terms of learning experiences. General education courses work well with a subject centered curriculum. Mental development becomes a primary goal of instruction. The mind is a real entity and needs optimal development. General education with its subject matter emphasis is well suited to developing the mind and intellect. Intellectual pursuits are in emphasis when general education, also called liberal education, is stressed. Liberation of the intellect becomes a primary objective. Mental development emphasizes thinking in the abstract when engaging in critical and creative thought. Mind needs to be stimulated and developed for the learner to become a good citizen in society. A quality curriculum and a highly competent academically inclined instructor are necessary in teaching-learning situations. Subject matter specialists on the national level must be involved in developing the adult education curriculum. Goals selected by the instructor should stress mental development of the learner. Learning opportunities chosen by the instructor need to relate directly to the chosen ends. Evaluation emphasizes using diverse methods to assess student attainment of objectives.

General education tends not to emphasise vocational course work. Training for a vocation or profession comes at a later time. But first, a quality general education must be in the repertoire of all students. For adults, general education may also be taken as course work to enrich the personal self, after retirement to fulfill desired goals, when retraining is necessary to secure a new job, to be a better educated person, and to improve oneself in the societal arena. A quality general education is prised highly in society, perhaps more so than vocational training. However, this distinction should not be made. Rather, each person must appraise the self and his/her opportunities in life to decide what kind of an education would best meet the needs of the involved person. The following, among others, would be salient questions to raise in furthering one's own programme of adult education;

1. What do I want out of life?
2. How do I attain these wants?
3. What would assist me personally to obtain the good life?
4. Where do I go for needed assistance in adult education?
5. What must I do to advance personally and in the economic arena?
6. Might personal development and work satisfaction be harmonised so that congruency between the two goals is possible?
7. How should one appraise situations to determine if there is harmony between the self concept and earning a living?
8. What makes for continuous growth and development in education so that life-long learning is in evidence?
9. What can be done to receive recognition by others for talents and abilities possessed?

10. What must one do to have personal needs met other continuously?

The adult in the educational arena must strive to achieve optimally and continually in knowledge, skills, and attitudes.

**Closing**

Students need to experience a meaningful curriculum in adult education. They must perceive purposes for learning to attain in a more optimal manner. There are numerous opportunities in the educational arena which provide occasions for learners to participate fully in. Adult learners should take advantage of these opportunities and take course work or engage in informal education to maximize one's own potentialities. Meeting security needs may mean upgrading or retraining to obtain a quality job or type of occupation. Adult education can minimize deficits one has personally in the workforce. Also, adult education assists one to be a better educated person such as taking classes in general education. A well rounded education such as in general education may guide in improving the self concept and increase feelings of self worth. One might then be able to participate more fully in clubs, organisations, and the societal arena in general. Informal conversation also stresses that individuals be knowledgeable and informed of the world surrounding the everyday affairs of human beings. Through contributions made, one might well develop and possess feelings of positive self esteem. No one basically desires to be an isolate in society but rather be an active participant in an atmosphere of respect. Both general education and vocational training are important to meet needs of each person. Neither is superior to the other. Rather, the adult learner must appraise the self in determining which paths to pursue to optimalize achievement.

# The Psychology of Learning and Adult Education

Educational psychologists have definite recommendations to make in guiding optimal adult achievement. Continuous education is important for all individuals. Society emphasizes a changing environment. Inventions, technology, and values seemingly change much in time and space. Thus, each person must modify, reconstruct, and evaluate the self to determine which goals need attainment in order grow, develop, and achieve. Changeless situations do not exist. Rather individuals must adjust to changes in society. Also, it is good to forecast changes so that one can be a leader in bringing new concepts and generalisations to fruition. Leadership is needed much in society to solve local, regional, state, national, and international problems. One should, of course, develop extreme proficiency in solving personal problematic situations.

## The Psychology of Instruction

Instructors of adult education should follow tenets of the psychology of learning to assist students to attain as optimally as possible. In a changing world which requires abilities to be developed as much as possible, learners in adult education must attain optimally. Quality attitudes assist in achieving as much as individual abilities permit. The instructor needs to guide students to develop attitudes which assist optimal attainment.

Thus, the instructor guides learners to be successful in coursework taken. Sequence in learning is based upon what learners have achieved previously. New facts, concepts, and generalisations obtained are related directly to what was achieved previously. With quality sequence and order in learning, the adult learner may attain feelings of success and develop a positive self concept. A good self concept guides students to achieve higher goals in life. Low self concepts greatly hinder students from attaining that which is possible. Objectives for student attainment should not be so high that failure to achieve is an end result. Nor should the objectives be stated at such a low level of complexity that a lack of challenge is in evidence. Challenge for learners is salient if they can be successful students in adult education.

Purpose for learning is important. Thus, adult learners need to accept reasons for goal attainment. To guide students to perceive purpose, the instructor of adult education must explain why it is important for learners to achieve each salient objective before it is being stressed in an ongoing lesson. A deductive procedure may be used in that the instructor explains to students why it is salient to achieve an objective. The explanation is provided by the instructor and exist for student use in developing purpose for learning. To use a different approach, the instructor may use an inductive method. With induction, the instructor asks adult learners why it is important to learn specific content and skills as stated in the objective being stressed for student attainment. Responses must come from students when providing reasons for learning. Questions raised by the instructor must relate directly to establishing reasons for adult learners to perceive purpose for participating in an ongoing activity. The activity to participate in and the goal to be attained become one and not separate entities. Active participation by learners to the questions raised by the instructor is needed. Inductive teaching stresses that students themselves are guide by the instructor to establish reasons for learning. Purpose for learning may also be emphasised through the use of extrinsic rewards. Thus, the instructor must praise learners for quality individual or group participation in ongoing activities and experiences. Praise received stresses feedback to learners that goal attainment by students is in evidence which should be purposeful to students. Instructors must not hesitate to praise students for achieving well within a class or course.

Interest in learning is a powerful factor in guiding students to achieve. With interest, the student attends to ongoing presentations. Attention is then focused on content presented by the instructor and from answers to questions raised by students. Active involvement by students is definitely preferable to a learner being a passive recipient of ideas and skills.

## Specific Psychologies of Learning

The instructor of adult education classes needs to study and implement selected tenets from diverse schools of thought in the theory of learning developed by educational psychologists. Behaviorism as one theory of learning emphasizes establishing precise objective prior to instruction for learner attainment. Each course then in adult education must have specific objectives which leave no leeway in interpretation. After instruction, the student has or has not attained a specific objective. With precise measurably stated objectives, the instructor must choose learning opportunities that relate directly to the objective being emphasised in teaching-learning situations. Activities chosen assist adult learners to attain that which is stated in the objective, neither more nor less. After instruction, the instructor measures which students have or have not been successful in goal attainment. Those learners who have been unsuccessful in achieving the desired goal need a different teaching strategy so they too can be successful in achieving stated ends.

Precise objectives (using behaviorism as a psychology of learning) need to be arranged in sequence so that adult students may attain as much as possible. The instructor arranges the objectives sequentially to secure optimal learner progress. A logical sequence is then in evidence when the instructor orders the objectives in ascending levels of difficulty.

When teaching toward objectives or ends, the instructor is stressing an outcomes based approach in adult education. Since measurement is frequent to determine if learners have attained each precise objective, measurement driven instruction is being stressed. Testing is a major means of ascertaining the amount of achievement each adult student is making. Results in testing from each student may be given as per cent or responses correct, percentile rank, quartile deviation, and/or standard deviation. Numerical results are then in evidence.

Reinforcement theory within the framework of behaviorism states that the instructor rewards students frequently. Praise for work well done by students can be an excellent way of reinforcing learning.

Toward the other end of the continuum, the instructor may use humanism as a psychology of learning to provide for individual differences. Humanism advocates heavy input from students in developing the adult education curriculum. Thus, the instructor invites questions from students in ongoing lessons and units of study. These questions may well stress problem solving and emphasize student concerns in adult education. Projects to be completed for the course should be determined by the learner with instructor guidance. Term papers and other written requirements need to involve the student when selecting topics to write about. The instructor decides upon the written work as a requirement, but the learner decides upon the topic and title to pursue within the framework of the course. At frequent intervals during the duration of the course, students within committees may decide content to be discussed. The content assists in clarifying course objectives, or it might guide learners to engage in depth thinking pertaining to vital facts, concepts, generalisations, and skills inherent in the adult education course. Critical and creative thinking should then be in evidence.

A contract system might also be stressed to emphasize humanism as a psychology of learning. The contract may be developed with each student somewhat toward the beginning of the semester or duration of the course. With background information, the student with instructor guidance plans what should go into the contract for the former to complete. Include in the contract could be the following;

1. Reading activities and their summaries.
2. Constructing projects related to the objectives of the course.
3. Drawings made of a procedure or plan of operation.
4. Developing a term paper on a self chosen topic stressing content relevant to the class being taken.
5. Tape recording a talk on a vital area of concern within the framework of content relating directly to course content.

Humanism as a psychology of instruction stresses learners being actively involved in choosing objectives, learning opportunities, and evaluation procedures in the ongoing course. Learning is its very own reward. Intrinsic motivation is then in evidence.

**Summary**

Using tenets of the psychology of learning when teaching students guides adult students to attain more optimally in the curriculum. Students individually need to achieve as much as possible. Thus, the instructor needs to determine when behaviorism or humanism should be stressed in ongoing activities. Both psychologies are highly reputable and should be used to guide optimal learner achievement. Instructors need to evaluate the self in terms of how well student achieve in the adult education curriculum.

# The Classics and Adult Reading Interests

Individual needs should be met as much as possible in reading. The adult reading curriculum should be no exception. In many communities, there are adults who desire to have a Great Books Club organised. Generally classical literature would then be read and discussed here. There are selected logistics which need to be followed in developing a Great Books Club for those interested. The following then need to be planned for and implemented:

1. Place and date of meetings
2. Books to be discussed sequentially
3. Necessary officers chosen to facilitate the work of the group
4. Records and minutes kept of ongoing procedures and discussions
5. Correspondence carried on to facilitate growth and communication of the origination (Ediger and Rao, 2000, Chapter Seventeen).

As the Great Books Club progresses, additional duties and responsibilities will accrue. These need to be discussed and problems resolved such as the availability of coffee to assist in being alert as well as refreshments if desired.

Notices need to be posted such as in a public library when organizing a Great Books Club. The Great Books Club is open to all who wish to participate. Members do have responsibilities to read the chosen book selected and be ready to discuss subject matter read in a given session.

**Discussion Settings of the Club**

A comfortable setting needs to be in the offing with members facing each other, seated in a circle. Face to face interactions make the setting for discussion a better place for interactive communication as compared to being seated in rows and columns. The latter has a tendency to leave out participants seated at the ends.

Selections for choosing a literary selection for group discussion should meet certain criteria. These include the following:

1. The books chosen should be decided upon by the group. If several groups of five members can be formed, then each should do their own choosing. Each group might then wish to share ideas discussed with others.

2. The chosen books should be available to readers in the group. If copies need to be ordered, ample time should be allotted for ordering and receiving these copies.

3. The chosen books should follow criteria for being categorised as Classical Literature. If recent writings are selected, they might well be integrated with classical literature.

4. The chosen books should have purpose or reasons involved for their reading. One purpose might be they are read for their own sake for enjoyment and appreciation.

5. The chosen books are of interest to readers in stimulating reading of other literary selections. This objective is important in that too frequently a Great Books Club does not survive. Initially, participants are highly interested in joining and attending, but this seems to diminish until the organisation dissolves. The holding power of the organisation must be great to

survivor and flourish (Ediger and Rao, 2003, Chapter Ten).

The goals of actual reading of the Great Books should emphasize selected objectives. Certainly, monetary ends are not there. Intellectual values, however, are salient. The curious mind needs to reach out and grasp relevant ideas of the past. These ideas have stood the test of time and are still highly significant. Curiosity in the great ideas of the past have cultural ends. The great ideas of the past are valuable in and of themselves in producing the cultured person who can communicate with others in terms of facts, concepts, and generalisations which have remained with us over the centuries. Many of the past writings have come and gone, no longer to be remembered. Sometimes a long ago written manuscript is found and there is much interest in its contents for a short period of time only. Recent writings, and there are many of these, will also be forgotten in time with a few of excellence surviving. The Classics have survived in time and place and will, no doubt, continue to do so (Adler,1981).

Classical ideas then have stood the test of time such as Plato's Republic. His theories on government have provided subject matter for discussion over the centuries. His ideal Republic or nation was to be isolated from other nations. Why? Plato seemingly feared or did not like *change*. New ideas might creep in from a neighboring country (See Hutchins, 1953).

Two worlds were in evidence, according to Plato. One was the real world (The Forms) which in reality appeared to be heaven. The Forms were above the here and the now which was called the apparent world. The apparent world where human beings live on the planet Earth was inferior to the Forms. The Forms contained the ideal plant, animal, person, and so on, whereas the apparent world experienced change in the here and the now. The Forms contained also the perfect government, changeless and eternal in nature. What is on earth is a model or copy of the ideal in the Forms.

The values and beliefs of the past are worth examining in terms of what was done when changes occurred and how selected enduring values survived. Examination of values is ongoing in society in that selected values have always been important as compared to needed modifications which may well be necessary in time and place (See Sahakian, 1968.

Higher levels of cognition are required for reading and discussing the classics. A major objective is developing and increasing the ability to think (See Adler, 1977). Critical thinking is needed when comparing, for example, the classification of workers given by Plato as compared to what is in evidence presently in society.

Thus, Plato advocated three categories of workers:

1. The rulers were at the apex of status in the Republic. These were the professional rulers who would govern the ideal society. They would be the last to drop out of Plato's educational system. The education obtained would be quite demanding whereby the future rulers would excel. The rulers studied much philosophy and would be those who could understand the Forms best.

2. The warriors would be in the middle of having status in Plato's Republic. However, all in society had salient roles to engage in. Differentiation of roles was necessary so that each category of workers could fulfill their responsibilities. The warrior protected the ideal nation from enemies foreign and domestic. The security of the Republic would depend upon the warriors.

3. The artisans would have the lowest status in the Republic. Their salient role in society was to provide the necessities of life for others. Thus, food production, clothing needs, and providing materials for shelter building would predominate (Ediger, 1995).

Plato's balance of roles for different categories of workers in society to fulfill was to make for a well functioning society. Plato's theory when compared to workers presently in society makes for incongruities and yet there are similarities. Making these contrasts and comparisons certainly would stress a high level of critical thought.

Creative thinking is also important. Novel ideas can enter into the Great Books discussion when a participant comes up with a completely new idea in making the comparisons and contrasts. Intellectual challenges occur when there is healthy debate on what Plato meant by discussing the Forms and the unchanging. Novel ideas do tend to emerge. An exciting discussion where participants respect each other is indeed an enjoyable experience!

Problem solving is another good thinking experience for individuals. There will be problems arising in viewing and understanding Plato's Republic which are perplexing. These problems need clarification so that necessary information may be located for the next Great Book's session. Hopefully, each participant will have access to classical writings which bear information sought in answer to the problem. Problem solving emphasizes seeking what is not known and yet needs to be found. Participants learn in the process to more fully understand what Plato had in mind in his ideal Republic. Problem solving emphasizes deliberation, thinking, searching for information, organizing, and evaluating that which was gathered. There are times, too, when brain storming becomes an important device to generate ideas. In brain storming, participants present as many ideas in a group about a dilemma as possible. One rule is to not ridicule any idea given since this might well hinder the free flow of ideas. Ideas given should be recorded on the chalkboard or overhead. Duplication of ideas is to be avoided. Thoughts should be brief so that they can be readily recorded. After no more contributions are forthcoming, the presented ideas may be regrouped depending upon the degree to which they might overlap. This will cut down on the number of separate categories or conclusions. Participants may notice how diverse the ideas are which came from contributors and how these can be combined, even if they are slightly different. For example, if participants are familiar with the concept of "heaven" in religious thought, they may brain storm the likenesses or differences of Plato's Forms with heaven.

A multicultural emphasis should also be stressed to include writings of diverse cultures such as Latino, African American, Native Americans, among others. The concept of "Great Books" needs to be open-ended in order to meet reading needs of participants. Nothing is carved in stone. Understanding and prizing other cultures is a part of being an educated person.

There are salient criteria for participants to follow when participating in a discussion of the Great Books:

1. All should participate when feasible.
2. No one should dominate the discussion.
3. Ideas need to be presented clearly and concisely.
4. Thoughts of others should be challenged politely, if needed.
5. Interrupting others should be avoided.
6. Politeness is important at all times.
7. Accepting others as colleagues must be emphasised.
8. No one should be left out of the discussion. Careful notice and assistance to bring each member into the discussion must be in evidence so that all develop feelings of belonging.
9. Putdowns (ridiculing others or their ideas) must be avoided; each person needs to have esteem needs met.
10. There should be opportunities for all to grow in knowledge and enthusiasm involving the Great Books!

It is important for the Great Books Club to have criteria such as those listed above to appraise the self and the group in terms of using these appropriate group processes (Ediger, 2003, 28-34).

**In Closing**

The Great Books Club may wish to have a resource person attend a meeting, perhaps at an initial meeting. University professors and high school instructors who teach classes in classical content may have valuable suggestions on implementing and sustaining a Great Books Club. Certainly, one needs to lean upon those who possess knowledge and skills in discussing ideas pertaining to the classics. Once the Great Books Club has met, then the momentum needs to be forthcoming. Enthusiasm and interest needs to be developed and sustained in any good organisation. What is more important than discussing values within their context for use in society. Furthermore, values provide guidance in life. Sometimes, outdated values are adhered to; whereas the new needs to be ushered in, making for modifications of one's value system. General education and the liberal arts are good for all to study. Great ideas of the past are then studied and these assist one to think and delve into that which has survived and endured in space and time (Ediger and Rao, 2003, Chapters one through six).

## References

Adler, Mortimer J. (1981), *Six Great Ideas*. New York: Collier Books.

Adler, Mortimer J. (1977), *Reforming Education*. Boulder, Colorado: Westview Press.

Ediger, Marlow (1995), *Philosophy in Curriculum Development*. Kirksville, Missouri: Simpson Publishing Company.

Ediger, Marlow (2003), *"Thoughts of some Prominent Educational Thinkers,"* Edutracks, 2 (8), 28-34.

Ediger, Marlow, and D. Bhaskara Rao (2000), *Teaching Reading Successfully*. New Delhi, India: Discovery Publishing House, Chapter Seventeen.

Ediger, Marlow, and D. Bhaskara Rao (2003), *Language Arts Curriculum*. New Delhi, India: Discovery Publishing House, Chap Ten.

Ediger, Marlow, and D. Bhaskara Rao (2003), *Philosophy and Curriculum*. New Delhi, India: Discovery Publishing House, Chapters one through six.

Hutchins, Robert Maynard (1953), "The Basis of Education," in The *Conflict in Education*. New York: Harper and Row, Chapter Four.

Sahakian, William (1968), *History of Philosophy*. New York: Barnes and Noble Books.

# Curriculum Design in Technical Education

There are selected issues which need to be addressed in technical education. Issues need studying, researching, and deliberating in working toward closure. Perhaps, educators will not agree on solutions, presently or in the future. People have had diverse background experiences and develop different philosophies. However, it is important to discuss solutions to problems and attempt to reach consensus. Achievement and growth occur when individuals in technical education listen to the thinking of others and arrive at the best curriculum possible.

## Who Should Select Objectives?

Objectives may be developed on the local level with heavy input from instructors in the surrounding environment. Here, instructors in technical education may met together in a planned series of meetings to choose the best objectives possible for learner attainment. Through quality discussions, participants share their expertise. Reference materials, consultant assistance, and supervisory guidance are available to stimulate thought and decision-making. Instructors then should be able to come up with a set of worthwhile objectives that provide for students of divers achievement levels.

Somewhat toward the other end of the continuum, objectives in technical education may be written on the state level. Representatives from selected areas who have a reputation for truly being professionals in technical education may select and write objectives on the state level. Guidance and assistance in this task is provided for on the state level. Objectives derived from participants are then available to instructors on the local level.

Thus, an issue in technical education exists in terms of who should select objectives for learner achievement.

**How Should Learning Activities be Sequenced?**

The instructor or teaching team need to determine under which sequence students attain more optimally. He/she may use tightly sequenced behaviorally stated objectives in the curriculum. Here, the instructor arranges objectives in technical education in a particular order for student achievement. Logical thinking by the instructor is used to place the objectives in ascending order of complexity. Toward the other end of the continuum, the student, in degrees, assists in sequencing objectives. Thus, the student helps in selecting and arranging objectives of instruction through the raising of questions in class, the use of a contract system which involves student-teacher planning to determine what the former is to learn, and learner choice as to what is to be learned from a set of learning stations developed by the instructor. In situations such as these, a psychological curriculum is in evidence. Here, the learner is involved in ordering his/her own activities and experiences.

Individual differences need to be provided for so that all may attain optimally.

**Evaluation of Achievement**

Evaluation is a critical area to truly determine what students have attained. The instructor needs to devise procedures of evaluation which are valid in that they measure what has been taught. Reliability is another key ingredient in the evaluative process, be it test-retest, split-half, and/or alternative forms of measurement devices.

A vital question pertains to who should appraise student progress. The instructor could do all the appraising of learner progress with the development and use of evaluative procedures. If precise measurably stated objectives have been used in the instructional arena, the instructor could complete and use criterion referenced tests. Should students be rather heavily involved in evaluation of progress, a portfolio approach may be used. Both the instructor and student select, after careful deliberation, what should go into the portfolio. From the port folio, the employer may appraise the quality of work done by the learner in technical education.

## In Closing

Three major questions must be raised in developing the curriculum. These are:

1. Who should choose objectives of instruction?
2. How should learning opportunities be sequenced?
3. Which procedures should be used to appraise learner progress?

The above named questions need very careful consideration so that the best curriculum possible may be offered to students.

# Leadership in Vocational/Technical Education

Leadership is needed in schools to overcome problem in the school setting. Richardson and others (1989) emphasised that principals be proactive and not reactive persons. Thus, problems tend to be identified before they happen rather than reacting to crises situations only. Ediger (1993) stressed the importance of administrators and supervisors being highly knowledgeable about the curriculum in providing for optimal learner achievement. Much parental dissatisfaction might well be avoided if leadership capabilities were used to guide each pupil to attain as much as possible.

## Knowledge of the Curriculum

To assist pupils to achieve as well as possible in the school setting, attempts need to be made to identify effective schools. This is indeed difficult. Wallberg (1979) identified more than 2,700 research studies that emphasised effective schools. Squires, Huitt, and Segar (1985) in summarizing research pertaining to effective schools raised the following questions:

1. Does the school leader have purpose in mind when administering and supervising in the school setting?
2. Are high academic standards being stressed?
3. Is the principal supportive of efforts in school improvement?
4. Are adequate staff development programmes in evidence to improve the curriculum?

5. Do faculty and staff work together to harmonize endeavors in instructional improvement and discipline of learners.

6. Is the principal visible to observe teaching and learning as well as to confer with teachers on curriculum and instruction matters?

Questions arise here as to what is meant by school and curriculum improvement, having purpose in mind in making changes in the educational setting, as well as which inservice education programmes to stress for faculty development. A need exists to make decisions based on theory. Something must provide direction and guidance in whatever is done in education, teaching, and learning. Writers frequently write about the necessity of theory guiding instruction. These writers tend not to state which theories should be emphasised in the curriculum. There are numerous recommendable psychologies and theories of instruction that can be emphasised in the school curriculum. I recommend strongly that all administrators, supervisors, and teachers become thoroughly familiar with each theory. Depth learning of each theory should be in the offing for educational leaders which includes classroom teachers. These theories have stood the test of time and tend to be classical in nature. I will discuss what I believe to be selected relevant theories of instruction which educational leaders must be able to implement in ongoing lessons and units of study.

Dewey (1916) emphasised problem solving approaches in teaching-learning situations. The problems need to be real and lifelike to pupils. Committee work to identify and solve contextual problems in a creative atmosphere was stressed. The teacher is a guide a resource person, not a dispenser of information.

Piaget (1950) stressed a developmental psychology by identifying four stages that most pupils go through as they progress from birth through the elementary school years. These developmental stages are sensorimotor (birth to two years of age), preoperational (ages two to seven), concrete operations (ages seven to eleven), and the stage of formal operations (age eleven and beyond). The ages given are approximate in Piaget's research findings.

Maslow (1954) emphasised a theory of motivation with its *hierarchy of needs* that individuals possess such as physiological, safety and security, love and belonging, esteem, and self actualisation. Personal needs of pupils then must be met if they are to do well in school. *Pupil teacher planning* of the curriculum is salient.

Bruner (1968) emphasised that a structure of knowledge be identified for each curriculum areas. These structural ideas represent key ideas or major generalisations as perceived by academicians in their respective areas of expertise. Leaders in education and teachers might well identify their own structure of knowledge to emphasize in teaching each curriculum area. Bruner's theory of instruction is practical since its implementation might well provide objectives, learning opportunities to attain the objectives, as well as evaluation procedures to ascertain learner progress.

Behaviorism, as a psychology of learning, has a long history of importance (Bobbitt 1916, W.W. Charters 1923, B.F. Skinner 1979). Behaviorism stresses the importance of *precise, measurably stated objectives* for pupil attainment, written prior to instruction. Mastery learning, instructional management systems, and criterion referenced testing are present day examples of behaviorism. Reinforcement theory is also directly relate to behaviorism.

The *basics* (Bagley 1905, Bestor 1953, Smith 1959) in the curriculum also has a relatively long history in education. It has never been determined at any age in time what is basic for pupils to learn. Former President of the United States Ronald Reagan and his Secretary of Education William Bennett continually emphasised that teachers should teach the basics and not waste time on the frivolous. They too did not define what the basics were that pupils should acquire. If we only could know what these are, much time would be saved in teaching learners. Too be sure, effort must always be put forth to determine what is basic and essential for pupils to achieve.

More is expected of administrators and supervisors than ever before. Knowledge of the curriculum is no exception. Missouri since 1985 with the Excellence in Education Act, among other states in the United States, mandates that principals evaluate each notenured teacher at least once a year and tenured teachers at lest once every three years. This means that principals need to have knowledge of the curriculum when appraising teaching performance. Teachers will grasp how knowledgeable the principal is during an observation to the classroom followed with a conference. The purpose of observational visits and followup conferences should be to improve the teaching knowledge, skills, and attitudes of the classroom teacher.

Theories of learning to provide direction in teaching-learning situations differ from each other. What then can be done to assist teachers and administrators/supervisors in providing for optimal pupil attainment in the classroom? Determine which theory or theories benefit individual learners in teaching and learning. Pupils differ much from each other and need guidance to learn as much as possible. Since pupils are human beings and are different one from the other, it behooves educational leaders to determine which theory in use will assist the pupil to attain as optimally as possible.

## Functions of the Educational Leader

Leaders in education must emphasize the importance of good human and public relations (Shoemaker and Fraser 1981). Principals and supervisors need to assist teachers to have pupils achieve goals. Assisting teachers can largely be done if there is mutual respect and acceptance between the leaders and the teachers. Hindrance in quality communication among participants results in a lack of sharing ideas, results, and work completion in the school setting. Oliva (1984) stresses careful attention be given to methods of nonverbal, written, and verbal communications skills.

Gestures, facial expressions, and body movements do convey something to the receiver of nonverbal communication. A friendly countenance emphasizing a willingness to work together and collaborate on salient tasks to improve the curriculum are musts. People realize rather quickly in most cases in which selected individuals indicate nonverbally that they do not wish to serve on a committee, nor give the time to do so, nor indicate feelings of cooperation in moving toward an ideal or have a vision of what should be accomplished in the school setting. The educational leader must present a role model here. The principal/supervisor sets examples for teachers to follow. His/her enthusiasm, knowledge, empathy, and understanding of teachers as human beings having much worth should be an inherent facet of the nonverbal role model. Written communication skills are further needed by the educational leader to convey, clarify, and confirm meaningful information to teachers be it in a bulletin, notices of staff development, trends in teaching for teachers to think about, and issues in the curriculum. Modern technology has made it so that word processors make the act of written communication easier, neater in the final copy, and more flexible in making revisions and modifications. Mechanical errors must be omitted in all written messages used to communicate to receivers of the message.

Verbal communication must be comprehendible with appropriate stress, pitch, and juncture used to convey information to others. Quality eye contact is a must in verbal communication. Ellis (1986) wrote that, in terms of research results from the studies of William Rutherford and associates, the most successful principals clearly communicated expectations, provided technical assistance, and monitored the results.

Being able to communicate well comes up again and again in research results pertaining to educational leaders. Hallinger and Murphy (1986) in emphasizing effective school research summaries list the following as being salient:

1. Determining and communicating the goals of the school.
2. Supervising and evaluation teaching and learning.
3. Coordinating curriculum efforts.
4. Developing high standards in the academics as well as high expectations.
5. Monitoring and evaluating student achievement.
6. Encouraging professional development of teachers.
7. Maintaining time on task for instruction.
8. Developing incentives for teachers and students.

Stocklinski and Miller-Colbert (1991) emphasize the Comer Process, a research based model for school improvement that has as its basis collaboration, consensus, and communications for the solving of problems in academic, social, and staff development areas. This process permits teachers, supervisors/principals, and parents to harmonize efforts in working together for the good of the pupil. Among other items of importance here is the emphasis placed upon quality *communication* to achieve goals of the school and of education.

**Traits and Characteristics of Principals**

More is expected in a complex society than ever before of school supervisors and administrators.

Duttweiler and Hord (1989) state that educational leaders who are effective desire a participatory style of supervision. These principals and supervisors want into from others, particularly teachers. Thus, there needs to be collaboration skills in working together for the good of the student. Skills in being able to foster cooperation among participants in selecting objectives of instruction, learning opportunities to attain the objectives, and evaluation procedures to assess progress are desired from school leaders. These leaders need to be able to motivate, encourage, and stimulate others in the school setting to participate in school improvement endeavors. Thus, principals and supervisors should be skillful in working effectively with others to achieve the goals of the school. An open school environment assists participants to become actively involved to improve the total school curriculum.

Society is continually changing. It does not stay stable. With the many societal changes, the school curriculum also needs modification and revisions. The world of work and the personal needs of individuals require that student competencies need developing in the areas of creative thing, problem solving, critical thinking, as well as reasoning skills (Dede, 1989). Educational leaders should think of change as being relevant in society. These changes have tremendous implications for objectives and goals in the curriculum, learning opportunities to attain the stated ends, and assessment procedures to determine how much pupils have learned and what is left to be done to guide more optimal learner attainment.

The new leader in the school setting must be:

1. Highly knowledgeable of workable procedures of teaching.
2. An effective leader possessing skills to work with others.
3. Able to motivate teachers and others in the school setting.
4. Proficient in curriculum development.
5. Knowledgeable of child development characteristics.
6. Proficient in a variety of communication skills.
7. Skillful in interpersonal relations.

8. Able to plan and implement decisions made through collaboration.
9. Knowledgeable of societal trends and quality school practices.
10. Able to apply technology to instruction and management.
11. Skillful in the use of political processes to attain objectives of instruction.
12. Knowledgeable about school site management and its implementation.
13. Secure parental cooperation and input.
14. Obtain information to use in making relevant decisions.
15. Empower individuals, especially teachers, in a rich school cultural climate.

**Summary**

Foresight of educational leaders is vital so that a vision of the ideal is possible. Efforts need to be made to achieve the vision. It is an ongoing process. Much knowledge of the curriculum is necessary to attain and grow. Purposes need to be involved in moving from what is to what should be. The educational leader needs to provide support to those working toward positive changes in curriculum improvement. Staff development is needed in making these changes. Collaboration among participants is necessary to work toward a desired curriculum.

Diverse theories of instruction that have stood the test of time may be sued by teachers to guide pupils to achieve as much as possible. The theory used must harmonize with what assist the learner(s) to attain and achieve. Each theory provides the teacher guidance and direction in making educational decisions.

Quality supervisors/principals are able to communicate well with others. Diverse forms of communication must be learning situations. Why is this necessary? Knowledge acquired must be used or it may be forgotten rather quickly. That which is learned then must have utilitarian values. Skills objectives stress that students use acquired knowledge. Quality attitudes must be stressed in the vocational curriculum so that students have an inward desire to learn, grow, achieve, and develop. Positive attitudes then assist in achieving knowledge and skills goals more readily. Students need to feel that life has its many opportunities to become a productive member in society. Each opportunity needs to be appraised and accepted as being worthwhile in and of itself. The vocational student must develop feelings of a an adequate self concept. He/she then can attain in more optimal manner. Lifelong learning is salient to a vocational student. Talents and abilities must be upgraded continuously in changing societal arena. Workers become outdated unless continuous education is involved. The academic areas of reading and literature, mathematics, science, social studies, the fine arts, and physical education need to be stressed as integrated course work with vocational studies. For secondary and post-secondary vocational classes, the student needs to avail the self of the many opportunities that are available for enrichment. If opportunities are not seized and accepted, they may not be available at a later time to the personal self. Richness of opportunities which are accepted as educational goals truly provide avenues to develop the self more adequately. Thus, the goals of being a competent worker as well as being a person of immense personal development should make for a more satisfying lifestyle. The supervisor of vocational education must stress both the objectives of the institution and personal development when providing leadership in the curriculum.

**Workshops and Vocational Education**

Supervisors of vocational education classes need to upgrade their own knowledge, skills, and attitudes in developing a quality curriculum. Faculty members also need to engage in continuous education for the best teaching and learning situations to accrue. A well devised workshop which meets the needs of participants can certainly improve the vocational curriculum for students. The workshop must have a relevant theme such as "Improving Instruction in Vocational Education." Otherwise, the learning activities can be quite open-ended for the workshop. All faculty and administration/supervision personnel should attend the general session. The general session stresses the identification of problem areas in teaching vocational courses. Input from each participant is a desired ideal in the general session. Participants need discuss their concerns in teaching students. The writer has noticed the following problems voiced by instructors in teaching vocational education:

1. How to secure learner attention in teaching-learning situations.
2. How to adjust objectives so that each student experiences continuous progress.
3. How to evaluate student progress in a valid and reliable manner.
4. How to guide learners so that they understand what has been taught.
5. How to use performance objectives in teaching.

After adequate discussion of problems faced in teaching in the vocational arena, participants may volunteer to serve on a committee to solve a problem area as identified in the general session. Not more than four participants should be on any one committee. Assuming four have volunteered to serve on the committee to work on the problem of securing learner attention in ongoing lessons and units of study. An adequate number of reference sources should be available for data gathering, be they reading, audio-visual, or human resources. If students attend to ongoing presentations a better chance of depth learning, retaining what has been learned, and transferring that which has been acquired to a new tasks will be more in evidence. In answer to the problem of securing learner attention, the following suggestions may have been acquired through the use of reference sources:

1. The teacher using voice inflection such as proper stress, pitch, and intonation to develop learner interest in the lesson presentation.

2. The teacher rewarding learners with verbal praise for quality responses given by students.

3. The teacher verifying methods of teaching used. Varied methodology might include inductive procedures, problem solving methods, deductive approaches, teacher-student planning of the curriculum in part, student selection of term projects that relate to the course content, and the use of measurably stated objectives.

4. The teacher using eye contact continuously in teaching-learning situations.

5. The teacher adjusting the curriculum to present individual levels of learner attainment with continual learner progress following.

Quality consultants need to be available to assist participants in the workshop to secure needed information. Consultants must be knowledgeable and be able to work harmoniously with each participant in the workshop. Consultants can be very helpful in guiding participants to clarify ideas, to think critically and creatively, as well as engage on problem solving. They may be excellent in assisting the workshop participant to appraise the quality of responses secured to problem areas. A supportive consultant is necessary to promote the goals of each workshop participant.

A good professional library should be available to all vocational education faculty during the entire school year. The library becomes crucial when a workshop is being conducted. Teacher education textbooks, video-tape, video-disks, pamphlets, brochures, research studies, among other reference sources, should be available to participant in the workshop. Supervisors of vocational education guide instructor proficiency by encouraging library use.

In addition to the general session and committee endeavors, participants should also choose a personal problem or area of difficulty to pursue in the workshop setting. Perhaps, a participant wishes to study approaches in appraising a student in an apprenticeship situation. The workshop participant with consultant leadership might study the use of quality criteria to evaluate a student at the workplace using instructor observation. Each criterion emphasised needs to reflect recommended thinking by specialists in evaluating student progress. Observations made should be reliable in that if a second observer evaluates the same student, consistency of evaluation results from the two evaluators should be in evidence. Should the two evaluators disagree much, one could develop no conclusions from observations made. It is only if consistency is in evidence that conclusions can be drawn pertaining to the quality of work done by the apprentice. Thus, interobserver reliability is important when appraising a single person in the workplace.

The workshop participant may also study the use of rating scales and checklists as means of evaluating individual student attainment. Standards on both the rating scale and checklist should reflect the latest trends in behavior that a good student or worker should exhibit to achieve optimally. The results from using the rating scale and the checklist can be filed and compared with future evaluations.

Additional evaluation procedures to use include teacher written test items such as true-false, multiple choice, essay, matching, and short answer test items. Each test item must possess clarity so that students understand that which is wanted in terms of responses. Tricky items on a test must be eliminated. Trivia has no place in test items that appear on a vocational test. Results from the test for each student should be used to reteach and modify needed knowledge, skills, and attitudes. Test results then have an important and integral role the teaching-learning process. Supervisors of vocational courses have an important role in guiding instructors to do a good job in evaluating student progress and using the evaluation results to improve instruction.

**Faculty Meetings**

Instructors need to share ideas gleaned from the workshop which were used in actual teaching-learning situations. Sharing can be done in series of regularly scheduled faculty meetings. Peers should want to learn how well new ideas secured from the workshop actually work in the classroom setting. Each instructor will need to adapt content secured from the workshop to his/her own plans for instruction. Adaptations also should be made to fit the categories of learners taught in vocational education, be they normal students or handicapped individuals. If a participant in the workshop acquired selected theories of learning in the vocational arenas, application of those studied must be planned and implemented. Theories need to be practical and guide instruction. Each theory provides guidance and direction to what is done in the instructional arena. Instructional procedures should not be left to chance but has a source which improves instruction. Thus, the supervisor of vocational education assists workshop participants to implement specific teaching suggestions as well as relevant theories of instruction. How well workshop ideas work in teaching-learning situations can be shared within the faculty meeting setting.

**Stimulus**

Response theory stresses that what students have learned can be measured through testing as well as through other objective procedures of appraisal. Numerical results only are wanted from students when they are being appraised. Percentile ranks, quartile deviation scores, standard deviation results, and stanines are acceptable examples of learner results from evaluation. Feedback to students in terms of achievement is then free from bias and the subjective. Objectives of vocational instruction are chosen well ahead of the time they are to be implemented in teaching-learning situations. Precision in writing the objectives is salient. Either a student attains or does not attain an objective, arragned in ascending order of complexity with other objectives. There is no leeway basically for interpreting the meaning of any single objective. Objectives in S-R theory of learning are clear, direct, and lack vagueness. The instructor of vocational courses may announce to students the objectives to be attained, prior to the lesson presentation.

Learners then knew what is expected of them as a result of instruction. Reinforcement of correct responses is very important, If a student responds correctly in diverse learning situations, he/she should be rewarded for doing well. Verbal praise can be an effective reinforce. Reinforcers can shape student behavior in a desirable direction. Continuous reinforcement can be very helpful in students developing quality attitudes and feelings toward the present course being taken. The learner should then put forth increased effort in learning. Not only are attitudinal goals attained more effectively, but also knowledge and skills objectives. Quality attitudes do affect the number of knowledge and skills goals achieved.

Supervisors of vocational coursework should also guide instructors to use problem solving procedures in teaching-learning situations. With problem solving, the instructor guides students to identify a problem within a contextual setting. Learners then develop one or more hypotheses in answer to the problem. A variety of reference sources are then used to check each hypothesis. Reference sources can consist of:

1. Vital textbook content for the course.
2. The instructor of the class or other knowledgeable people.

used to achieve purposes in the school setting. The goals and objectives of the school need communicating to parents and the lay public. Learning opportunities being emphasised in the school setting should harmonize with quality goals and objectives. Monitoring of learner progress in goal attainment is must. There need to be high standards for pupil achievement with time on task involved. Incentives for learning and for teaching should be in the offing.

Society changes rather continuously making it necessary for the school curriculum to change. Higher levels of cognition must be stressed in teaching-learning situations. Knowledgeable, skillful leaders should possess abilities to work effectively with others, especially teachers. These leaders must be proficient in curriculum development procedures. Child growth and development characteristics should be used in improving teaching and learning. Good interpersonal relations are needed to guide staff development efforts as well as involve parents in matters pertaining to curriculum improvement.

There are principles of learning from educational psychology which teachers and educational leaders tend to agree with. These principles of learning provide guidance in choosing objectives of instruction, learning opportunities for pupils to achieve the objectives, as well as appraisal procedures to ascertain what pupils have learned. Ediger (1994) lists these principles of learning as follows:

1. Pupils need to attach meaning and understanding to ongoing loessons and units of study.
2. Pupils need to experience interest in learning.
3. Pupils need to perceive purpose in learning.
4. Pupils need to experience sequence in learning opportunities.
5. Pupils need to experience rational balance among objectives in the curriculum, such as knowledge, skills, and attitudinal goals.

**The long range goal of educational leaders is to assist teachers in guiding pupils to achieve more optimally. Supervisors/principals need to challenge teachers to provide the best curriculum possible for pupils in the school setting.**

## References

Richardson, M.D., and others, "A Descriptive Analysis of Kentucky Elementary School Principals." *ERIC Document Reproduction service* #ED 311557.

Ediger, Marlow, "Goals of School Administrators," *Machigan Principal,* Fall, 1993, pp. 12-14.

Wallberg, H., and others, "The Quiet Revolution in Education Research," *Phi Delta Kappan,* November, 1979, pp. 179-183.

Squires, David, and others, *Effective Schools and Classrooms: A Research Based Perspective,* Alexandria, Virginia: Association for Supervision and Curriculum Development, 1985.

Dewey, John, *Democracy and Education.* New York: The Macmillan Company. 1916.

Piaget, Jean, *The Psychology of Intelligence.* New York: Harcourt Brace Jovanovich, 1950.

Bruner, Jerome, *Toward a Theory of Instruction.* Cambridge, Massachusetts: Harvard University Press, 1968.

Bobbitt, Franklin. *The Curriculum,* Boston: Houghton Mifflin Company, 1918.

Charters, W.W. Charters, *Curriculum Construction.* New York: The Macmillan Company, 1923.

Skinner, B.F., *Beyond Freedom and Dignity.* New York: Alfred Knopf, Inc, 1979.

Bagley, William, *The Educative Process.* New York: The Macmillan Company, 1905.

Bestor, Arthur, *Educational Wastelands.* Urbana: University of Illinois Press, 1953.

Smith, Mortimer, *Diminished Mind.* Chicago: Regency Press, 1959.

Shoemaker, J., and Fraser, H.W. "What Principals Can Do: Some Implications from Studies of Effective Schooling," *Phi Delta Kappan,* November, 1981, pp. 178-182.

Oliva, P.F., *Supervision for Today's Schools.* New York: Longman, 1984.

Ellis, T.I., "The Principal as Instructional Leader," *ERIC Document Reproduction Service* #ED 274 031, 1986.

Hallinger, P., and J. Murphy. "Instructional Leadership in Effective Schools." *ERIC Document Reproduction Service* #ED 309 535, 1986.

Stocklinski, J., and J., Miller-Colbert, "The Comer Process Moving from I to we." *ERIC Document Reproductive Service* #EJ 419 920, 1986.

# 30

# Supervision in Vocational Education

The supervisor has a leadership role in improving the vocational education curriculum. He/she is able work harmoniously with others in the school and societal arena. The supervisor places high priority upon being above to stimulate instructors to teach well. He/she realizes that instructors must guide learners to attain the goals of the institution as well as meet their own personal needs. The institution has its definite goals for learners to attain. These goals represent knowledge, skills, as well as attitudinal ends. Each of these types of goals are salient for students to obtain. Instructors need to be held accountable for guiding student goal attainment. Students individually need to attain as much as possible. Vocational education instructors also have personal needs, wants, and responsibilities. These need to be given adequate attention so that the personal dimensions receives its fair share of time. Thus, a proper balance must be maintained between the demands of the institution with its instructional goals for students to attain and the instructor as a person attempting to meet personal needs.

## Instructional Goals of Vocational Education

Institutions stressing goals in vocational education must emphasizes vital objectives that stimulate, encourage, and challenge each learner. Thus, each objective needs to be scrutinised carefully before its implementation in the curriculum. Careless selection of objectives might stress the trivial and the unimportant. Time is then wasted in teaching and learning situations. Rather, the instructor must assume responsibility for choosing carefully that which is salient and worthwhile for students to achieve. Much must be learner by each student in vocational course work. Vocational course need to be demanding so that learners are being trained and educated for the world of work. The vocational curriculum and the societal arena of work should be integrated and not separated from each other. Supervisors of vocational educational must assist instructors of choose vital goals for student, attainment.

Objectives selected in terms of knowledge, skills, and attitudes for student achievement need to be sequenced properly. Quality sequence in teaching-learning situations guide learners to attain more optimally. If objectives are too difficult to achieve, students might well experience failure. Should the objectives be excessively easy to attain, learners may become bored with the curriculum. Objectives then must be sequenced or ordered properly so that continuous progress of students is an end result. Vocational students need to feel successful in each lesson and unit taught. Feelings of success spur learners on to greater and higher levels of achievement. Feeling of failure tend to lower the self concept of the involved individual.

Depth teaching of knowledge, skills, and attitudes should be in the offing. With depth teaching, students achieve objectives with better understanding as compared to survey procedures. In emphasizing the former, students experience a variety of learning opportunities to attain each objective. An adequate amount of time is spent on learners achieving individual objectives. In survey methods of teaching, learners experience a more shallow approach in achieving each objective. Skimming of content, abilities, and feelings in a vocational course is more in evidence in survey as compared to depth teaching in ongoing lessons. There are many facets of determining objectives in the vocational curriculum that supervisors of instruction should assist in.

Rational balance among knowledge, skills, and attitudinal objectives should be in evidence in teaching-

3. Relevant audio-visual materials, brochures, and pamphlets, among other relevant sources.

Following the gathering of data, the hypothesis is evaluated. The hypothesis may then be modified if needed. Instructor observation is necessary to evaluate how well learners are engaging in problem selection, developing hypothesis, checking each hypothesis, as well as modifying the hypothesis if needed. The instructor then must appraise student attainment in the classroom setting or in the work place in noticing how well learners are achieving in real life-like situations. Thus, in a hands on approach, students are appraised in terms of criteria emphasised in problem solving. Problem solving stresses a psychological sequence in that learners are heavily involved in sequencing or ordering their own activities with instructor guidance.

## Closing

The supervisor of vocational education has many salient responsibilities. He/she provides guidance and direction to instructors in updating the objectives of instruction, choosing learning opportunities for students to attain objectives, and selecting evaluation procedures which truly appraise learner achievement.

The supervisor provides leadership to make necessary changes in the vocational curriculum through the use of workshops and faculty meetings. Inservice training and educating are needed continually to develop a quality vocational curriculum for students.